P9-CQI-419

Call To Action

Secret Formulas To Improve Online Results

Bryan Eisenberg &
Jeffrey Eisenberg

Wizard Academy Press
Austin, Texas

Call To Action: Secret Formulas To Improve Online Results
Copyright © 2005 by Future Now, Inc

All rights reserved. No part of this book shall be reproduced, stored in a retrieval system, or transmitted by any means, electronic, mechanical, photocopying, recording, or otherwise, without written permission from the authors. No patent liability is assumed with respect to the use of the information contained herein. Although every precaution has been taken in the preparation of this book, the publisher and authors assume no responsibility for errors or omissions. Nor is any liability assumed for damages resulting from the use of the information contained herein.

International Standard Book Number: 1-932226-39-7
Library of Congress Control Number: 2005922802
Printed and bound by RJ Communications, LLC
Book Design and Layout by Lisa T. Davis
Cover Design by Janet Tingey

We dedicate this book to our parents
Esther & Fred
and to the memory of our uncle,
Morris I. "Pocho" Eskinazi

Foreword

Bryan and I had an entirely different book in mind only a few months ago. As often happens, we were ahead of ourselves. In almost seven years of client work, research and software development, we have developed some radically advanced thinking about online persuasion and conversion. We have so many more insights we want to share with all of you, and we will eventually, but this key information can't wait – so this is the book that needs to be published now. Online marketers need a book that deals fundamentally with the principles and concepts of conversion.

When we started Future Now, Inc. in 1998, full of naïve enthusiasm crusading for higher online conversion rates, we were a voice in the wilderness. In those days of absurd dot-com valuations based on eyeballs, we believed it would be only a "couple of years" until our business flourished. It wasn't until 2004 that online marketers started to include conversion rates on their radar. If it weren't for the early adopters, our clients and friends, we would never have learned what we're sharing with you now.

This book is a compilation of some of our *GrokDotCom* articles, *ClickZ* columns, seminar presentations and training materials, as well as contributions by our staff and colleagues. We hope you will get from these pages as much as we have put into them.

I wish you all happiness, prosperity and health.

Jeffrey Eisenberg
New York City, February 2005

Acknowledgements

We made a business decision not to list every contributor as an author but if anyone else deserves to be listed as an author it is Lisa Davis. Her contributions go well beyond the over 200 articles she's authored, her editing skills, her counsel, her insight and her loyalty.

We offer a heartfelt thanks to the members of our team for making this book possible: Holly Buchanan, Anthony Garcia, Dave Cadoff, John Quarto-vonTivadar, Howard Kaplan, Esther Eisenberg, William Schloth, Rich Brant, Cindy Kaplan, Danielle Delgado and John Walsh.

We thank Roy H. Williams and Pennie Williams, our partners, for being such good friends and believing in us way before it made any sense to.

We owe a great big thanks to Amanda Watlington, the editor of this book and her husband Mal Watlington for all the late nights and the mad rush to the finish line.

We are grateful for all the work of our ClickZ editors: Rebecca Lieb, Pamela Parker, and Erin Brenner.

We thank Corrine Taylor for her patience and friendship.

We thank Sean Taylor of Wizard Academy Press for all his help.

We thank Mike Drew of PromoteABook.com for all his book marketing advice.

We must not forget to thank our past and present clients and readers for everything they teach us.

We also want to acknowledge:

Our Contributors: Tamara Adlin, Andy King, Jason Burby, Dave Cadoff, Sam Decker, Lauren Freedman, Ashley Friedlein, Anne Holland, Sean D'Souza, Brett Hurt, John Marshall, Gerry McGovern, Jim Novo, Lonny Paul, Jared Spool, Jim Sterne, Nick Usborne, Dr. Ralph Wilson.

Our Web Analytics Friends: John Simpson, Brent Hieggelke, Anne Lindberg, Sue Burton, Greg Drew and the rest of the crew. Rand Schulman, Erik Bratt, Olivier Silvestre and the rest of the crew. Brett Hurt, Jane Paolucci, Joe Davis and the crew. Josh James, John Pestana, John Mellor, Matt Belkin and the crew. Jim MacIntyre, Terry Lund, Dylan Lewis and the rest of the crew. John Marshall and his crew. A special thanks to the Web Analytics Association Board members: Jim Sterne, Seth Romanow, Andrew Edwards, Andrea Hadley, Rand Schulman and Greg Drew. And a special thanks to all the committee chairs and members of the WAA.

Our friends at JupiterMedia/ClickZ: Eric Peterson, Danny Sullivan and Alan Meckler.

Other friends: Hal Alpiar, Anne Holland, Brad Powers, Mike Sack, Betsy Weber, Jason Ciment, John Morana, Maheesh Jain, David Galland, John Marchese, Valerie Marchese, Dr. Richard Grant, PHD, BJ Fogg, Frederick Marckini, Rob Murray, Sage Peterson, Larry Kerstein, Craig 'CC' Chapman for getting the Grok emailed out, Iva and Rob Koberg for their LiveStoryboard CMS, Nathan Stewart, many of the graduates of the Wizard Academy including the W.B. crew, Chris Maddock, Juan Guillermo Tornoe, Hal Helms and Larry Chase.

We thank our family for their patience and love: Mom, Dad, Abuelita, Stacey, Cindy, Hannah and the little one on the way.

We are sure that we've forgotten somebody else important and we apologize to them.

TABLE OF CONTENTS

"Humanity is acquiring all the right technology for all the wrong reasons." - R. Buckminster Fuller, Michael Moncur's (Cynical) Quotations

Prefatory

"Spending a fortune to drive traffic to your website – when most of it never does anything while it's there – results in high customer acquisition costs and hurts profitability." - Anonymous

One Step at a Time

Years ago, the famous marketing theorist Theodore Levitt pointed out to the rail barons that they were in the transportation business, not just railroading. Following Levitt's lead, we'd like to point out that Web marketers are not just traffic drivers. They are customer acquisition managers. They must manage the process from the point at which the customer first enters the conversion funnel until they exit.

Trying to increase sales simply by driving more traffic to a website with a poor customer conversion rate is like trying to keep a leaky bucket (your sales funnel) full by adding more water instead of plugging the holes. Instead, work on keeping more of your visitors from falling out of the funnel on the way to the close. Here are five great reasons to focus on increasing your conversion rate:

1. You don't just get more sales — you get more sales from your existing traffic. There's no need to increase your marketing expenses to attract more traffic.
2. Your customer acquisition cost goes down.
3. Your customer retention rate goes up.
4. Your customer lifetime value goes up.
5. The effect is permanent. It outlives any particular marketing program.

There are five discrete areas where improvements can be made that will increase closing/conversion rates: planning, structure, momentum, communication, and value. We have organized Call to Action into these areas of improvement so that you can get the most benefit from this information.

Planning

Planning involves everything that happens before your prospect reaches your website, from how you get traffic, to developing your UVP (unique value proposition), to planning the elements for the clickstream and storyboard of your website, to understanding your marketplace, customers, brand and brand positioning. Planning is about understanding your visitors, so you can anticipate their knowledge levels, moods and mindsets.

The organization must understand the distinct roles of those involved in planning. Central to that understanding realizing that the functions and capabilities of marketing and sales are not the same. Marketing drives traffic; sales converts traffic into revenue. That being said, the organization must accept it is impossible to maximize your sales without using expert selling principles and processes. Unfortunately, most companies do not have any one person who is directly responsible for the sales effectiveness of the company website.

Structure

Troubleshooting the structure of a website includes analyzing and evaluating the effectiveness of the navigation; information architecture; design/style; color; copy versus images; layout; technology; font (size, style, and color); speed; and the perception of speed.

By understanding your website's sales metrics you can identify what part of your website structure needs help. For example, you may note that your website has a low website engagement rate. Getting to the products requires too much drilling down into the website. By removing just one step in the process, and delivering traffic right to the product page, you may increase sales. One of our clients increased sales by 39 percent through just a single change. How many sales are you leaving on the table?

Momentum

The elements motivating visitors to go from one page to the next and eventually take an action on your website are "momentum." To build momentum, use AIDAS, the 5-step sales process (See chapter "Is Your Home Page Helping or Hindering Sales?"). To improve momentum, focus on how to get people to take action at the points of action. If you want your visitors to do something, don't just hope they'll figure it out; tell them (e.g., "Click Here"). You must go beyond usability. This isn't simply removing obstacles. It is creating the desire that drives action. To achieve momentum you must make sure there are clear calls to action on every page. This means locating important information at the point where it will have the most impact. For example, it may be premature to put your guarantee policy on your home page; but not putting it on your checkout page is a big mistake. You must balance opportunity with overload and prevent "analysis paralysis." This happens when prospects are so overloaded with choices that they become overwhelmed and freeze or abandon your website.

Communication

The Internet is a powerful, fast, and flexible communication tool. Communicating effectively involves improving your writing and writing style, evaluating your balance of images and copy, expressing value, setting the appropriate mood, developing policies and procedures that instill trust, selling style versus substance, timing your messages for best effect, incorporating scannable and skimmable text, effectively managing your follow-up communication, knowing when you should use long or short copy, and much, much more. You must pay attention to every nuance, because communication isn't what you intend, it's what your customers perceive.

Value

Value is not the same as price, and price alone is actually a lower priority for most buyers. Whether you will get the sale and your "buyer" will turn into a "customer" is determined by the value the customer finds. Customers search for products, but they buy value. Are you effective at selling your product's benefits instead of just its features? Does the style of your website equate with your UVP? Do you delight customers with the way you fulfill their orders, or do you merely satisfy or, even worse, disappoint them? Do your website's products and/or services address your customers' deeply felt needs, or are you trying to push something they may not even want? The customer must be able to readily determine your value, not have to guess at it.

Call to Action includes what you need to know if you want to achieve dramatic results from your website. You will be able to see if you are planning for top performance. You will have the tools to know if you are evaluating your performance accurately. You will find tips for building a structure that supports your sales. You will know what you must do to achieve the momentum you need to get the results you want. And, you will have lots of helpful information for how to effectively communicate your value proposition. Read on! This is your *Call to Action*.

Conversion Tip

6 Dell Principles for Improving Conversion

Dell pioneered use of the Internet as a sales channel beginning in 1996, becoming the first company to record $1 million in online sales in 1997.

If I were asked, "what was fundamental to our improvement", I wouldn't respond with one or two initiatives. In lieu of a best practice case study, I'd suggest we look at the several principles and processes we use to run the Dell.com Home & Home Office site and merchandising. Part culture, part methods, the entire team understands how to continuously improve our site, day by day. Here are a few that make a big impact to ongoing improvements.

Metrics Rigor

The fundamental 'blood flow' of Dell is our metrics. We are always looking to optimize and improve, and use metrics to understand the heartbeat of the business down to the capillary. As such, our online metrics are part of daily conversations about the site, but more importantly, included when we discuss the entire business. Traffic and conversion are part of a daily discussion, and many diagnostic metrics are used to understand customer behavior and opportunity.

The rigor is around the frequency and use of metrics to report the status of customer experience and the business. Definitions are important, so we make sure everyone understands what the metric means and how it impacts the business. We use dashboards and operation reviews to update management and staff on progress against goals. We 'democratize' access to the data so that people throughout the company can diagnose and analyze customer behavior and business impact.

Focus and Ownership

We created a position called the Web Producer, who really has two jobs. First, he or she is the 'site manager' for a particular part of the site, managing the workflow, content and merchandising decisions for a part of the site. But perhaps more importantly, they are given ownership of a metric, such as conversion. This ownership means they're accountable for meeting goals, and puts them at the hub between product managers, brand managers, developers and senior management for all activities to drive that metric. They report weekly to senior management and partners on progress against aggressive goals, and the status of initiatives planned to improve.

Start Small…Go Big

Perhaps what's different is the extent of our nature to second guess our opinions with testing. Because the data is there, and we're data fanatics, we use testing to justify investment. We start small by piloting new technologies, new merchandising, layout, navigation, and content. On projects we prioritize using NPV (Net Present Value) net of launch and sustainment costs. So, by testing — starting small and going big — we make sure whatever we do has a demonstrable impact on conversion (or any metric that helps the business).

Designing on Purpose

Site decisions are balanced between user goals and business goals. We look at multiple data points to understand what customers want and what they do (note: these are not always the same). We triangulate insights from many sources: entry/exit surveys, focus groups, usability studies, phone data, financial results and of course web metrics. Then, we can modify promotions, merchandising, and real estate allocation to improve conversion.

For example, through site pathing and usability studies we found users had no problem finding the financing information. Yet, when people reached the page, we would see high abandonment. So we surveyed what information people were looking for, which of course was how to find their potential monthly payment. So we added an interactive flash calculator to determine payments for any price point. Interactivity is always a conversion booster, but it met a need. Abandonment was cut in half.

Driving Urgency

Urgency is also a well-known direct marketing concept. So for years we have been offering time-limited promotions with purchase of a computer. To make sure that's the reason to buy now is clear to our users we use several tactics:

- Urgency copy — using words such as "Click here now," "Limited Time Offer," and "Last Day" in the promotion message
- Clear Action — On every promotion offer, you can't miss the "More details" link.
- Cross-off pricing — we make it clear to the user how much they are getting off the regular price by crossing out the original price and highlighting the sale price.
- Deadline — We try to always add the date the promotion, and give a countdown — "2 Days Left" or "Ends Today".

Frequency and Consistency

You'll notice throughout Dell.com, that we merchandise promotions on multiple pages with a consistent layout. The message is treated in the same way on the home page, product page and configurator. Since many users come into our site at different levels, it's important that we repeat these important messages on several pages so they are not overlooked. And, for users who go through the entire site, this ensures that if they leave Dell.com they remember there are some good deals available at Dell. The concept of frequency and consistency throughout the site, in message and treatment, also works for other messages we want to be sure consumers remember.

- **Sam Decker** spent four years overseeing operations and product management for Dell's consumer e-commerce and e-support sites. His expertise in operations, user experience, financial management, process, and technology helped drive growth in Dell.com conversion rates and consumer online sales.

"To win the customer's attention, we must surprise Broca's area with sensory stimuli other than that which was expected." - Roy Williams, The Wizard of Ads

20,000 Leagues into the Brain

To understand persuasion you must have a rudimentary understanding of the physiology of the human brain. At the front of the brain, right behind your forehead, is the prefrontal cortex, which is the center for planning, emotion, and judgement. Its job is to give the signal to the motor association cortex, located adjacent to it, to coordinate behaviors, and then initiate voluntary movement (take action). Until your marketing message has reached the prefrontal cortex, all you have done is take up space and make noise.

The shortcut into the human brain is the ear. The auditory cortex is right next door. Raw sound enters the auditory cortex, and spoken words, melodies, rhythm, laughter, and jingles are stored in the auditory association area. That's why you can remember hundreds of songs you never intended to learn ("You deserve a break today...").

To test the power of sound and auditory reception for yourself, try this. First, watch your TV with the sound off, then listen to your TV with the picture off. You can prove to yourself in just seconds, that when it comes to conveying information, affecting emotions, and causing action, sound beats pictures hands down. Where is the sound in your website? It's in the words, which we understand by "hearing" them in our minds.

In 1861 Paul Broca identified the section of the brain involved in speech production. It assesses the syntax of words while listening to and understanding what is structurally very complex. Partially, the brain does its job by learning rules about how we talk and then almost skipping over the parts of what we say that are predictable based on those rules. According to Roy Williams, the Wizard of Ads, success in advertising (and marketing) is about surprising Broca's area, and you can best do that by using sound.

It seems almost too obvious; after all, humans are drawn to things that are surprising, shocking, catastrophic, and chaotic. Anything predictable is boring. Yet "predictable" describes most marketing and ads, doesn't it? A century and a half after Broca's discovery, some people still aren't paying attention.

According to cognitive neuroscience, our thoughts are composed of neither words nor pictures. Human thought is a speed-of-light progression of mental images, each one a complex composite of sound, shape, texture, color, smell, taste, and mood. Different words are attached to these mental images in an area of the brain called Wernicke's area. This is the area responsible for naming, for associating nouns with objects. Once a word has been attached to each mental image, the whole verbal jigsaw puzzle moves to Broca's area. There the words are arranged into understandable sentences.

The problem for marketers is that when the Wernicke area attaches the "usual" words and the Broca area arranges them in the "usual" order, the result can be painfully predictable and, therefore, eminently forgettable. Only when you break the pattern of predictability do you achieve impact and memorability.

Words - the Magic Potion

Williams believes that the secret of persuasion lies in the skillful use of action words: "The magic of advertising is in the verbs... Describe what you want the listener to see, and she will see it. Cause her to imagine taking the action you'd like her to take, and you've brought her much closer to taking the action." The success of Williams' own ads, as well as the ads created by those he has mentored, speaks for itself.

Sound is invasive, intrusive, and irresistible. Driving sound through Broca's area allows us to cross the bridge to the dorsolateral prefrontal association area, otherwise known as the imagination.

So what does this mean for marketing your website? It means you will be most successful when you use words that cross from the ear almost directly to the prefrontal cortex, the decision part of the brain. The killer app in web marketing is not sight, it is sound, whether heard directly (audio) or mentally (ad copy). It is not the design of your website that sells. It is the content — the words.

Are there exceptions? Of course! But don't bet your budget or your business on them. Choose your words carefully. Every word you use on your website is a drop of the magic potion.

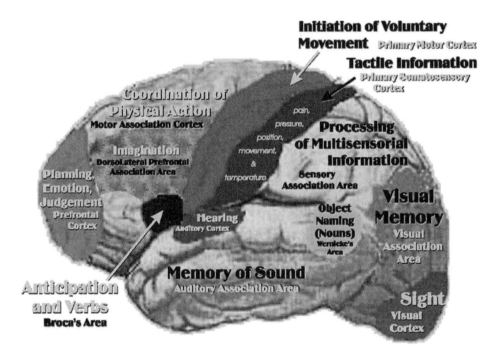

Concept by: Silvia Helena Cardoso, PhD
Center for Biomedical Information, University of Campinas, Brazil

Brain Map Review — Wizard of Ads Academy

"For a time commentators thought flair should mean only "a sense of smell," as it does in French. But in English today it is Standard meaning "a special talent, ability." - The Columbia Guide to Standard American English, Kenneth G. Wilson, lexicographer

Map Scent Trails That Lead to Better Conversion

We're always alert to new research uncovering the patterns users follow while searching on the Internet. One of the more popular information-foraging theories currently being proven confirms what we've known for quite some time.

As early as 2001, a Xerox Palo Alto Research study indicated humans track information in a manner similar to how animals follow a scent. According to an article on the study:

People... engage in what [Dr. Ed Chi] calls "hub-and-spoke" surfing: They begin at the center, and they follow a trail based on its information scent . . . . If the scent is sufficiently strong, the surfer will continue to go on that trail. But if the trail is weak, they go back to the hub. "People repeat this process until they're satisfied," Chi said.

Knowing how people hunt and sniff around for info is certainly useful, but that usefulness is limited until you determine more about what a person is sniffing for.

What Visitors Sniff Around For

At User Interface Engineering, Jared Spool conducted a study with his team. Participants had to try to find, on a website, a specific item that interested them. They were given detailed descriptions of what they were looking for before searching. Each website they were asked to search did contain that information. Spool cites the results:

It turned out that users were far more successful at finding their targets when the description words, which they told us before they saw the website, appeared on the home page. In the tasks where users successfully found their target content, the description words appeared on the home page 72% of the time. When users were unsuccessful, their words only appeared an average of 6% of the time on the home page.

In the persuasion architecture process, extensive research is conducted to reveal and learn everything possible about a website's customers. The process takes into account:

- Topographics, the competitive environment and the users' behavior within the environment.
- Pyschographics, what customers do psychologically as part of their buying processes.
- Demographics, the customer's attributes and how they affect the buying processes.

We also study a website's Web analytics, specifically keyword referrals and a handful of other key metrics. All this information is used to create a set of robust, three-dimensional personas. Once the personas are created, only then do we begin to build information scent trails that will lead visitors down the road to conversion.

The Trail of the Perfect Diamond

During the Leo Diamond redesign project, we researched and created a persona we dubbed Natalie. She is an attractive, 29-year-young, high-end department store buyer. She earns about $42,000 a year. She is recently engaged and plans on telling her fiancé exactly what she wants in an engagement ring. Natalie comes from a family with means and was denied nothing growing up. She has a deeply-seeded motivation to impress. Status and name brands are of paramount importance to her.

Not until we're armed with this information can we begin to plot an information scent trail for Natalie. Her motivations reveal likely search terms, keywords, and trigger words that communicate a sufficiently strong scent to motivate, propel, and guide Natalie through the conversion process. Spool writes:

First, users expect to find "trigger words" in the links. A trigger word is a word (or phrase) that causes the user to click. When the trigger words match the user's goals, they find those words right away and the links make them more confident that they are going to find their content.

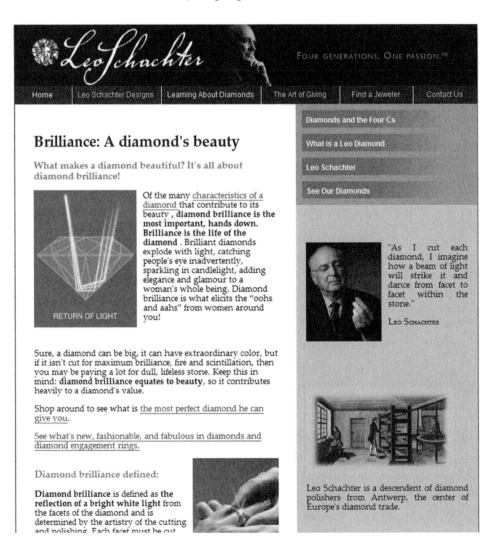

We know Natalie wants the perfect diamond, one that will never fail to impress, a diamond worthy of her. To convert Natalie, we must get her to the store locator page where she'll send her fiancé to purchase her engagement ring.

We created specific pages to provide Natalie with the information she needs to determine the Leo Diamond is the correct choice for her.

A Forest Full of Scents

On websites such as Amazon.com, information and products fall naturally into categories that are more or less distinctive to the visitor. Search, navigation, and product descriptions help users stay and orient themselves on the scent trail. In the case of the Leo Diamond website, the scent trail is less distinctive and obvious; the entire website is about diamonds and packed with diamond information. Helping Natalie sniff her way to relevant information is a more subtle, complicated process.

The nature of the website makes it unlikely that Natalie (or any other persona) will stay on a predetermined, linear conversion path. We also don't want to force Natalie into a hub-and-spoke cycle. Natalie, an impatient, competitive type, will bail, unable to participate in that cycle for long.

How do we keep Natalie from getting lost in a forest of scents?

Using resolving door links, we can better manage Natalie's experience on the website, ensuring that whatever page she's on, she can pick up a relevant scent trail leading toward conversion.

The pages she'll visit contain two types of hyperlinks: call to action and point of resolution. She'll go round and round through her points of resolution (or resolving door) until we provide her a call to action.

Natalie's resolving-door pages contain information that may be important to Natalie but isn't critical. By providing links to pages with critical information on these pages, we can let Natalie wander around the website and never completely leave her conversion path.

Scent: Another Term for Relevance

What we find most exciting about current information-scent research is it forces the question, "What's most relevant to the customer?" The end result can only be a website that contains not only the relevant product or solution but also the relevant scent and content to get the customer to it.

"For a salesman, there is no rock bottom to the life. He don't put a bolt to a nut, he don't tell you the law or give you medicine. He's a man way out there in the blue, riding on a smile and a shoeshine. And when they start not smiling back—that's an earthquake. And then you get yourself a couple of spots on your hat, and you're finished. Nobody dast blame this man. A salesman is got to dream, boy. It comes with the territory." - Arthur Miller, Death of a Salesman

Is Your Website Your Digital Salesperson?

Can your company's sales only be made by a salesperson? Do you expect your website to be little more than a company brochure? Or, do you still believe that b2b sales cannot be made through the Web? If these are your beliefs or even myths you've heard, let's reevaluate them and take an informed look at the role of the salesperson and the website.

When a company has a need to fill, recognizes a problem, or identifies an opportunity, potential purchasers try to recall advertising that says who can solve their problem. Or, they'll ask friends and colleagues if they know who can fill their need. They may even consult the yellow pages.

Would they look for a solution on the Web? After all, companies only have websites to show to friends, enhance prestige, and increase IT expenditures, right? "Everyone has a website, so I've got to have one, too," goes the thinking. A website makes you appear up-to-date, even hip. Rarely, you think, will anyone ever actually see the website. It's like a novelty T-shirt you wear under two layers of clothing.

Even if prospects search the Web for alternatives, they may never find your website. A website is a needle in a haystack, isn't it? If prospects don't know the URL when they start, how would they ever find a website in the wide ocean of porn, sports scores, and spam that make up the Web?

If somehow they do find your website, it's impossible for it to qualify a visitor's need well enough to present the right information, or so the thinking goes. It's nothing more than an electronic brochure, right? Only a salesperson can properly qualify a prospect and deliver the right information at the right time, the way prospects want it. A properly trained salesperson can discern prospect personalities and speak to them in their language.

The Salesperson Does It All. . . Right?

A salesperson can develop a presentation that explains everything prospects are curious about, and answers every question they might pose. Prospects never need to visit a website. They won't need any reassurance beyond the salesperson's words. The in-depth presentation prepared by the well-trained salesperson answers all their concerns and leaves no stone unturned. That's something a website could never do!

Once they receive information during the presentation, prospects understand everything. They'll perfectly recall and explain it to their colleagues and managers. They require no supplemental information. Their colleagues will never go to the website to learn more, because the prospects who heard the original presentation will have explained everything exactly the way the salesperson did.

Even if the website attempts to answer visitor questions with hyperlinks, it's unlikely anyone will click. Who has the time? Who wants to get carpal tunnel syndrome surfing some company's website?

If the website owner knew in advance the order in which prospects would pose specific questions, the marketer could come up with a bleeding-edge presentation to address them as they arose. The website would provide answers for prospects as, or even before they formed their most penetrating questions. Yet that would be impossible. So the question remains: Is there any need for a website? Certainly! Competitors have them. So, everybody must have one, too.

Do people remember everything the salesperson presents? After a salesperson finishes the presentation, is it guaranteed that prospects won't seek out a competitor's website for alternative answers? Surely they see no value in what a competing website can teach them. After all, only a live person can provide all the in-depth answers.

A website could never become a digital salesperson, replacing a real, live human being. Something as lifeless as a website can't beat a live person's communication skills. After all, a live person flawlessly duplicates their presentation each time with all the nuances and subtleties. All the different questions prospects may ask are answered the same way every time. And the answers to their most burning questions are always at the salesperson's fingertips.

Maybe a website alone can't make a sale, but can a website help lose a sale? If you are one of those who believe that your product can only be sold through your sales force, think through your entire sales process. Reconsider all your customers' needs and responses before you answer.

Conversion Tip

Make Your Website About the Customer Instead of About the Company

Was your website designed around your corporate structure? Is there any way in the world that potential customers can know ahead of time that your widgets are sold out of one division and your gadgets out of another? You have lots of different customers with different needs. To help them do what they had in mind, forget how you are organized, and focus on helping them get in, buy and get out quickly by:

- Making it obvious which button to click.
- Making sure each major button or link is made up of as few words as possible that complete this sentence: "I want to _____."

Remember, nobody wants to "click here." They want to:
- Find the right bike for me
- Buy a bicycle
- Get my bike fixed
- Ask a question
- Find my order
- Find a store

This applies to the rest of the links on your site as well. The "Buy Now" button is not pushy salesmanship - it's a clear message to the visitor who is desperate for clear messages. Make your site about the people who visit it and "customer experience" will improve overnight.

- **Jim Sterne**, author, consultant and producer of the Emetrics Summit.

"When the conduct of men is designed to be influenced, persuasion, kind unassuming persuasion, should ever be adopted. It is an old and true maxim that 'a drop of honey catches more flies than a gallon of gall.' So with men. If you would win a man to your cause, first convince him that you are his sincere friend. Therein is a drop of honey that catches his heart, which, say what he will, is the great highroad to his reason, and which, once gained, you will find but little trouble in convincing him of the justice of your cause, if indeed that cause is really a good one." - Abraham Lincoln

When Visitors Achieve Their Goals, Conversions Increase

Anything resulting in a lower level of customer satisfaction or a lost customer is a defect — a flaw in your website, sales process, product/service or fulfillment.

When a visitor doesn't convert, your website has a service defect. You don't deliver on promises made to customers or prospects. Conversion rates reflect your ability to persuade visitors to take action, and customer satisfaction. The only way to achieve your goals is if your visitors first achieve theirs.

Forrester's Harley Manning once asked over 10,000 people how satisfied they are with their most recent online purchase. Respondents were grouped into three buckets: dissatisfied, neutral, and satisfied. The groups were then asked how likely they would be to return to the website they purchased from. Here are the results…

Of those in the dissatisfied group, 39 percent said they'd return (I don't fully understand why); 47 percent of the neutral group said they'd return (not a major improvement). However, 93 percent of the satisfied group said they would return. The survey data is self-reported so there may be some biases, but it is directionally correct.

Dissatisfaction Results in Lost Sales

While performing a conversion assessment for a well-known online retailer, I logged in and looked at the top entry pages to look for high abandonment rates or single-access views. Sure enough, one page had a 93 percent abandon rate: a category page of $15-30 products. Something on the page was defective.

I found the page on the website. So many things were right. The company has over 24,000 stock keeping units (SKUs) in this category and provides easy access to its in-site search solution. There was a list of new offerings and top-sellers, as well as some featured picks.

Where was the defect? It was subtle. The in-site search box was in a banner area above the rest of the page's content. Half the banner area was a promotional image; the other half was the search field. Defect? The promotional image spoke about offerings for kids. Unless the user was interested in this offering, the search field appeared invisible and irrelevant. Visitors immediately became dissatisfied. This made it look like the category didn't offer much of what users wanted. As soon as the client changed the image to focus visitors on the 24,000 SKUs available, the abandonment rate plunged to 53 percent.

There was even more room for improvement on the page, but applying this one improvement to this and other website pages resulted in a positive return on investment (ROI) for our engagement.

Identifying Defects, a Continuous Cycle of Improvement

Are you looking for and measuring defects in your website, sales process, or customer's post-purchase experience? Have you implemented a process for doing it? What defects have you found and corrected? What defects do you ignore? Are you involved in a continuous improvement process, or is the status quo good enough to satisfy you?

Conversion Tip

For Heaven's Sakes, Let Them Pee

Imagine you are sitting in a car in the middle of a long road trip. You really have to pee. It's all you can think about. Your eyes are peeled for the nearest rest stop. You're spending all of your cognitive cycles trying to calculate how long you can hold it before the situation becomes dire and you're starting to weigh the pros and cons of pulling over to the side of the road. It's bad. Meanwhile, your beloved is sitting next to you, chattering on about how lovely the scenery is. Needless to say, you're not that interested nor are you being even remotely attentive. Your beloved begins to get irked. Things start to escalate and both sides get irritated, each convinced they are 'right' to be doing what they are doing.

Why am I asking you to imagine this? Because I think that many visitors to online retail stores are on a long road trip and they have to pee. They have a goal and they want to be successful in that goal; they aren't looking to be distracted until their goal is satisfied. Perhaps they want those cool sneakers but they want them for less. Maybe they're trying to find a replacement for the CD they broke yesterday. Maybe their needs aren't quite as pressing as the one I described above, but they are there nonetheless. And what is their experience at your store? My guess it's almost exactly like our poor driver's experience: they're trying to ignore information that is distracting, annoying, and, as far as they're concerned, completely irrelevant to their goal. They're wading through banners and sale stickers. They're searching through a sea of chattering navigation links. They're typing something in search and wondering why they didn't get what they wanted.

Ask yourself: when she arrives at my store, does my customer have to pee and, if she does, am I letting her? Or am I trying to force her to think about things I think are important and interesting about my store? Can I understand the reasons my customer came to my store in the first place, help him or her achieve those goals, and then introduce all the "wonderful scenery" when they are ready to listen? Examine the who, what, where, when, and why of the messages on your site. Respect the fact that many customers have something in mind when they arrive and that they're not looking to be distracted. When they arrive, let them pee. You'll be amazed how interested they get in the scenery once they're done.

- **Tamara Adlin**, Senior Usability Specialist of a major online e-tailer and co-author with John Pruitt, *The Persona Lifecycle: Keeping People in Mind During Product Design*, Morgan Kaufmann Press, summer 2005.

"Congratulations! Today is your day. You're off to Great Places! You're off and away! You have brains in your head. You have feet in your shoes. You can steer yourself any direction you choose." - Dr. Seuss, Oh, The Places You'll Go!

Ending the Single Page Visit

The importance of a customer's past experience cannot be underestimated. According to research on WebSideStory's StatMarket data:

- 74 percent of visitors reach websites by direct navigation (type the URL) or bookmarks.
- 16 percent of visitors reach websites via links from other websites.
- 11 percent of visitors reach websites via search engines.

Commenting on the data, WebSideStory's CMO, Rand Schulman, observed, "The days of Web users randomly 'surfing' to websites are ending. Now more than ever, people know exactly where they want to go on the Web. This does not mean search websites or other Web links are now less important, because users still have to initially find a website before they can bookmark it. However, having a website worth returning to is becoming increasingly important to businesses."

If thousands, even millions of unique visitors think of your website as the one that could meet their needs or solve their problems, why do most leave after the first page or two? Why do conversions remain at an anemic 2-5 percent? Do you offer a solution or product that could meet the needs of more than 5 percent of your market? Can visitors find that solution on your website? Do they understand your offer's value? Was it made at the right time? Are you sure they're coming back?

Of foremost importance, if you had the opportunity to engage one-on-one with each of your visitors, and each honestly expressed her needs or wants, what percentage would you be able to satisfy?

Internet Marketers Ineffectively Engage Visitors

If your call center employees only converted 2 percent of qualified prospects, you'd probably fire them all. So what makes that 2 percent rate ok for a website? A OneStat.com study of typical metrics for a large sample of websites illustrates the level of disengagement visitors have as measured by page views:

- 1 page view: 9.52 percent
- 1-2 page views: 54.60 percent
- 2-3 page views: 16.56 percent
- 3-4 page views: 8.75 percent
- 4-5 page views: 4.43 percent
- 6-7 page views: 1.41 percent
- 7-8 page views: 0.85 percent

- 8-9 page views: 0.68 percent
- 9-10 page views: 0.51 percent
- More than 10 page views: 2.69 percent

TYPICAL WEBSITE TRAFFIC DROP-OFF

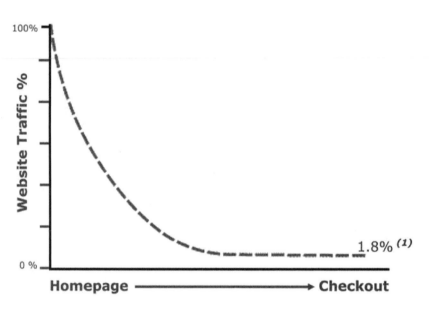

(1) Shop.org members report an average conversion rate of 1.8%

This behavior isn't unique just to the users in OneStat's study. We've observed similar behaviors across hundreds of websites.

Perhaps it takes visitors a page or two to figure out they're in the wrong place, but this is doubtful. Over half of visitors are interested enough to click one or two steps deeper before bailing. Clearly websites fail to provide enough "scent" (motivation, persuasion, value) to the majority of their visitors to keep them going in the process. Websites apparently just don't meet their needs.

Search Only Gets You Visitors

Based on the WebSideStory data presented above, over a quarter of all visitors reach websites via links or search engines. Search engine marketing (SEM) focuses on increasing link popularity and visibility in search engines and extends to advertising on search properties. Over 550 million searches are performed each day.

Typical searcher behavior is to enter a search phrase in a query box, click on a search results link, view the page, and decide whether it's worth investigating. If not, the searcher clicks back and goes on to the next link in the results. Obviously, the first view of the landing page is incredibly important. If the visitor clicks back, no other website pages are viewed — a classic one-page visit.

Online marketers are typically so busy fiddling with their search marketing and PPC search advertising campaigns that they've lost sight of their bigger problem: Their websites have low conversion rates.

Usability Equates with Use

Many marketers expect usability studies to answer their marketing questions. Yet every usability study starts with a website as a given. If someone commissions a usability study, the website is the target .

Usability studies suffer from one major flaw: They never study the most important aspect of visitor behavior. The neglected aspect is the visitor's initial impression of the website relative to other available choices — its competitors.

Online behavioral specialist Jim Novo says, "They only study committed behavior, once the visitor has decided, 'OK, this is the website I'm going to drill down into.' All they are studying is what happens after the most critical event — getting chosen relative to a list of other websites in a search engine."

There's nothing wrong with usability per se, but it only addresses a small portion of the entire picture. One option is to have the usability study test a bunch of competitor websites, including the target website. The test may not even get past a quick view of the entry page. That's the ultimate usability test, isn't it? What if the user preferred other websites and never even "used" yours? What value is a usability test then?

It's Navigation, Not Traffic

Navigation is the biggest challenge websites face. The issues are: What to do with the traffic once it lands on the website? How to get visitors to take the first action and click deeper? And once there, how to induce visitors to click to the next step, and the next, and the next?

There are dozens of books dedicated to website navigation. Gurus lecture on information architecture. Usability wonks pontificate at conferences about how visitors can find your links. None ever deals with what motivates visitors to click on a link that will guide them to the persuasive path you want them to take. That path takes visitors on a journey from the initial landing page through the pages they find most relevant to their needs to the thank-you-for-ordering page. It creates, at the minimum, a click-through experience evocative of your brand.

Persuasion architecture links a visitor's buying experience to your company's sales process. It bridges the buy/sell processes in a holistic, contextually sensitive, and measurable way. You must know how users behave to generate sales and maximize return on investment (ROI). If you can influence visitor behavior and empathize with visitor motivations, you can influence results to provide a better experience and more frequent, effective conversions.

"Strategy without tactics is the slowest route to victory. Tactics without strategy is the noise before defeat." - Sun Tzu

A Solid Foundation

There are three fundamental ways to increase your website revenue:

1. Increase Traffic. With this technique, you drive more visitors to your website, on the theory that more visitors will translate into more buyers. Most of the tactics for increasing traffic require that you spend more money. Tactics include advertising, positioning in search engines, public relations campaigns, viral marketing, and encouraging customers to return.

2. Merchandise. Another way to increase your revenue is to encourage your paying customers to spend more money per visit. You can accomplish this in many ways: cross-selling, up-selling, evaluating your most effective price points and margins, providing extra services at discount, bundling products or services into "packages," and stressing benefits rather than features. Even something as basic as improving the quality of your copy can have a dramatic impact on your results.

3. Increase Your Conversion Rate. If you concentrate on improving your website's conversion ratio (the number of unique visitors who actually buy divided by the total number of unique visitors), you will get much-improved results without having to spend more money to drive more traffic. There are literally thousands of adjustments, many of which cost practically nothing, that will increase your results dramatically. These include removing unnecessary steps in the checkout process, clarifying your Unique Selling Proposition, redesigning your navigation scheme or prominently displaying your privacy assurances and guarantees. All these adjustments take into account the interrelationship between consumer buying behavior (consumer psychology) and the professional sales process.

To build a stable and profitable online business, it is necessary to focus on all these areas. If you neglect any of them, then you are building a structure without a foundation. The only way to build a successful, long-term business is to understand the interrelationships of all the parts.

Exhibit 1: Conversion Pyramid

To build a solid structure, you must first build a website that focuses on maximizing conversion, then improve its merchandising, and only then undertake to drive more traffic. It is the only sane and logical order - the way you can build a business to last like the Great Pyramids of Egypt, rather than one that crumbles under the weight of its own inefficient "design."

The bottom line is that to be successful online, you must make conversion your first priority. Only when you have a successful, efficient "machine" that gets the most from your existing traffic do you have an enterprise in which it makes sense to invest further marketing capital.

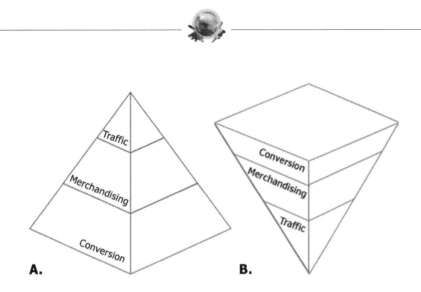

A.   B.

Some Thoughts About Conversion Rates – The Numbers

Conventional wisdom seems to convey the notion that conversion is a low-scoring game. Depending on whom you ask average conversion rates are between 2 and 4 percent.

By today's standards, you get bragging rights and the full dose of hero treatment if you can maintain a conversion rate of 5 percent or above. You have deity-like status if your conversion rate approaches double digits. The world's finest players sport double-digit conversion rates of somewhere around 12-14 percent.

Of course, we're referencing top-line conversion: The number of visitors who take the macro action you want them to divided by the total number of website visitors.

A double-digit conversion rate seems unimaginable to some, but experience demonstrates it's certainly possible. We've seen it happen time and again.

But, you might say, look at those who still don't convert! Even with an awe-inspiring 12 percent conversion rate, it's a little painful to consider 88 percent of visitors still don't convert. That's quite a mound of traffic. But it's understandable why many feel content with these conversion rates. Even when a dismal 2 percent conversion rate is elevated to 4 percent, that constitutes a 100 percent increase. This usually leads to profitability. One hundred percent growth tends to make people fat and happy.

That's one reason why the conversion rate game is only played on a portion of the playing field. Most websites optimize and test paths leading from the home page to the shopping cart (or lead-generation form). Many have milked their Web analytics dry and can only squeeze out another few drops of conversion here and there. Others have A/B tested everything they can think of, with only incremental improvements. Still others see so many opportunities, they don't know how or where to start or, more important, how to manage multiple conversion paths.

If conversion rate optimization were a football game, most teams have been trying to get to the end zone only with a simple, straight-up-the-middle running play offense. No wonder they can't move the conversion football more than a few yards at a time.

If all your visitors were exactly the same in personality, product need, and buying preference, you could use this simple conversion strategy and theoretically achieve as close to a 100 percent conversion rate as possible.

Current conversion rate optimization deals with and measures what is. It can tell you what's going wrong, and where. In some cases, it can indicate why things happen on your website. But you must also take into account what could be.

Take a more inclusive, holistic approach to converting more visitors. In other words, instead of trying to drag a 12 percent conversion rate, kicking and screaming, up to 13 or 14 percent, put the ball in the air and aim to convert all your potential customers.

Even if your website is among the best performing, 88 percent refuse to tread down the same, tired conversion path you've been optimizing for a year or two. If that path were the one they wanted to click through, don't you think they would have by now?

Just Keep Experimenting

There are truly thousands of improvements, big and small, you can make to improve your conversion rate. Some are obvious and should be made immediately, and many of them cost nothing to implement.

Nevertheless, you should focus on changing one thing at a time. If you change too many things at once, you may see a net increase in sales, but a change that had a negative impact may have diluted a change that had a positive impact.

The best strategy is to make one change, see that it gives you "X" percent increase in sales, and then make another change. If you start losing sales after the second change, just undo what you did and try something else, always moving your conversion rate up.

"...a fixed aim furnishes us with a fixed measure, by which we can decide whether such or such an action proposed is worth trying for or not, and as aims must vary with the individual, the decisions of any two people as to the desirableness of an action may not be the same." - Anna C. Brackett, *The Technique of Rest*

It's All about Testing and Metrics

The Butterfly Effect, familiar to those who have even a passing knowledge of Chaos Theory, grants the power to cause a hurricane in China to a butterfly flapping its wings in New Mexico. If the butterfly had not flapped its wings at just the right point in space/time, the hurricane would not have happened. This theory should be familiar ground for Internet marketers, who understand that small changes can lead to drastic changes in results. It is often the very small variations, infinitesimally minute, possibly unobserved, like the butterfly flapping its wings that can have extraordinary impact on the final outcome.

Do not assume that any of the basic elements of your website, buttons, background colors or a couple of words, are unimportant. Many marketers treat these as incidental design decisions, but they actually can't be ignored as they are all part of your persuasion architecture.

How do you know which elements are important. Test everything! And then keep testing some more (sometimes a change that had a dramatic impact one week can fizzle out the next). The process we advocate is an ongoing system-wide process of measuring, testing and optimizing for conversion. This will provide those little victories that lead to "the winning edge".

"The winning edge" is what makes a winner a winner whether the winner is your website or an athletic team. The winning edge is what will determine if your website is a winner or a loser, whether it engages your traffic to take the action you want (converts, or not). Remember no detail is too small. Everything on your website and every element of your shopping cart either adds to or detracts from its ability to convert your traffic.

What Should Be Measured?

There are just ten business metrics or operating measurements that an e-tailer must track to measure performance: visitors, conversion rate, sales, average sale, gross revenue, margin, gross profit, overhead, net profit and growth.

Of the ten metrics that you need to track, only these five are key metrics:

- Visitors
- Conversion rate
- Average sale
- Margin
- Overhead

Why are these five the key metrics and not the other five? Simply because the key metrics are the only ones you can do anything about. You have absolutely no control over the other five metrics. They are simply the mathematical results of the key metrics. By exercising control over the key metrics, you can improve your business. The starting point is to make the decision and then put someone in charge. Then, establish and use a "system" for measuring, testing and optimizing your website.

Using a system can help you:

- Get more and better qualified visitors
- Learn what visitors really want
- Present better and increase your conversion rate
- Price more accurately
- Increase the effectiveness of your merchandizing
- Understand your errors and learn from your mistakes
- Train others

Should you use such a system? Of course. It makes good business sense. Did you know there are still many businesses that rigorously measure their key metrics offline, but don't apply the same discipline online? There are businesses that do not know how many visitors their website gets in a given month and have no idea how many visitors made a purchase. Without this information, they have no idea if it is the persuasion architecture of their website or the marketing that is working or not working. This information is far more important than the forensic data of revenue and net profit that come after website results.

What we advocate is a system similar to what the Japanese call kaizen; steady, regular, incremental, unrelenting growth. More visitors, higher conversion rates, bigger sales and fatter margins are the payoff. Focusing on the five key metrics is how you can achieve triple digit gains from single digit improvements.

It takes more patience, a high degree of planning and more work up front to get results. It is why so many businesses tread water or produce anemic results. They simply lack the corporate stamina to take on the task. It's the exceptional manager or entrepreneur who is willing to roll up her sleeves, question the value of the business and commit to constant improvement. That is what it takes to be successful. It won't come out of a black box, you can't buy it from a consultant and it will be more painful, at first, than profitable. Ask yourself; are you ready to commit to success?

"Trust men, and they will be true to you; treat them greatly, and they will show themselves great, though they make an exception in your favor to all their rules of trade." - Ralph Waldo Emerson, Prudence

Persuasion — Moving Beyond Trust and Credibility

Trust and credibility are vital to making a website persuasive. If you can't establish trust and credibility, your website won't persuade. But there's an even more important element in the persuasion mix, as we'll soon show.

Persuasion is impossible without appealing to a person's emotions. No decision, no matter how logically justified, is made without emotions. Even the most logical decision is a source of pride, satisfaction, happiness, and/or beauty to the decision maker. At a 2001 scientific conference, Dr. Dean Shibata presented a study based on brain activity imaging that reveals emotions are inextricably a part of the decision process. According to Shibata, "If you eliminate the emotional guiding factors, it's impossible [for people] to make decisions in daily life."

People with damaged prefrontal lobes — where emotions are processed — are completely stymied when making decisions such as determining what to buy.

So what's more important than trust and credibility? Confidence! Without confidence nobody is willing to buy anything. According to The American Heritage Dictionary, confidence is "a feeling of assurance, especially of self-assurance."

How often have you gone shopping only to return home empty-handed? You weren't sure at that time that you'd found the right thing, but later you bought the item. Did the item improve? No, you became confident enough that the item would meet your need or solve your problem. The best forms of persuasion are never based on pressure, deception, trickery, or gimmicks. True persuasion is nothing less than a transfer of confidence.

The trust and credibility your website communicates is critical in helping visitors feel confident in purchasing from you. For example, I trust Citibank and its credibility beyond reproach. But I wouldn't look to Citibank for advice on my dog's nutritional needs. No matter how easy Citibank's dog food was to find, how quickly the information downloaded, how beautifully presented the merchandise was, or how inexpensive it was, I still wouldn't purchase. Why? It has to do with my dog-food buying process.

I buy the same brand of dog food out of habit. There was a time when I was in the market for dog food and was persuaded to buy a certain brand. Would I change brands? Perhaps, but the competition would need to introduce a threat or an opportunity that would make me lose confidence in the brand I currently buy.

Building your visitor's self-assurance is based on answering the questions visitors are asking. The more relevant the information you present, the closer it matches how visitors want it presented, the more confidence you help build. Only by applying persuasion architecture can you plan with empathy exactly what it will take for visitors to feel confident about choosing your product or service.

Put yourself in your potential customers' shoes. If the shoes are too tight or too loose, brush up on your empathic skills and approach your website just as they would — without your level of knowledge. Be honest with yourself. Are you giving visitors that extra edge? Are you telling them that piece of information they haven't found in your other literature? Are you talking to them in a way they appreciate? Are you presenting to them differently based on what their needs are? Are you in fact inspiring their confidence?

Persuasion vs. Basic Optimization

As we've said, clicks are people. Each has different needs, capabilities, preferences, and expectations.

The same conversion goal, or a singular conversion path, for everyone is foolproof recipe for mediocrity in website performance. Instead, use scenario design to help create, define, and measure more effective conversion paths.

Different visitors are in different stages of the buying cycle. They need different volumes and types of information. Does your website account for these variances? Do you even have the answers and information each type of visitor may seek?

Some visitors have drastically different motivations for buying. Have you addressed each motivation in your copy and trigger words?

Some visitors require multiple visits before they're ready to convert. Have you planned proper first, second, and beyond visit conversion scenarios and strategies for them?

Have you sorted out the types of hyperlinks you should include on pages? Do your point-of-resolution links create resolving doors for point-of-action links?

Then, there's audience segmentation. Visitors enter your website from several channels, carrying different expectations based on the channel that got them there. Have you planned appropriate paths (not just landing pages) for those who enter your website organically? For those who enter from banner ads, e-mail, or media campaigns?

Many companies establish conversion funnels for measuring performance for these channels but put little thought into how a conversion path may need to be planned differently based on context. In such cases, scenario design will rationalize all on- and offline sales efforts into a seamless whole, consistently relevant across all channels.

Using Web analytics and A/B testing exclusively for conversion rate optimization is better than doing nothing. But it's still entry-level persuasion.

And finally, remember that persuasion isn't site-wide. It applies to outside elements, such as pay-per-click (PPC) ads, e-mail, banners, and offline collateral. Explore every possible question or issue. Architect those persuasive paths to a close.

"Every man, who knows to the minutest details all the complexity of the conditions surrounding him, cannot help imagining that the complexity of these conditions, and the difficulty of making them clear, is something exceptional and personal, peculiar to himself, and never supposes that others are surrounded by just as complicated an array of personal affairs as he is." - Leo Tolstoy, Anna Karenina

Does Sales Complexity Really Make a Difference?

We recently overheard a fellow talking about "the simplicity of the B2C sale." He was comparing it to the complexity of the "considered purchase," B2B sale. We were amused, not at the thought one sale might be more complex than another, but at the thought that B2C sales, simply because they are B2C, are inherently less complicated. We wondered if that guy has ever bought a house or a car, booked a cruise, applied for a loan or tried to research dietary strategies that might remediate cancer.

Your business category is not the issue. The complexity of your sale is not the issue. Whether your sale is "impulse" or a "considered purchase" is not the issue. Buying into these notions as determining factors when it comes to your ability to design persuasively is thinking that will lead you down the garden path.

Understanding and managing your sale as a persuasive process is the only relevant issue.

Does "Considered Purchase" Make a Difference?

Let's take a closer look at what many consider a complex sale category, the "considered purchase." Ever try to get a handle on what, exactly, constitutes a considered purchase? Most folks agree it doesn't include the impulse buy, but beyond that, things get pretty confusing. I did a little Google search on "considered purchase" and discovered the following, in no particular order:

- It includes the things you might find listed in comparative consumer reports like travel, electronics, furniture, and high-end cookware.
- A considered purchase costs more money, has less market competition, and is a more unique product.
- One business described their service as follows: "With content that ranges from food to furniture and from exercise equipment to electronics, including consumables, durables, daily needs, and considered-purchase items, [we] can help the consumer with all of her shopping needs." So, that means consumables, durables and daily needs aren't considered purchases?

Does B2B Make a Difference?

Very often you will find a fuzzy sort of thinking about the distinctions between B2B and B2C:

One thing differentiating business to business marketing from consumer marketing is a product's price tag. B to b purchases, like machine tools or enterprise software, usually start in the six-figure range. This is why the average b to b sale involves seven decision makers ... [and] why b to b marketers call them "considered purchases." Consumer goods are a bit cheaper and less risky to buy. [1]

In business to business, most transactions are a considered purchase. Example: no one runs out and buys 13 jet engines on a lark. There are no frequent buyer programs for $250,000 machine tools or $500,000 enterprise software solutions. A mentor distinguished consumer purchases from business to business purchases like this: "Buying the wrong toothpaste leaves a bad taste in your mouth. Making the wrong business to business purchase can cost you your job." And that's just one reason why these sales are complex. [2]

How much time do you want to spend debating the classification of your sales process? Does it really make a difference if it focuses on considered sales or B2B? It is certain that it won't bring you an inch closer to being able to design an effective, persuasive website. And since nobody seems the least bit clear when it comes to classification schemes, I figure it falls into the realm of utterly pointless activity.

Forget the categories. Think in terms of your persuasive process.

The Persuasive Process

At the most elemental level, commercial websites come in four flavors (we bother with these categories only because they help shape the nature of the Web analytics we employ to test, measure and optimize) – every commercial website you'll come across is a subset or combination of one of these four variations: e-commerce, content, lead-generation and self-service.

And here's what every online business has in common:

- Each business has an ultimate conversion goal.
- Each business has a series of steps (each one of these a separate point of conversion) that ideally help folks achieve that ultimate conversion goal.
- Each business has an audience made up of folks who have their own agendas and their own ways of satisfying their agendas.

Once you've figured out what you're trying to accomplish through your website – your business objective – you turn to understanding your persuasive process by answering these three questions:

- Who needs to be persuaded? When you know whom you need to persuade, you can create personas that allow you to design meaningful navigation scenarios.
- What actions does this person need to take? Not all actions will be direct functions of your sales process; many will be actions your personas need to take to satisfy their buying decision process.
- How will you most effectively persuade that person? Knowing "who" and "what" helps you create persuasive copy and content.

Persuasive Momentum — Every Click Requires a Decision

The essence of the Internet experience is how visitors click from one hyperlink to the next. How they feel about that experience is determined by whether each click fulfills the visitors' expectations and needs. Satisfaction with each click (a micro-action) increases their confidence they'll get what they came for (the goal or macro-action).

The click, then, is the essence of your persuasive process. Every click represents a question your visitor is asking. It represents your visitor's willingness to try to stay engaged with you (for now). It represents a unique point of conversion. It represents continued persuasive momentum. If your visitors don't click, communication ceases and persuasive momentum evaporates.

No matter how complex the sale, every persuasive process unfolds click-by-click, one micro-action conversion at a time.

The Militating Factors in Your Sale — Things That Really DO Make a Difference

No two sales are alike. But whatever you sell, certain factors pertain to the buying decisions your audience has to make. These factors are critical to shaping your persuasive process, and are the most important reasons why you have to map your audience's buying processes to your selling process. These are the factors that will determine the intricacy of your website's persuasive process:

- Knowledge. How difficult is it for prospective buyers to understand the nature of your product or service, or the procedures for buying? What do they need to know? Your persuasive process must eliminate the friction generated by confusion or lack of knowledge. Knowledge dimensions for the buying decision can differ based on who is doing the buying: is the customer buying for herself (she will be the end user) or is she buying on behalf of another (as in the case of a purchasing agent)? The knowledge assumptions and language – especially jargon – that work for one may be totally inappropriate for the other.

- Need. How urgent is the need for your product or service? How fast are prospects likely to make their decisions to buy? Will the need be satisfied by a one-time purchase (impulsive or momentous) or is the need on-going? Prospects might be willing to compromise their thoroughness for a casual one-time deal. But if that one-time deal is something like a house, or if they are choosing a long-term relationship to satisfy an on-going need, things get significantly more complicated.

- Risk. How risky, especially with respect to issues of finance, is the sale? While price may not be an ultimate decision factor in a purchase (for many, safety and trust trump price), increasing financial risk necessitates a more intricate persuasive structure. Risk may also be associated with compromises to health, as when individuals or medical professionals have to make treatment choices. Or even, for that matter, when someone simply evaluates the safety of an herbal remedy.

- Consensus. Just how many people do you have to persuade? An individual? An individual and her significant other? Several end-users and heads-of-department? Your ability to understand who is involved in the decision-making process allows you to provide copy and content that appropriately informs, reassures and persuades.

These factors apply differently depending on the nature of your sale. For example, home computers aren't a terribly high-risk product anymore, but lots of consumers find them unfathomable beasts, and they'll take their time acquiring information before deciding to buy one (unless their one and only computer upon which their sole-proprietor business depends just got zapped by lightning and must be replaced by tomorrow noon).

By the same token, you might take a while to consider the purchase of a water-heater if you are building a new house, but if your existing water heater goes up the spout, you need to replace it pronto. Almost no one would say a pencil is a considered purchase – knowledge of pencils isn't much of a problem and there's generally no risk associated – but if the purchase of a case of pencils or a single pencil from a new vender requires several departments to sign off, consensus is an issue.

These factors can also be interdependent. Take knowledge. The more you know about something, the more you may perceive the risks involved. Conversely, more knowledge may afford you the perception of less risk. The individual facing heart surgery will consider the relationship between knowledge and risk differently than will the heart surgeon. As will the individual investor staking his life earnings on options, compared to the options trader for whom these transactions are daily occurrences.

B2C, B2B, impulse purchases, straightforward purchases, considered purchases, non-profit, lead-generation . . . it doesn't really matter. If you understand all the elements that make up your unique persuasive process and if you understand your audience, you will be able to apply persuasive principles to greatest effect. You, too, can have your website converting like a wild thing. Trust me. Persuasion isn't just the best game in town . . . it's the only game in town!

[1] Strategic Public Relations. http://prblog.typepad.com/strategic_public_relation/2003/08/the_considered_.html

[2] Strategic Public Relations. http://prblog.typepad.com/strategic_public_relation/2002/08/

"The philosopher believes that the value of his philosophy lies in its totality, in its structure: posterity discovers it in the stones with which he built and with which other structures are subsequently built that are frequently better—and so, in the fact that that structure can be demolished and yet still possess value as material." - Friedrich Nietzsche

So, What Is Value?

As we discovered in the previous chapter, value is not directly connected to price. If value is not price, then just what is it? Alas! It has many faces. So how would you define this elusive value that your visitors are finding at your website? Can you provide a definition that supports and reinforces your persuasive process? It's a trick question. There is no one way of looking at value, but there are qualities in the broad concept of value that your particular business will answer differently for each of the different visitors to your website.

If there is no perception of value, the visitor is gone. But you ... stick around! Mohanbir Sawhney, McCormick Tribune Professor of Technology at Northwestern University's Kellogg School of Management, organized his ideas on the nature of value into seven over-arching qualities. The words (abridged) are his.

Value is customer-defined. Never forget that value is defined by those who use and those who pay for it. To understand the true nature of value, you need to get inside the minds and hearts of your customers, whether they're internal or external. Vendors must communicate the value of their products not in terms of what these products do, but what they do for customers, expressed in a language that customers can relate to.

Value is opaque. An important consequence of value being defined by customers is that it is very difficult to quantify. You need to understand all factors that customers take into consideration in assessing value, and you have to understand the relative importance that customers place on each factor. In the absence of this understanding, you are shooting in the dark. Once you understand the factors that specific customers consider when making decisions and how they make trade-offs, you can develop a better understanding of the value propositions that might appeal to each one.

Value is multi-dimensional. A common myth in business is that decisions are made solely on functional value, that is, a product's features and functionality. Value has two other dimensions as well: economic value; what these features and functions are worth to customers in terms of time and money and psychological value; the emotional benefits that customers get from your products or your company.

Value is a trade-off. Value is the perceived worth of something in relation to the total cost that customers pay for it. This definition underscores the fact that value is a trade-off between costs and benefits.

Value is contextual. You cannot divorce the value of [something] from the context in which it will be used . . . . Unless you understand the end-usage context, you run the risk of creating value propositions and offerings that are irrelevant for customers.

Value is relative. Customers never assess the value of an offering in isolation. They always consider value relative to alternatives. These alternatives may not be other products or systems, but other ways of accomplishing the same goals or doing nothing at all . . . . By understanding competing alternatives, you will also be able to focus on points of differentiation relative to these options and ignore points of parity that clutter and dilute your value proposition.

Value is a mind-set. The value mind-set is grounded in the belief that the sole purpose of a company is to create value for its customers and to be compensated equitably for its efforts. Therefore, everything the company says and does should revolve around its customers, not its products. This is a radical shift in perspective, and few companies truly embrace this idea despite their claims of being customer-focused. [1]

And, The Value Is?

The value of whatever you are doing in cyberspace lives solely in the minds of your visitors. They decide what value means to them, and then they look to you to see if you provide it. So ask yourself if your persuasive system identifies the qualities of value that are important to your visitors. And then ask yourself if your website truly communicates these values effectively. As you read the rest of Call to Action and begin to implement changes on your website, always ask: "Is this adding value for my customer – however value is defined?"

Conversion Measures Defined

Conversion rate is one of your most important key performance indicators (KPI). While it's certainly not the only measure you should use to ascertain website health, its value cannot be overestimated. Given the emphasis on conversion in this book, we believe it will be helpful to provide some definitions up front. You can refer to this tip whenever you have a question regarding what's what.

Conversion Rate: The number of visitors who took the action you wanted on your site divided by the total number of visitors. It is, in essence, a measure of your ability to persuade visitors to take the action(s) you want them to take.

Macro-conversion: End-goal conversion, like a purchase, which may be composed of many other conversion points (Micro-conversion).

Micro-conversion: One of a series of decisions taken by the visitor on the way to Macro-conversion. The evidence of a micro-conversion is clicks (measurable Micro-conversions).

Overall conversion rate: Total number of actions considered conversion divided by total number of visits. This is a site's overall effectiveness rating for getting visitors to fulfill your goals within a single visit. However, it should be used with caution, since it doesn't account for people having numerous goals (not identical to yours) when visiting a Web site. It provides a less accurate picture of how effectively a Web site serves people and accomplishes your goals on a per-visit basis. Its best use is for evaluation of broad, sweeping changes. Use it to evaluate the results of a site redesign, a specific marketing campaign, or new site-search technology.

Scenario conversion rate: Total number of visitors starting a specific scenario divided by total number who complete it. Scenario conversion rates enable you to quickly identify specific conversion processes (e.g. marketing campaigns, affiliate relationships, or pay-per-click (PPC) search engine keywords) that require improvement or ones whose successes should be modeled. Everything on your site: new content, navigation, new link anchor text, promotions, calls to action, or merchandising, can be measured to determine if it contributes or detracts from the scenario conversion rate.

There are two types of scenario conversions:

- Linear — Created when visitors need to complete a registration process or checkout process.
- Non-linear — Created by visitor segments as they navigate your website. These scenarios can either be explicitly planned or implicit. Measurement begins where people start the scenario (the driving point) and ends where they complete the intended scenario (conversion point) and whether or not they hit key value pages. Explicitly planning these non-linear scenarios is what we call "Persuasion Architecture."

Conversion over time: Several measures that reveal a site's effectiveness in generating conversions over time. Use this for situations where conversion is likely to occur over time or multiple visits. This is why measuring conversion rates as buying sessions over total sessions is not always the best way to calculate conversion rates.

To understand conversion over time for your site, these visitor history measures are useful:

- Days between first visit and first purchase. "Purchase" can be any form of conversion you define, such as collecting lead-generation information.
- Number of visits between purchases. How many visits occur before more purchases are made? Use this to understand repeat buying behavior of audience segments.
- Days since most recent purchase. How recently have visitor segments made purchases?
- Number of total purchases (purchase count) and lifetime value. How many purchases have visitors made, and what is their lifetime value?

Other measures that may prove helpful in addition to the ones provided above include visitor frequency, recency and latency by purchase count, and lifetime value. More information will be provided about these later in the book.

---

1 "Fundamentals of Value: To achieve a value mind-set, focus relentlessly on customers." Mohanbir Sawhney. CIO. http://www.cio.com/archive/070103/gain.html.

"If you don't know where you're going, any road will do" - Lewis Carroll, *Alice in Wonderland*

Planning

Planning involves everything that happens before a visitor reaches your site. It includes steps that you take to get traffic to your site — the creation of the elements for the clickstream and the storyboard of your site that guide visitors once they are there. It includes strategic marketing planning, such as the development of your UVP (unique value proposition), based on your understanding of the marketplace and targeted customers, and your brand and brand positioning. Planning is about understanding your visitors, so you can anticipate their knowledge levels, moods and mindsets.

Planning also includes making conscious distinctions concerning the roles of those in marketing and sales. It requires an understanding of where these two disciplines complement one another, and where they make related yet very separate contributions to an organization's business success.

In short, planning is "getting your act together" before putting resources in motion. Good planning not only brings good results but provides good results while maximizing return on your investments of time, energy and dollars.

"Every time a message seems to grab us, and we think, "I just might try it," we are at the nexus of choice and persuasion that is advertising." - Andrew Hacker, Professor of Political Science, Queens College, New York Times

The Incredibly Condensed History of Persuasion and Sales

Virtually all web sites have a persuasive purpose; to get someone to subscribe, to register, to inquire or to buy something. To better grasp the concept of persuasion and sales we need to trace back through time and observe the evolution of sales. Notice how each step in the evolution of sales seems to make the purchase easier for the buyer and harder on the vendor. Each step seems to remove some of the friction buyers feel and makes the purchase process smoother for the buyer.

Depending on your religious persuasion you may or may not believe that the first sale involved an apple; if not, sales of some sort is certainly the world's oldest profession even if it involved some form of inexact exchange in the form of barter. In ancient times someone would have chickens, and you would have cows; and we would decide how many chickens were worth exchanging for a cow. Obviously, this system was inefficient for both parties; since one party might have needed ducks and not chickens. This is how trade fairs and open marketplaces developed, so that many trades could be made simultaneously until each party got approximately what they came for. Until money came along, goods and services were difficult to value since barter required so many trades and middlemen.

Money became the standard, and this evolutionary step made it easier to exchange value since every product and service had a monetary value assigned to it by the free market. You either paid the value or not. Eventually, vendors decided it made sense to aggregate in one area, so that all the buyers could meet them. This created a larger market for the vendors but also opened them up for competition on price and selection. Even then merchants would develop reputations for expertise in one product line or service line.

Eventually the market evolved to where open air vendors established specialized stores. Stores were able to offer greater convenience and more inventory because they no longer had to travel around. Stores became bigger and concentrated in commercial districts and that, of course, led to malls. So now in addition to a large selection of stores that offered one-stop shopping, buyers could also be fed and amused.

When catalogs appeared, they offered specialty products the stores couldn't carry and remote shopping for those buyers who did not have stores near them. The Sears catalog was transported along railroad lines. The catalog brought the far-away nearer to the buyer so they could shop from home.

If people could buy from their homes, then why not take the old "barker" style of selling and present it to them right through their television, while they were feeling comfortable. That's exactly what QVC & HSN offered. These elaborate interactive catalogs were a huge success with buyers who could now buy while they sat on their sofas with a phone in one ear and a remote control in their other hand.

In the late 1990's the Internet was going to change everything. The promise was to trump QVC and HSN with interactive, on-demand catalogs that would be available 24/7, 365 days a year, with unlimited options to choose from, lots of competitors to decide between and all the strangest things you could imagine waiting to be found (check out eBay). This was simply one more foreseeable evolutionary step for buyers.

The next phase of online sales history is going to belong to those who grasp and correctly apply the concept of what might be called a digital salesperson: a website that: performs all the functions an expert human salesperson would in the real world; is able to guide the prospect through all five steps of a professional sale; acknowledges how different people want to be sold; and can adapt to those needs.

The bottom line: each evolutionary step forced the merchant to work harder to remove friction from the buyer's experience in a systematic way. The Internet offers a virtually frictionless way for consumers to buy, which means that we must work that much harder to persuade and inform buyers since they are only one-click from your competitor across the globe. As a merchant you have to decide if you will: do the hard work; leave it up to the buyer; or let your competitor do it. It's up to you; the buyer is always one-click away from goodbye.

"He had noticed often that even in actual praise, technique was opposed to essential quality, as though one could paint well something that was bad." – Leo Tolstoy, Anna Karenina

Web Marketing Fundamentals #1:
Accidental Marketing (or Seduced by Technique)

It's frightening to watch people get all excited about new technology that allows them to perform miracles and then track the results of their miracles with thousands of metrics — when those miracles have little or nothing to do with actually converting traffic or closing a sale.

So what's wrong with the latest and greatest marketing tools? Nothing at all is wrong with them per se. However, we'd like you to picture the following scenario:

We decide to get into the entertainment business, perhaps making movies, since conventional wisdom says you can make big money from it. We find some investors, buy some great real estate for the studio, buy all the latest equipment, negotiate awesome distribution deals, contract with some high-priced talent (how about Tom Hanks and Julia Roberts — let's not spare a dime), then spend like mad on advertising for a movie about. . . how wall paint dries differently in different climates.

Can you imagine how unsuccessful we'd be? It's not the tools of the trade (the "how") that would cause us to fail but rather the "what" and the "why." The two questions we failed to ask are, "What will people perceive as valuable enough to pay for?" and, "Why can we provide it better than the competition?"

It's obvious, at least to most of us, that even if we buy the same basketball shoes as Michael Jordan, that alone won't give us his abilities.

Great marketers, like great athletes, aren't born that way; they are trained to develop their natural abilities and hone their skills. Persuading people to take action is both an art and a science requiring lots of intelligent planning by professionals trained in the fundamentals of marketing and in exactly how marketing needs to be done to support sales.

Here's the definition of marketing according to the American Marketing Association:

Marketing is the process of planning and executing the conception, pricing, promotion, and distribution of ideas, goods, and services to create exchanges that satisfy individual and organizational objectives.

Did you notice how broad that definition is? Is that what you think of when you think of marketing? In most companies, the marketing department is dominated by either creative or analytical personalities. Instead of looking at the marketing process as a holistic strategy concerned with the objectives of the larger business, the process becomes tactical and emphasizes analyzing or separates it into parts. It's this sort of myopia that is the leading cause of accidental marketing, which is getting customers in ways that have nothing to do with, or even in spite of, your marketing program.

By now you may be anxiously thinking, "How can I tell if my business is practicing accidental marketing?" As you continue to read, be brutally honest with yourself about your responses to the following questions:

- What came first, the idea for your product or service, or the understanding that there was a market need that needed fulfilling? If you answered the idea came first, that's a big red flag.
- Who are your customers?
- What do they really need?
- What benefits (not features) of your product or service satisfy the real needs of your customers?
- What about your product or service is unique, and how can you answer the customer's question, "Why should I buy from you?"
- What other options does a customer have to buying your product or service (including doing nothing at all)? Are they better options, or worse?
- How does a customer make a decision to buy products or services like yours?
- What does your customer need to know before he or she will buy from you?
- How does your customer perceive not only your product, but also your company compared to your competition?
- What is the process a customer goes through before buying your products or services?
- What is the value of your product or service to the client? (This is not the price.)
- What would a customer say if a colleague asked him or her to recommend your product or service?

If you and your marketing department don't have detailed answers to all of the above questions easily rolling off your tongues, then you are most likely engaged in accidental marketing.

Also, if you have one or more of these symptoms, you are engaged in "accidental marketing":

- More effort is spent discussing how things look than what they convey.
- More effort is spent tracking metrics than understanding what they really show of customer perception and customer behavior.
- More effort is spent explaining what you offer than listening to what your customers want.
- More effort is spent attracting prospective customers than figuring out how to convert the ones you already get to customers.
- More effort is spent attracting new customers than keeping existing ones.
- More effort is spent looking for and implementing the latest and greatest technical gimmick than adapting time-tested persuasion principles that have been proven to work.
- Marketing doesn't talk to sales or doesn't respect its input.

Whether "accidental marketing" becomes a buzzword any time soon really doesn't matter. What does matter is that those who persist in practicing it won't be around long — and those who don't won't miss those who do.

"Who is it in first place, my lord?" In a halting voice the Marquis replied, "I'm sorry to report, Madam, it seems it is the yacht America." "The yacht America" asked the Queen, "Then who is in second?" The Marquis, in a restrained voice filled with that profound respect an English gentleman reserves for his Queen, answered softly, "Madam, there is no second." – Queen Victoria, on learning that England had lost the first America's Cup race

Web Marketing Fundamentals #2: Looking for the Winning Edge

Your pulse races and your hands are fastened onto your ticket as the chestnut 3-year-old flies into the homestretch. You whisper a prayer as you watch her cross the finish line. You listen anxiously to the announcement. It's a photo finish, too close to call. She almost won the race. She lost by a nose. Disappointed and frustrated, you rip up your ticket.

The first-place horse won 10 times the prize money that the second-place horse did. That's just how the purse gets divided. Have you ever considered why this is? Was the winner 10 times better than the second-place horse? Hardly, the win was only won by a nose. What makes the winner a winner is a concept called "the winning edge."

I read an excellent article by Allen Weiss of MarketingProfs.com entitled "Why Marketing Is Soft, but Hard." It reminded me of the concept's importance. I was introduced to the concept when I was first learning about sales and marketing. One of my early mentors drilled it into me that "everything you do either enhances or detracts from your ability to close the sale. No detail, however minute, is neutral." I was intrigued by that concept, and he recommended that I listen to an audiocassette by Brian Tracy titled "The Psychology of Selling: The Art of Closing the Sale." It's Tracy who drilled that horseracing image indelibly into my mind.

As Allen Weiss explains in his article, it's hard to really understand simple ideas. In fact, it's often harder than remembering complicated ideas. With complicated ideas, like those in mathematics, software coding, and finance, we tend to really "get it" because we spend so much time trying to understand the ideas.

With simpler ideas we tend to spend little energy (often because we think that it warrants little energy to understand) and often mistakenly think that we understand something because it appears to be simple.

In a lot of ways marketing is simple. For example, the basic ideas behind branding are actually very few. Still, people like to see these same ideas presented in thousands of different ways. People want thousands of different examples that expose the same basic idea — isn't this a waste of time and money?

The reason for this seemingly strange inefficiency is that marketing is based on tacit know-how. Tacit know-how is difficult to write down and can only be learned by doing. Learning to play an instrument is based on tacit know-how, as is learning to cook and virtually every other practice that requires reading/learning and then doing (many, many times) before you really understand it.

We are constantly researching and testing concepts and techniques that produce exceptional results. You don't have to read about consumer psychology, social anthropology, usability, chaos theory, physiology, color theory, perception, sales, marketing, information architecture, and all the various other materials that we read. And why, you may ask? It's simple. We want you to develop the winning edge.

All the information you need is out there. That doesn't mean you may not occasionally need some help, and, if you'd like us to, we're happy to provide it. What we mean is that if you have the burning desire to win, then it's up to you to gain that winning edge by constantly improving your website's conversion rate.

Remember that no detail is too small; everything on your Web site either adds or detracts from its ability to convert your traffic. And remember, too, that the one in second place is the first loser. How badly do you really want to win?

". . . the widow walked up to him with the acidulous sweet smile of a cautious shopkeeper who is anxious neither to lose money nor to offend a customer." - Honoré de Balzac, Old Goriot

Web Marketing Fundamentals #3: Acquiring and Understanding Customers (Plus Thoughts on CRM)

Have you been bombarded with the latest buzz suggesting we should spend time, resources, and money on online customer relationship management (CRM) software? Talk about putting the cart before the horse! Oh, the idea is pointed in the right direction, all right — but don't you think you first need a satisfied customer base to manage?

Your goal, of course, is lots of satisfied customers — happy ones who become loyal, repeat buyers as well as active referrers. But just because they bought from you once, doesn't mean you have a relationship with them — yet. In fact, for all you know, they're not coming back and maybe for a very good reason.

First, you have to create an online shopping experience that plants the seeds of a real relationship. Then, you have to nurture those seeds with outstanding fulfillment and customer service. Building a relationship takes time. Shoving some tech-heavy CRM application at your customers is more likely to push them away than draw them in. If you want to get it right, you need to follow not CRM, but MRC: Manage your e-business correctly so that you can establish a relationship in which you can develop a delighted and loyal customer. Only then can all the other stuff you do have the impact you want.

Lots of e-businesses have the software to facilitate CRM, and lots of software vendors would love to sell you some if you don't have it yet. Nevertheless, most businesses don't have the in-depth customer knowledge they need to use the technology effectively. They wind up getting carried away with trying to manage what they don't actually have.

According to David Sims, a smart customer relations expert with common sense:

Everybody who profits from CRM has their own definition of what it is, but they're agreed as to what it is not: CRM isn't about technology any more than hospitality is about throwing a welcome mat on your front porch.

Properly understood, CRM is "a philosophy that puts the customer at the design point, it's getting intimate with the customer," [in the words of Liz Shahnam, CRM analyst with the META Group]. Mike Littell, president of the CRM division of EDS, agrees: "We view CRM more as a strategy than a process. It's designed to understand and anticipate the needs of the current and potential customer base a company has." Once you nail that, Littell says, there's "a plethora of technology out there that helps capture customer data and external sources, and consolidate it in a central warehouse to add intelligence to the overall CRM strategy."

In short, first get a happy customer base, and then you've got something to manage. To put it more bluntly, poor customer service can lose you a customer and leave you with nothing to manage.

Almost every one of us has had the following problem: You go to a website, run into a snag making a purchase, and decide to call customer service. But the lines at customer service are all busy. Do they put you on hold? No! They tell you to go to the website! Didn't you just come from there?

So, before you go spending your money on CRM, spend a little time — no, a LOT of time — considering how effective you are at MRC — Managing your e-business correctly so you can establish a Relationship from which you can develop a delighted and loyal Customer. Only then can all the other stuff you do have the impact you want. That's where it all starts, and if you get it wrong, that's also where it all ends.

"Dogs, when they have lost scent, "cast for it," i.e. spread out and search in different directions to recover it." - E. Cobham Brewer, Dictionary of Phrase and Fable

Site Planning #1: What to Do When the Customers Show Up (Clue: Don't Frustrate Them)

Do you ever get really frustrated? We sure do. One thing that frustrates us big-time is when we read all the e-commerce and Internet-related newsletters in our inboxes (about 50 per day) droning on about technology solutions.

Hey, we're not Luddites. We enjoy the benefits of technology and think it's a wonderful thing. Nevertheless, technology is much easier to come by than common sense.

Every time we see a website that sucks, we can hear in the background the happy chatter of its designers, developers, and programmers: "That's really cool. The customers? They'll figure it out. In fact, once they do, they'll love it." These well-meaning people sure put a lot of faith in the patience, motivation, and resilience of their visitors. Yet despite their best intentions, they're actually hurting sales, not helping them. They seem to forget that customers are always one click away from goodbye!

Picture This Trip

Let's imagine that you excitedly head out in your car to go shopping. You know exactly what you want to buy and where you'll find it in stock at a great price. Along the way, though, you get stuck in a really bad traffic jam. Your car overheats, and your air conditioning quits. After several long hours of sweltering in the heat, you eventually get the problem fixed.

You're back on the road, but what's that? A detour ahead? You thought you followed all the signs, so how come now you're lost? Another hour of wandering and, at last, you locate the store. Naturally, the parking lot is full, and you have to park eight blocks away. Now, you're finally at the front door.

How are you feeling? How tolerant are you going to be if the shopping experience is anything less than delightful?

The Online Equivalent

Now, here's the cyberspace equivalent for most (let us repeat, most) consumers. First, they have to figure out how to use a PC, not to mention the operating system, which is just sooo intuitive. Then, they need to get online, which is a breeze; no learning curve here and no busy signals or disconnects either, right? Then, finally they figure out how a browser works. But, what then?

They now have to figure out how different websites use different navigation methods, hyperlinks, icons, conventions, jargon, frames, and forms. They even have to figure out when to use the "Back" button on the browser as opposed to a link on the page.

For those who need more examples, we've compiled a list of online roadblocks, things that get in the way of customers en route to buying from you:

- Getting on-line. What's an ISP? What do I really need? Why can't I just plug it in and go?
- Learning to use e-mail. Okay . . . I get the bit about not needing stamps . . .
- Learning to use a browser. Omigod, if I click will I cause the Fall of Western Civilization? Whew, I'm there but… how the heck do I get back?
- Learning to use navigation, hyperlinks, frames and forms. Go where …do what … how? How come this flashes at me? Hey, it changes color! Where the heck am I? You want me to give you this information? Why? You just fed the whole form back to me. What did I do wrong?
- Learning to download. What am I letting onto my computer? I go where to install? Help!
- Learning to use plug-ins. I need what to do this? Says who? That's what they think (said while clicking off to the next competitor)!
- Learning about pop-up boxes and drop-down menus. Whoa, where did this come from? What am I supposed to do? Why won't it stay on my screen?
- Deciphering cryptic error messages. It killed my computer! Error 404? Get me out of here!
- Differentiating legitimate business from scams. Who am I to trust when there aren't any faces?

Only after negotiating all these hurdles (and maybe a glass of vodka on the rocks or two) do they arrive at your website. Give them any reason to leave, and they will.

Your customers want to be shopping and buying. Isn't that what you want them to be doing, too? Instead, they're trying to figure out "Where do I go?" "What do I do next?" "How did I get here?" "How do I get back?" And, if all that's not enough, you have to help them get past some well-founded fears in this age of worms, viruses and spyware.

Give them any reason to leave, and they will.

Now, do you have a better appreciation of what your customers are up against? You can't do anything about the frustrations they have endured before they find you. But, once you've finally hooked up, you need to be especially kind to them.

The Majority Rules

The whole trick is realizing your customer is Mr. or Ms. Basic User — not Mr. or Ms. Techno-Whiz.

The Techno-Whizzes will buy no matter what, so you lose nothing by not being too cool for your own good. And, they're the minority. The Basics are the majority, by far. If you want them to stay on your website and buy from you, you have to keep it simple, clear, and consistent.

And no, that doesn't have to mean boring.

Also, contrary to semi-popular belief, people do not want to be surprised while shopping online. They want an experience that's delightful but also predictable, comfortable, and safe. Nor do they want to be entertained. If that's what they want, they'll go to an entertainment website. Adding stuff just for entertainment value only slows the download and distracts from buying. Other than that, it's a great idea…

Remember: While you're (always!) one click away from goodbye, your competitor — who has taken the time and made the effort to create a smooth, simple, consistent, safe, and delightful experience — is just one click away from hello.

Conversion Tip

How Much Are You Leaving on the Table?

Imagine I have a magical device that tells me when anyone who is in a 2 mile radius of where I'm sitting has run out of milk. I drive to their apartment only to find them sitting there with a empty carton of milk and a dry bowl of cereal. I put them into my car and drive them to the nearest 7-Eleven. And, just to ensure they purchase, I give them the money to buy their milk. What are the odds that this person will buy milk in this instance? 100 percent, right? The 7-Eleven would really have to screw up big to not sell milk to this person at this moment.

This is what my company does online. We find people who need products. We bring them to sites that have those products. We give them the cash to buy the products. And we watch to see how the site does at selling the product these people want to them.

The average e-commerce website only manages to sell someone a product they really want, under these odd conditions, 30 percent of the time. 70 percent of the time, the customer who knows exactly what they want runs into some show-stopping obstacle that prevents the purchase.

Look at your annual revenue from your site. Assume that only represents the 30 percent who are successfully purchasing. That means there is another 70 percent (more than twice your current revenue) who is trying to buy from you, but failing. That's the opportunity that you're currently leaving on the table.

We're not even considering the people who haven't decided what they want yet. We're only talking about those people who are ready to purchase from you. There's a very good chance you could double your revenues just by figuring out what is stopping your purchasers from purchasing.

- **Jared Spool**, Usability Guru at User Interface Engineering

"If we all worked on the assumption that what is accepted as true is really true, there would be little hope of advance." - Orville Wright

Site Planning #2: Getting Past the Assumptions That Kill Sales

People make assumptions. It's human nature. It happens based partly because of our experiences, but altogether too often from our impatience ("Hey, I know this already. Let's go on to . . ."). And you know what happens when we assume: some very strange things. Experts and specialists don't have all the answers (In the best cases, we have most of the questions.). But we'd like to clear up some assumptions about on-site sales conversions right now.

Assumption: If you're so good, you can sell me.

False! People who challenge you to sell them are setting a trap for you. Don't fall into it. Our own website includes the words, "The Conversion Rate Specialists: Persuading your visitors to take ACTION." But who are your visitors? Where do they come from? How qualified are they? How motivated are they? Are they able to act on your offer if they want to? Of course, you have to make your offer attractive, even compelling, and you have to provide a clear call to action at the right point of action. But even when you do, not everyone will want what you are offering, and some who do may still not be able to act for reasons that have nothing to do with you. Even those who challenge you to "sell me" may just be asking you to spin your wheels. Target your efforts at prospects that both want and can act on your offer. Don't waste your valuable time and money on the rest.

Assumption: They're on my website, so they must be interested in my product or service.

False! There are four types of Web site visitors:
1. Those who know exactly what they are looking for. For them, your navigation needs to be excellent in order for them to find what they want and buy quickly and easily.
2. Those who are browsing and have a general interest in your offerings. You must give them a strong value proposition that tells them why they should buy from you — if not today, then when they return.
3. Those who are looking for something and are not sure what it is they want. You have to do everything right to sell to them, using the five-step sales process and AIDAS in order to sell them anything. Unfortunately, this is the case with the majority of website traffic.
4. Those who have no interest in your offerings. They arrive out of curiosity, by mistake, or from overly aggressive search engine optimization or other promotional efforts.

Assumption: The Shop.org average customer conversion rate of 1.8 percent is "normal."

False! It's a good reference point, but this statistic drives us crazy. We have clients with conversion rates from 0.35 percent to 77.28 percent. There are so many variables involved. Here's a list with some of the most important variables (in no special order):

- Your brand
- Your offer
- Your perceived value
- Your price
- Degree to which your traffic is targeted
- The season
- Your copywriting
- Your website's usability
- Your website's design
- Your website's navigation
- Your shopping process
- Your policies
- Your guarantees
- Your page layouts
- Your competition (online and offline)

It's a complicated issue, and a simple numerical answer as to what constitutes a good conversion rate misses the point. A good conversion rate is one that at least makes you profitable. A smart business is one that is constantly working to make its conversion rate even better.

Assumption: If you do it right, you can sell anything.

If your value proposition doesn't make sense, or if you're trying to solve a problem nobody thinks they have, or if your service stinks, or if your prices are out of this world, or (insert your favorite business obstacle here) — you don't stand a chance. We constantly get inquiries from companies like WeCanSellOverpriced-IceToEskimosBecauseWeHaveAWebSite.com; they are beyond help. Don't be one of them.

Just because you've migrated to the web, don't forget to incorporate the five key steps (for any type of sale) into your selling process. What are the five steps? Prospect, Rapport, Qualify, Present, Close. If you don't prospect, you have no customer to build rapport with. No rapport = no trust = no sale. As you build rapport you then can qualify your customer and know both what that customer wants and what kind of presentation will work best. This leads to the presentation of the product in the way that works for the customer. If they want data, why make them stare at testimonials? If they want price, why make them sit through a flash demo? If they're ready to give you their money and get the satisfaction of buying, why stop them suddenly and demand a bunch of profile info? Which is more important to you, their data or their purchase? Then, when you've laid the perfect foundation, you close the sale. You don't have to just hope your customer will buy; in fact, you can't afford to.

Assumption: You can't afford to focus on your conversion rate until you have more sales.

False! If you can't afford to focus on your conversion rate right now, then what are you doing? Is it that your customer acquisition cost is already too low? Are you making too much profit and looking for a net operating loss to offset it?

We doubt it. It is more likely that you just haven't taken the time to understand that investing in improving your customer conversion rate right now has a return on investment that not only is huge but also keeps paying you back again and again with every marketing campaign you run. Not doing it, on the other hand, is like trying to keep a leaky bucket full by pouring in more water rather than fixing the leaks.

"Do the browse pages and search pages on your website look so different that it's clear they are owned by different groups in your company? If so, your corporate underpants are showing. Customers don't think about shopping as a series of 'pages' or 'features.' They think of the holistic experience. So humor them. Create the holistic experience before you add more features. Erase all signs of your corporate underpants. Present an integrated site design." - Tamara Adlin

Site Planning #3: Building in Customer Service Where it Counts

You go into a great big department store, and at the very back of the second floor there's a little office suite called "Customer Service." Most of us don't give it a second thought . . . we simply think of it, if we think of it at all, as the place we go to wait in line when things go wrong.

E-tailing is a different world. Your customer service, the degree to which you keep your customer delighted, starts the instant he or she lands on your website. In e-business, customer service isn't where you go when you have a problem, and it certainly isn't what happens after the sale is completed. It is everything that goes into creating a superior online shopping experience from start to finish.

Think about it. You don't have any online sales people moving about, interacting with your clients and representing your products, your sales philosophy, your guarantees, or anything else that is distinctive about your business. You rely exclusively on your website to do this (even if you are an acknowledged brand in the bricks-and-mortar world, you can fail if you don't rethink your online approach to customer service). A prospect arrives at your home page (or somewhere within your online store) and is immediately in need of customer service.

During shopping, customers use service to find or inquire about products. Do you have this item? Is this sold separately? How much comes in one of those bottles? Is this product compatible with that product? A host of questions is behind even a single purchase. So how are you going to help them get the answers they need so they want to make the purchase from you and not from one of your competitors?

During the buying process, customers need service to explain billing issues, receipts, payment options, and the checkout procedure. This is a critical point for most shoppers, and you don't want them abandoning their shopping carts in confusion, frustration, or because they don't trust you.

Once the order is placed, customers need to be able to check the status of an order being processed. They want their purchase acknowledged, and they like follow-through. They may even want to track its shipping status. Give them everything they need so that they have the cyberspace equivalent of carrying the item home.

When the item is received, customers may have questions about how it works. Something may be missing. They may decide the product isn't suitable. They need service to handle exchanges or returns. Do you give prompt, knowledgeable and complete responses to questions? Do you answer questions, or do you point them somewhere else, making them do more work and causing them to get more frustrated? Do you quickly, efficiently and cheerfully honor your guarantees? Assist with billing errors?

The keys to great customer service are in the things I've mentioned before:

- Make it simple and easy for your visitor to find information and navigate your website.
- Give them helpful and descriptive information about your products or services.
- Prominently display your toll-free number and other help tools.
- Make it clear and simple to buy from you.
- Give the customer a reason to place his or her confidence in you — inspire trust.

Customer service on the web is a comprehensive package, and results in an on-going dialogue with your shopper. Don't miss out by thinking it's a little office hidden at the back that the customer calls when there's a problem after the sale. By then, it's much too late.

Conversion Tip

Merchandizing to All Customers

Utilizing multiple-channels with interspersed entry points; delivering a message to consumers which is universally understandable; providing helpful materials which provide both the educated consumer brain food and the uneducated consumer a new understanding — is not an easy task.

Today's marketplace exists at only two levels of consumer merchandising: Either a 'broad stroke' methodology, providing the same interactions for all users; or a uniquely customized approach, catering to every perceived whim to buy, read and talk about. While the personalized approach is a means to provide guidance to the meek and uninformed while providing an outlet for 'fame' from the 'geek,' the moderate to high-end consumer is annoyed by this overkill of personalization.

The level of interactivity that Amazon.com has provided on their site has nearly turned to clutter with the huge array of options to buy, sell, read, upload manuals, view images, see "lists" of products which the 'power users' see as being important in some type of list, and even see similar products purchased by people who live in the same zip code I do — a list of content areas and related 'products' as endless as the number scrolls it takes to reach the bottom of a page.

I'm a big fan of great content — in moderation. Some product categories share basically the same content across the entire retail platform — such as movies, music, books and software. These pages are only enhanced by associated information and sometimes integration of external data. Other categories, such as hardware, home goods, computers and electronics – seem to cater to, once again, one end of the spectrum or the other.

The majority of online retailers must assume that people are aware of all the features and options available with a product they are contemplating purchasing, or that they are so daft that they don't want to know anything about the product other than it's price or even care to see more than a front and maybe a side photo of the product. A brief paragraph and a few part numbers should do the customer just fine.

I beg to differ. The key to product merchandising is the presentation of adequate materials to provide product specifications, educate and even entertain your visitor during their stay. If they have everything they need right where they are, they do not need to stray away to find out the one piece of information that they really need to make this purchasing decision.

Chances are that the visitor will be referred to another site which either sells the product or provides links to places that do after opening a new window (or simply abandoned their session on your site and used the same browser window to conduct a websearch) to a website which could provide them the information that they needed.

The association in the consumer's mind is that they provided the critical missing purchase information, they were satisfied and feel warm and fuzzy. Now, they want to stay here and shop. Even if it costs more.

On the opposing end of the spectrum, other sites pile on content until your eyes nearly bleed. The overwhelming placement of content within a single product page is just too much for anyone. The information must be segregated and placed within the appropriate context for presentment. There is no need to have every single image of a product available, in full size, on one page. Perhaps thumbnails from which I can choose, or upon hover show me the large image in a layer. Why do I need a pop-up? In fact, pop-ups these days are far less impacting than ever due to the default installation of at least one "pop-up blocker" program on the average computer.

Consumers became tired of the tirade of pop-ups in 2001-2003 thanks to several software applications, including "Gator eWallet" (from Claria) and the ever-popular P2P file-sharing software Kazaa. Must they endure more? Utilization of layers is a better option, and is quite elegant.

Provide convenient content navigation to the consumer, allowing them not to wander too far from point of purchase, but far enough to utilize related topics and product information.

Merchandising compatible and complimentary products in the proximity of purchase is critical. The ability to add multiple products when making the 'Add to Cart' decision is absolutely necessary. Save your consumer time and they will always buy more.

I find that when something is easy to do, like using a website to research domain names, being able to simply click away on boxes and add them to a basket in one click enables me to order more. It's easier and I actually sometimes get carried away. In the end, the domain merchant is the winner because it is easier and I am able to add 100 domains to a basket in the same time. Being able to submit 100 at the same time makes me drunk with power. They have my money, and I have a bunch of domains I would have otherwise not purchased. A traditional site would have me tired of pressing back and forth over and over again and checking out with 20 or less domains in the basket.

Providing consumers the ease of knowing exactly what products are compatible with others provides the unknowing shopper guidance needed to make a purchase. This is accomplished by providing a proximal placement of compatible products without obstructing the order path.

Most merchandising opportunities need to be common sense. If a consumer clicks on "Notepads" you should not be featuring a new Tablet PC. Sure, it's a notepad at a stretch, but turning a three-dollar purchase into a $2,500 investment is not reasonable.

Innovation is not a critical asset to your website. Do what you know well and leave the rest aside. Visitors are on your site because they believe you can satisfy their need. If you cannot, you have lost a customer. Innovation has its' place; take a long hard look to see if you have something not short of revolutionary and understandable. If you do, then more power to you.

- **Lonny Paul**, Director of eCommerce for a top ten eCommerce site with decades of experience in multi-channel marketing.

"Advertising is fundamentally persuasion and persuasion happens to be not a science, but an art."
- William Bernbach

Site Planning #4: The Artful Science of Conversion

Come along with me as we take a little journey in time . . .

March 2000. Venture capitalist Bill Gurley, formerly one of Wall Street's top Internet analysts (he was the lead analyst on the Amazon.com initial public offering), wrote that conversion rates are "the most powerful Internet metric of all" in a Fortune magazine article.

Fast-forward to June 2001. The business gurus from the Wharton School at the University of Pennsylvania, in an article titled "Getting Clicks With Casual Customers," wrote that "the study of conversion is in such an early stage that there are no firm rules about what works and what doesn't."

Rewind to January 2001. ClickZ, recognizing the value of bringing its audience leading-edge information, starts the Converting Web Site Traffic (now ROI Marketing) column written by the good folks at Future Now, Inc.

Rewind to March 2000. The first issue of GROKdotcom, our company newsletter, is published.

Fast-forward to today. As illustrated by the developments I've mentioned, you can see there has long been a debate over the nature of conversion marketing online but only recently has it come to the forefront.

Are there rules and science influencing our understanding of conversion practices? Let's review some facts, and then you can decide for yourself. Many readers have successfully implemented some of the techniques I write about, and their documentation provides a persuasive argument. So am I claiming to have invented the science of conversion? Hardly. Conversion is part science and part art that relies on understanding the psychology and process of persuasion and adapting it to the online medium.

Why does paying attention to the point of action (POA) increase conversion rates? Because you answer objections at the point the customers are getting ready to take an action. That is where they experience their greatest cognitive dissonance, and so that is where your answers have the most impact.

Why does applying the 'AIDAS test' improve your website's conversion rate? Because marketers have long known that any time you want to make a presentation, it should follow the format of attention, interest, desire, action, and satisfaction.

These are just two out of over 1,100 variables we have identified that influence conversion. These include factors ranging from font size and text color, to the message you place on a button, to how effectively you convey your unique value proposition, or UVP. (One of our clients just added a great one to its website, and the conversion rate doubled.)

Still think the science of conversion sounds theoretical? Let's take a look at how a real-world e-tailer takes advantage of this science. The Sharper Image, which began selling on the Internet in 1995, has been profitable since the day it started. One of the reasons for the company's success is that it does everything in-house, and the same people are responsible for making sure stuff sells in the catalog, in stores, and on the Web. Mollee Madrigal, a spokesperson for The Sharper Image, explains by saying: "The copy and creativity for every channel are the responsibility of our wonderful senior VP of creative services and his great team. He even writes the copy for many of the products himself." Strong copy that engages a prospect's senses and stimulates his desire until he takes action... hmm, it sounds like there is a process going on here.

Eliminating extra steps in the buying process improves conversion rates, and The Sharper Image even has a formula for displaying images on the home page. Madrigal explained: "The home page always includes the number-one best seller and a sales driver." In simple English, The Sharper Image is leading the prospect down a path of her choosing.

Another strategy The Sharper Image uses to increase conversion rates is something called "dynamic browsing." Dynamic browsing allows visitors to explore the online store and quickly scan an ever-changing selection of products. "Dynamic browsing is an effective merchandising tool," says Madrigal. "Just as in our stores or our catalog, products have characteristics that we would want displayed near to each other. We've tried hard to translate this to the Web effectively." For example, in a clothing catalog you would see a whole outfit — not just all the shirts, then all the pants, then all the shoes, and so on. "Whenever dynamic browsing is activated, the product is displayed with three related products and others that have weighted attributes towards the product selected." Sure sounds like The Sharper Image has some firm rules as to what works and what doesn't.

Are you wondering why we chose The Sharper Image? Why not Amazon.com? Certainly Amazon.com is applying scientific techniques to increase conversion. But what I wanted to illustrate is this: The Sharper Image is applying scientific techniques that were developed well before the Internet became commercial.

Should you go out and duplicate The Sharper Image's website? No, like every website, it's a work in progress — it needs continual improvement. And it's optimized for its business, not yours.

Also, the company hasn't yet successfully translated to the Web everything it does so well in its stores and catalogs. But that's the core of what the company is doing, and it'll get there. The marketing folks know what direction to take because they know their consumers haven't changed — only the medium has. What they do specifically has a lot to do with their products, services, and their powerful brand — all variables that may not apply in your situation. But the foundation, the "artful science" of understanding how to improve conversion rates, applies to us all. Let's get back to the fundamentals. That's where the results are.

Conversion Tip

Marketing in 2005 and Beyond

The Age of the Baby Boomer ended in 2003. The torch has been handed to a new generation with new ideas and values. Sure, we Boomers still hold the power at the top, but the prevailing worldview that drives our nation is completely other than the one we grew up with. Businesses that don't get in step with the new world order are going to find it increasingly difficult to succeed.

Being a Baby Boomer isn't about when you were born. It's about how you see the world. Baby Boomers were idealists who worshipped heroes, perfect icons of beauty and success. Today these icons are seen as phony, posed and laughable. Our cool as ice, suave lady's man James Bond has become the comic poser Austin Powers or the tragically flawed and vulnerable Jason

Bourne of The Bourne Identity. That's the essence of the new worldview; the rejection of delusion, a quiet demand for gritty truth. We're seeing it reflected in our movies, our television shows and our music.

Baby Boomers swayed back and forth to the lyrics of a 1971 Coke commercial featuring teenagers from around the world singing, "I'd like to buy the world a home and furnish it with love, grow apple trees and honeybees and snow white turtle doves. I'd like to teach the world to sing in perfect harmony, I'd like to buy the world a Coke and keep it company…" The idea was pure and wholesome, but it required no action other than belief. Today's generation would retch if that ad were aired, saying, "What has Coke actually done to promote world peace? Nothing. They're a bunch of phony posers." Consider the lyrics to the Grammy-winning, Record of the Year for 2004 by Coldplay: "Come out upon my seas, cursed missed opportunities. Am I a part of the cure? Or am I part of the disease?"

Baby Boomers believed in big dreams, reaching for the stars, personal freedom, "be all that you can be." Today's generation believes in small actions, getting your head out of the clouds, social obligation, "do your part."

A Baby Boomer anchored his or her identity in their career. The emerging generation sees his or her job only as a job.

Baby Boomers were diplomatic and sought the approval of others. The emerging generation feels it's more honest to be blunt, and they really don't care if you approve or not.

Boomers were driven, self-reliant and impressed by authority. Emergents are laid back, believe in working as a team, and have less confidence in "the boss."

Idealistic Boomers had an abundance mentality, believed in a better world, and were opulent in their spending. Emergents see scarcity, believe in doing what it takes to survive, and are more fiscally conservative.

Based solely on the core values of the emerging generation, here's what I believe we can expect to see beginning to happen during the next 3 to 4 years:

1. A decline among prestige brands such as Rolex, Harley-Davidson and Gucci.
2. The end of "upwardly mobile" as a slang expression.
3. A decline in the effectiveness of traditional advertising.
4. Comparison-shopping to be done increasingly online, though purchasing will remain in brick-and-mortar stores in many product categories.
5. An increase in volunteerism and donor support to socially responsible organizations.
6. A slow increase in the popularity of labor unions.
7. A slight decrease in the divorce rate as couples become increasingly committed to family unity and fall less under the spell of idealistic "true love."

Here's what these things mean to the business owner:

1. Don't count on prestige brands to be the future strength of your identity, as they have been in the past. Craft an identity that doesn't depend on the vendor lines you carry.

2. Investigate the values of the new "upscale" customer of tomorrow and get in step with those new values.

3. Focus less on instant-response, promotional advertising and become the store customers think of immediately when they need what you sell. The new trend in advertising is away from hype and romanticism and more toward facts and truth.

4. Have an informative, user-friendly website that allows customers to learn all the details of your product or service they would have traditionally learned from a salesperson. Don't expect tomorrow's customer to call you or come by your store "for more information."

5. Pick an organization or a cause you believe in and support it openly.

6. Speak less often to self-image and prestige as a motivating force in your customer. Believe it or not, people are becoming concerned about a world outside themselves.

These are the things that are coming, but remember: Changing too much too soon is almost as dangerous as changing too little too late. The adoption curve of the new values by the mainstream of society began in 2003 and will be complete by mid-2008 or early 2009. You have plenty of time to get in step with tomorrow. But you need to get started today.

- **Roy H. Williams**, Sept. 28, 2004, www.WizardAcademy.com

"Common sense is the collection of prejudices acquired by age eighteen." - Albert Einstein

Site Planning #5: Tips, Ideas and Helpful Hints

We've talked about a bunch of issues associated with improving the conversion rate on your website, from little tweaks to major overhauls. Prior to that, we provided a top level view of planning from a marketing perspective. Let's conclude this section on planning with some helpful tips — a summary, if you will, that will give you a place to start making a difference.

Clarify Your Value Proposition

If you haven't done it yet, you definitely want to take some time to identify just what makes you and your business valuable to your customer. From that, you can craft a concise and compelling message that communicates your value to your customers, perhaps even one that distinguishes you from the crowd. Your message answers the question, "Why should I buy from you and not one of your competitors?"

Refine Your Logo

Take a good look at your logo; does it needs a lift? That can easily get overlooked when it comes to thinking about improving your conversion rate. Your logo is the fundamental graphic representation of you and your business. Make sure the design is clean, professional, and evokes a positive and useful "first mental image" about your business.

Spruce Up Your POAs

You want to be certain your customers will be able to clearly identify all your points of action (POAs) and that it is immediately obvious to them what they need to do. Pair your POAs with appropriate statements that address your customers' concerns, particularly their worries about privacy (and mean what you say!). If an action requires the customer to provide information, be sure you ask only for the bare minimum and always make sure there is a clear exchange of value offered with subsequent requests for information.

Get Your Assurances Up Front

Don't forget to let your visitors know that they can shop on your website with confidence, that you offer safe and secure transactions and hassle-free guarantees. They won't buy from you if they don't trust you. An ideal place to locate some of these assurances is on the right side of your webpage — a place your customers are always at least peripherally aware of. Also, as customers move further into the sales process, you have to adjust your assurances to coincide with your customers' changing needs at each point.

Make Sure What They See Will Be What They Get

Beyond the adjustments to your website, now is also the perfect time to stress-test your back-end processes. Don't forget the importance of fulfillment and customer service to the digital sales process. Sterling service and satisfying fulfillment are what your customers expect from you — and they are typically less forgiving of glitches during the holiday shopping frenzy. Be sure that your systems, digital and human, are ready — ideally, eager — to cope with the load.

Ensure What YOU See on the Site is What THEY See

It's really dangerous to assume that your customers will get everything on your site the way you and your staff intend. In fact, you can take it to the bank (or, actually, not to the bank) that they won't. Ask yourself "Could your mom shop your website?" There is no substitute for third-party testing, and then learning from and applying the feedback. Testing does not have to be extensive or expensive or even professional. A few friends or family members and a couple of pizzas can get the job done.

So there's your recipe for success. Refine, tweak, and do the simple and quick stuff you can do right now to up your conversion rate. If you haven't tried this already, you'll be pleasantly surprised; even small changes can yield great results.

Conversion Tip

35 Quick Ideas to Improve Online Conversion

My strongest advice to grow and sustain online results is to understand your customer (and act accordingly), and to build a culture of strong measurement, rigor and accountability (Must read book: "Execution").

However, if you're looking for some quick ideas to improve conversion, below are some ideas I've seen work...

First, some context... There are essentially 5 customer purchase questions that are critical to answer if you want to improve conversion:

Can I find the item I'm looking for? – The benefits of search engine marketing is that most visitors come to your site to find a specific item or shop a category. Product selection and brand choice aside, the easier it is for them to find this first product they are shopping for, the less 'leakage' you will get.

Can I find something that interests me? – Whether visitors start looking for a specific item and continue to shop, or someone comes to your site on to do 'shopping', you need to make sure they find products that are tempting to buy. Products that are popular, cool, interesting, differentiated, and low priced.

Do I really want this product? – In the process of "A.I.D.A.", this is "Desire" stage. Do visitors really have the desire to buy that product. You obviously have to answer all relevant questions, but moreover, provide the details in a compelling way to persuade a customer to buy. Why this product, how does it help me, and why now?

Can I get it for the right price? – Let's face it, the Internet is the great price equalizer. Have you seen Froogle, epinions, shopping.com, deal.com, and the popularity of coupon sites? So, you need to have a good price, but moreover, can do a few things to convince prospects you have a great price...no need to go elsewhere.

Can I trust this company? – Unless you're like Land's End, enjoying 70% repeat business from familiar customers, you have to convince new prospects that you are a trustworthy company.

Online shopping is growing fast, but shoppers are still afraid of working with a no-name brand, especially if the site looks 'sketchy'. Familiarity and trust in a brand is one of the top 3 obstacles to buying from an online retailer.

Can I buy easily?

This is where usability and the art of persuasive reassurance are critical, starting from the home page and ending at checkout thank you page. There are many opportunities for the visitor to rethink their purchase along the way. The above questions are critical to resolve, but along the way, if the visitor gets stuck, none of the work you've done will make a difference. It's just too easy for a frustrated online user to decide 'to come back later' — unfortunately, they rarely do.

Within these questions, or stages of purchase, here are some top suggestions to help increase online conversion:

Can I find that item I'm looking for?

* Tune your internal search engine to match top search terms to product pages
* Put top sellers on home page. People buy on impulse or recommendation.
* Match the landing page to the marketing campaign. Use vanity urls for offline advertising.
* Test your categories, naming and navigation with customers. They're less intuitive than you think.

Can I find something that interests me?

* Put top sellers on home page
* Add related items to a product view
* Add relevant, topical-based shopping navigation or search
* Add interactivity to pull visitors into your site or a page

Do I really want this product?

* Display larger product pictures
* Show the product in action
* Headline the results your product promises
* Feature benefits in the copy
* Make it easy to read — bullets, short sentences/paragraphs, conversational.
* Add substantiated recommendations ("4 out of 5 dentists…")

Can I get it for the right price?

* Add a limited time promotion to a product or category
* Use Free Shipping (#1 online promotion)
* Show a good, better, best options
* Show comparisons to competitors
* Slash through pricing
* Repeat the deal or promotion on every page

Can I trust this company?

* Clean up the site design
* Add testimonials
* Add security certifications
* Add affiliations
* Get listings in BizRate, Froogle, Epinions, etc.
* Show your personality
* Increase the font size
* Less is more
* Highlight your money back guarantee
* Include privacy, contact us, about us pages.
* Add a phone number

Can I checkout easily?

* Add a call to action on every page
* Copy the best-practices in cart and checkout
* Add reassurance statements (security, guarantee, etc.)
* Add a phone number on every page

- **Sam Decker** spent four years overseeing operations and product management for Dell's consumer e-commerce and e-support sites. His expertise in operations, user experience, financial management, process, and technology helped drive growth in dell.com conversion rates and consumer online sales.

"Technology is a way of organizing the universe so that man doesn't have to experience it." - Max
Frisch, Michael Moncur's (Cynical) Quotations

Structure

Over the years, there has been plenty of debate concerning the definition of information architecture.
We pulled the following definitions from Peter Morville's blog, Semantic Studios:

From the Asilomar Institute for Information Architecture:

- The structural design of shared information environments.
- The art and science of organizing and labeling web sites, intranets, online communities and software to support usability and findability.
- An emerging community of practice focused on bringing principles of design and architecture to
  the digital landscape.

From Information Architecture for the World Wide Web (2nd Edition):

- The combination of organization, labeling, and navigation schemes within an information system.
- The structural design of an information space to facilitate task completion and intuitive access
  to content.
- The art and science of structuring and classifying websites and intranets to help people find and
  manage information.

And on the lighter side from The Devils Dictionary (2.0):

information architecture, noun -A vital component in the development of Web sites, used to round
the budget up to the next hundred thousand dollars.

Kidding aside, we've found that employing the right information architecture is serious stuff. Applying
the principles of good IA not only keeps visitors on your website, it makes it possible (and compelling) for
them to take actions which benefit both the buyer/visitor and seller/website owner.

The following section sets out what we believe are the guiding principles of good information architecture, and introduces the idea of persuasion architecture, which is central to our work.

"Architecture is to make us know and remember who we are." - Sir Jellicoe Geoffrey, International Herald Tribune

From Traditional to
Persuasion Architecture – Lessons Learned

In "Learning From Traditional Architects," Lorraine Johnston writes,

History records the architect as being the original master-builder .... During the eighteenth and nineteenth centuries, the role of the architect changed, becoming less personal. The builder now controlled the craftsmen, and the architect visited the building site less frequently .... The period saw the divorce of design from construction .... When the industrial revolution brought the need for different types of buildings, such as factories, mills and warehouses, architects tended to have little interest in coping with the construction needs of the industrial age.[1]

Architects, who originally were responsible for synthesizing a solution that could resolve multiple requirements, became more interested in style. The actual design choices for these business interests fell into the hands of the civil engineer, who inherently embraced a scientific approach to the new forms of buildings and materials.

As you might guess, we're introducing a metaphor (architecture) that's going to provide the foundation for this section of the book. To extend the metaphor, start thinking of the architect as a marketer responsible for the bottom line of the company's website and the civil engineer as an ace technical programmer who has developed the website.

Lots of things come to mind when I think of "architecture": design, intention, function, beauty, structure, movement. I think of how a museum is very different from a fast food joint which is very different from a house. Architecture as a discipline is a merger of science and art, joining the breadth of engineering and aesthetics with human use.

Ms. Johnston continues, "While the architectural champions of Gothic and Classic were making the head-lines, hard-headed practical and industrious men were quietly changing the face of Britain with their railway stations and their viaducts, their mills factories and housing estates ... architects followed classical design principles and left others to deal with the requirements resulting from the industrial revolution."

In short, somewhere along the line, architects started to overlook "the real needs of users, and technologists took over during the industrial revolution." The result? The birth of the urban slum and a general decline in the quality of construction and usability.

By the early twentieth century, architects were growing familiar with the new materials and engineering techniques, and "realised they had a vital role to play in bringing order and humanity into an increasingly chaotic world."

As an example of the new approach to architecture, the architect Frank Lloyd Wright wrote:

A building should contain as few rooms as will meet the condition which give it rise and under which we live, and which the architect should strive continually to simplify; the ensemble of the rooms should then be carefully considered that comfort and utility may go hand in hand with beauty.[2]

It's a cool article, especially if you replace "website" for "building," "web page" for "room," "call to action" for "door," think of "nature" as "functionality" and "materials" as the inherent character of the medium. You get the idea.

Look also at the development of Landscape Architecture, particularly through folks like Frederick Law Olmsted (best known for his role in shaping Central Park in New York):

Olmsted applied these principles of separation and subordination more consistently than any other landscape architect of his era. Subordination was accomplished in his parks where carefully constructed walks and paths would flow through landscape with gentle grades and easy curves, thus requiring the viewer's minimal attention to the process of movement. At the same time, many of the structures that Olmsted incorporated into his parks merge with their surroundings. Separation is accomplished in his park systems by designing large parks that were meant for the enjoyment of the scenery. Smaller recreational areas for other activities and where "park ways" handle the movement of pedestrians and vehicular traffic offset these large parks.[3]

Even more explicitly, the purpose of this form of architecture was to create space that shaped and guided the "user's" experience. Intention was integral to the design — when you stepped over here, you were supposed to see this; when you moved further down that path, you were presented with a secretive opening you simply couldn't resist investigating.

Here's the ethic of the modern architect in a nutshell:

The way clients are looking to the future requires that we study our client's situation more than we have ever done before. If we are to succeed, we must learn a great deal about how clients are organized and what strategies underlie their way of doing business.

So let me illuminate the comparison for you, the marketer: when you are in charge of the bottom line, it is your necessary role to provide the order, the comprehensive vision and an understanding of the human dynamic during the development process of your Web site.

Introducing Information Architecture

To get visitors to take action online, you practice Architecture: construction as the result of a conscious act; the creation of a unifying or coherent form or structure.

Information Architecture is definitely a piece of the puzzle, even if folks have often used the term in a vague sort of way. In our opinion, the best definition (and much shorter than those at the beginning of the chapter) comes from Louis Rosenfeld:

Information architecture involves the design of organization and navigation systems to help people find and manage information more successfully.[4]

Information Architecture is all about helping folks find the information they are looking for. It's about how you optimize your website's search engine so visitors can find products, how you categorize your supplemental navigation in ways that make sense to your visitors and reflect how they might look for your stuff. It's the rudiments of the Qualifying part of the sales process. Actually, brilliant Information Architecture is like a top-notch reference librarian.

But you don't only want to help people find your stuff and make it easy for them to interact with your site (the usability part of the puzzle), you want them to take action. You want them to buy, or subscribe, or qualify themselves as a lead. So you need to do more than allow them to act; you have to persuade them!

And that's where Persuasive Architecture comes in. It's the aesthetically appealing and functional structure you create to marry the organization of the buying and selling processes with the organization of information. It's the only way your website is actively going to influence, the only way you will pull (never push!) your visitors along the paths they need to walk to accomplish their goals — and yours.

From Information to Persuasion Architecture

Uncovery, Wireframing, Storyboarding, Prototyping, Development and Optimization. These are the critical steps that make up MAP™ (an acronym for the Minerva Architectural Process™), our iterative process of creating Persuasion Architecture.

The design or redesign of a website requires the input of many specialists, including technical programmers, information architects, copywriters, designers, usability folks, marketers and people who understand the consumer psychology of selling and buying. But it also needs the synthetic, coordinating abilities of an architect.

No detail that affects customer response should be left to chance — from the integration of the marketing message into the website's fabric, to e-mail marketing campaigns, to sales, to CRM, to the minutiae of customer response communications. What every company could really benefit from is a Chief Persuasion Officer, a Persuasion Architect - someone who embraces the global perspective of a business' effort and integrates all the parts toward the creation and maintenance of an effective, holistic persuasive system.

We can't put this any better than the woman who posted to a discussion topic on the Asilomar Institute for Information Architecture members-only mailing list. She created a little seminar demonstration to explain to participants the value of a synthetic coordinator:

> I split the content developers up into 6 groups and had each group pick a room in a house and 'design' it. They picked the type of room, size, color, scheme, style and layout, and drew it on a piece of paper. I then had one representative from each group come up to the front and try to put a house together using those rooms. Needless to say, we ended up with no bathrooms and 3 living rooms and a huge mess. I explained that there needed to be someone 'designing the house' first - an architect, if you will … I'd never seen so many light bulbs go on.[5]

Think about your website. Consider how many people have input into making it what it is. Need an architect?

Conversion Tip

Answer Questions Before They're Asked

There's a reason for the development of the FAQ. 80% of site visitors want to know the same stuff. So:

- Don't make them hit the Contact Us button. That's frustrating for them and costly for you.
- Don't even make them plow through your FAQs if it can be avoided.
- Figure out what people want to know and put it in your body copy, headers and sub-heads and in your banner ads.
- If there are simply too many questions, create a variety of FAQ's.
- Consider employing one of the wonderful customer service tools that let a customer service representative (CSR) call up the next question, answer it, and identify it as something new - something to be swept into the searchable database that can be accessed by customers and CSR's alike.

You want more customers buying? Give them answers.

- **Jim Sterne**, author, consultant and producer of the Emetrics Summit

[1] "Learning from traditional architects." Lorraine Johnston. Swinburne University of Technology, School of Information Technology. Hawthorn, Australia.

[2] "In the Cause of Architecture." Frank Lloyd Wright. Architectural Record . March, 1908. Reprinted in Frank Lloyd Wright, Collected Writings. vol 1. pp 87-88.

[3] http://www.fredericklawolmsted.com/Lifeframe.htm.

[4] "Information Architecture Revealed!" John S. Rhodes.

[5] "IA & usability" topic. Cindy Pae. AIFIA Members-Only Discussion List 3 January 2003.

"A good plan is like a road map: it shows the final destination and usually the best way to get there."
- H. Stanley Judd

MAP™ Your Path to Success

We really enjoy opportunities to solve problems through synthesis ... bringing together ideas from lots of different sources that help reveal a different, coherent way of looking at things – something that is more than the sum of its parts.

As a result, we've put our best thinking together into a tool that enables our clients to synthesize all the things we've been discussing over the years. We call this framework Persuasion Architecture. And associated with this framework is our process for persuasive design: the Minerva Architectural Process™ (MAP™).

You guys know online success isn't about sitting there twiddling your thumbs hoping the traffic that makes it to your website takes action. You have to be an active agent in the exchange – you have to persuade your visitors by interweaving the selling process with the buying process, consistently applying AIDAS as you answer the WIIFM question, all the while incorporating tenets of usability and information architecture. These are the critical elements behind any form of sales or conversion.

MAP™ is the process of making sure the design of your Web site has a solid foundation, so it persuades and converts your visitors more effectively.

The Phases of MAP™

Uncovery. Skillful uncovery is the first necessary step toward designing and developing effective persuasive architecture. Neglecting this phase would be the architectural equivalent of constructing a building but omitting the footers! Uncovery is responsible for mapping objectives, developing strategy, understanding the customer's buying process, understanding and refining the sales process, researching keywords and key phrases and defining the key business metrics you will use. If you don't get the uncovery part right, you won't be able to define or measure success. Uncovery is completed with the development of personas and narratives describing how the persona buys and what you would do to persuade them.

Wireframing. Wireframing defines the WHAT of the creative process. It's a structural representation of every click-through possibility and path your visitors might take: a map of interactivity. No pictures, no graphic design, just bare bones text and hyperlinks. You can click the links and see where you go; you can get a feel for the process of the website and help generate useful feedback at a time when changes and multiple iterations are a snap. When you wireframe, you evaluate the entire website and all its interactions before you enter the more costly phase of programming. Saves you time, saves you money! Wireframed web pages ideally contain the answers to the three questions essential to the persuasive process:

- What actions satisfy the objective?
- Who needs to be persuaded to take action?
- How do you persuade them most effectively to take action?

Storyboarding. Storyboarding focuses on HOW you go about accomplishing the WHAT. It's the way you begin to flesh out your wireframe. When you storyboard, you develop the persuasive copy that is going to grab your visitors' attention and motivate them through your website. You begin to consider the graphic mockup, paying careful attention to scanning and skimming, the eight second rule, the priority of content and KISS. Your first storyboards should appear in grayscale, so you can evaluate the composition and process without the emotional influence of color. You then proceed to a color mockup and finally, an HTML mockup in which you also consider download speeds, browser compatibilities, style sheets and tabular formats that help search engine spiders crawl your site.

Prototyping. As you iteratively storyboard your way along, you eventually get to the point where you have a finished prototype of your website that will be identical to the actual final product. It will meet the needs of the various personas who visit your site. It will offer them paths through the various scenarios that reflect their needs in the buying and selling process. It will communicate relevance at every turn.

When both the client and the developer agree prototyping is complete, you freeze the prototype. No other changes can be made – at least not in this version.

Development. Now, and only now, do you begin coding. Every detail is specified in the prototype. There's no need for guesswork. Just keep in mind: programming costs considerably more than planning – every hour you spend planning saves you roughly three hours in coding. The developers don't need to make choices for you – ones you'll probably have to fix later on — they simply get to do what they do best: code.

Optimization. The website works. Just as you intended it to. You unleash it on the cyber-public, and then the fun begins. If you've followed the process methodically and thoroughly, if you've completed each phase in order without rushing the process or meandering through it, then you have a starting point for testing and measuring that will allow you to adjust your tactics to maximize your effectiveness. Establish and consistently follow a disciplined strategy (a six-sigma approach) for monitoring your web analytics and continuous improvement. It's really the only way to come full circle in the process, to determine how closely you meet your objectives and how you can improve your results on every page that doesn't meet its responsibility.

And that's MAP™ in a nutshell.

"We find the fullness of life not only in options, but in commitments." - George W. Bush, First Inaugural Address

A Good Metaphor for MAP™

A while back, a number of books were published with multiple choice endings (Julio Cortazar's Hopscotch comes to mind). Readers were asked to 'turn to page 121 if you think A, turn to page 84 if you think B...' etc." There are a number of scenarios on each page. Persuasive writers would be able to channel readers towards the right decision.

Now, we all know reading a book isn't exactly the same thing as working your way through an ecommerce website, but the "multiple-ending book" is a remarkably clever metaphor for exactly what Persuasion Architecture hopes to accomplish: helping your visitors to achieve their goals (not always The End and absent the connotation of right or wrong) in the ways that suits them best.

Everything you do is about pulling your visitors along, motivating them to take the next step. It's not about pushing them, or requiring them to accommodate your master plan of what they need. So, until you present your entire conversion system from your visitors' points of view, you will never be as persuasive as you could be. And that means you will always be experiencing lower conversion rates than are possible.

Think folks are doing a good job pulling their visitors merrily along their way? Not according to a March 2004 study by OneStat.com. They evaluated Web metrics for a number of websites and determined the number of pages a visitor went to:

- 1 page view 9.52%
- 1 - 2 page views 54.60%
- 2 - 3 page views 16.56%
- 3 - 4 page views 8.75%
- 4 - 5 page views 4.43%
- 6 - 7 page views 1.41%
- 7 - 8 page views 0.85%
- 8 - 9 page views 0.68%
- 9 - 10 page views 0.51%
- more than 10 page views 2.69%

Think about those numbers a minute (you've seen them before). You might say it took folks two pages to figure out they were in the wrong place. We don't think so! Almost 55% of folks were interested enough to click one or two steps deeper into the process before bailing. This is a pretty clear indication that the sites are failing to provide a majority of their users enough "scent" (motivation, persuasion, value) to keep them in the process. Needs aren't getting met, and lots of websites aren't meeting them!

One of our friends, Chris, says it better than we could:

Persuasive design links the user buying experience to a company's sales process, theoretically bridging the buy/sell vacuum we see so often. You really need to know how users behave to generate sales growth - and surely if you can influence that behavior then the journey from the landing page to the 'thank you for your order' page should happen more frequently and more effectively.

By considering the user journey at a micro-level it is possible — given some time to research, implement and experiment - to turn more users into customers, to keep them happy and to ensure that they stay with you for longer.

How can one seemingly tiny element of a webpage prevent a user from reaching the checkout? How might one poorly constructed sentence have a disproportionately large negative impact on the decision to buy? How is it possible to act on what you know about your users, given that they must all be different people with different wants and needs? It sounds impossibly complex to bring all these things together, but surely it is more about attention to detail, good copy and perhaps a sprinkling of user-guided personalization?

It does seem impossibly complex when you think about it from the big picture point of view. But it isn't any more complex than lots of other constructions. When you design persuasively by following a logical methodology (MAP™), things can actually get pretty obvious.

Just like the type of book we spoke about at the beginning of this section, Persuasion Architecture is fundamentally about designing individual scenarios (navigation paths) into your conversion system. These let folks interact with you in ways that are meaningful to them. These make it more likely folks will take action on your site. These will improve your conversion rates.

Keep in mind that everyone on your website is involved in a journey. You just need to make sure the journey is as satisfying as reaching the goal. Because without the journey, they won't get to The End.

Conversion Tips

3 Tips for Converting Visitors to Subscribers

Tip #1: Maximizing conversion rates for selling content online

- Ensure your users can find what they want on your site (Internal search clarity, email and alert relevance)
- Make sure visitors can see enough of a preview of your paid content to make a purchasing decision. This can be aided by free samples, testimonials, money back guarantees and graphics even for text-based content.
- Make the payment process as painless as possible.

Tip #2: Maximizing conversion rates by cutting out irrelevant traffic

The easiest way to increase conversion rates is to reduce the number of visitors whilst maintaining the same number of conversions. Whilst this doesn't help total sales, or value creation, it does make the important point that quality is much more important than quantity.

- When site visitors climb, but sales stay level, check to see if feeds you are using are properly segmenting traffic.
- Trace irrelevant traffic, calls and emails to the source.

Tip #3: Don't overlook your site infrastructure

As a marketer, you might think that the speed of your site isn't your responsibility. But a slow site has a number of very bad repercussions:
- Less pages viewed per session, leading to lost revenue if you're selling ad space.
- Fewer search referrals when search engine spiders and bots may give up trying to index all your content
- Lower conversion rates.
  To address the speed issue:
- Monitor site speed at peak times, for example when you send out an e-mail promotion and get a spike of response.
- Employ one or more of the inexpensive and easy-to-use tools and services to monitor your site's performance.

- **Ashley Friedlein**, CEO, E-consultancy.

The Romans called her Minerva; the Greeks called her Athena. Born from Jupiter's (Zeus's) head and commonly known as the goddess of war, Minerva was also the goddess of arts, industry and handicraft, as well as the deity who presided over wisdom, study and intelligence. In Homer's Odyssey - where she appears as Athena, her Greek name - she disguises herself as a man called Mentor and advises Odysseus' son, Telemachus. Mentor has entered our language as the word for a wise and sympathetic guide. In this process, let us be yours! - The Grok

Mapping the MAP™ Process – A Look at Uncovery

How come folks do business with you? Because you're a family owned and operated company? Because you've been slogging along for 126 years? Because you have sterling customer service? Great prices and cool sales assistants? You may have all these things going for you, but it's probably not why your customers come to you. And it's not the stuff that's really going to persuade potential customers to do business with you.

There's something special about your business. You know what's special about you – trust me. It's just that you don't know you know it, or you don't think it's important enough. So it isn't something you communicate to your potential customers.

That's where the process of Uncovery rushes in to save the day.

No doubt you recall MAP™, our methodology that guides you through developing the persuasive architecture of your Web site? Uncovery is the first phase in the process:

"Skillful uncovery is the first necessary step toward designing and developing effective persuasive architecture. Neglecting this phase would be the architectural equivalent of constructing a building but omitting the footers!

Uncovery is responsible for mapping objectives, developing strategy, understanding the customer's buying process, understanding and refining the sales process, defining personas, researching keywords and key phrases and defining the key business metrics you will use. If you don't get the uncovery part right, you won't be able to define or measure success."

What is an Uncovery?

Most folks don't really know why people do business with them. They suffer from an "inside the bottle" mentality that keeps them from seeing what's truly going on around them. There are often crucial pieces of information that are hidden to them, and thus hidden to their potential customers. The purpose of uncovery is to root out that information and share it with everyone.

One of the best models to understand what the uncovery process accomplishes is the Johari Window, a communications model invented by Joseph Luft and Harry Ingham in the 60s. It describes the process of human interaction. If you can apply this as a model for interaction design, it is even more pertinent for the Web.

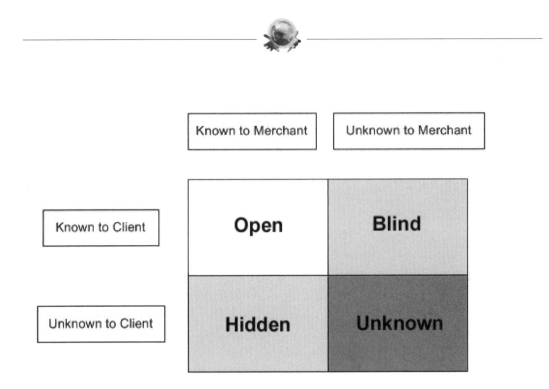

Let's talk about the Johari Window. "Self," that's us, and we are whiz-bang tax lawyers. "Others," that's you, our customers and potential customer base.

The OPEN quadrant represents all the information we both know about my business. It's the stuff we acknowledge about ourselves and put into brochures, or magazines, or newspapers, or on television so that you know it too. We share this information. It's OPEN.

Then there's information you know about us that we don't ever get to learn. You might have heard someone complain because we wouldn't let him itemize a deduction the way he wanted. Your neighbor may have had several experiences she's happy to share with you. You know this stuff, but we don't. We are BLIND to it.

The information that neither of us know is UNKNOWN. It might not always stay UNKNOWN as we continue along the path of doing business together, so it basically represents future possibility.

What You're Not Saying is What Matters

The critical piece we need to grasp for our web efforts to be most successful is the HIDDEN area, the part that we actually know about ourselves and you're really desperate to know.

Think about this. When was the last time you made a considered purchase? It probably took a lot of time – you probably spent a lot of time researching and shopping around. And eventually, still with unanswered questions, you came to the web hoping you'd find reviews and opinions that provided the answers you needed to discover.

This is the main reason why many visitors come to the Web to do business with you, and this is the area you want to open up as much as possible. By being the resource that finally answers the questions your visitors can't get answered anywhere else, this is where you can really maximize the ROI of your website.

After all, the more you are able to help your visitors meet their goals, the more you will meet yours.

"It forms the quality of light within which we can predicate our hopes and dreams toward survival and change, first made into language, then into idea, then into more tangible action." - Audre Lorde, Poetry is Not a Luxury

Explorations in Uncovery

In the previous section, we looked at the communications model of the Johari Window and related it to the critical process of Uncovery. The goal? To help a business uncover information about itself that is unknown to its potential customer base. Not just any old information, but emotionally powerful information, the kind that potential customers would find persuasive. This is the information that provides the foundation for a business's online objectives and suggests the strategies and tactics that will work best.

Suppose we sit down with you, and ask you why folks do business with you. You'll probably swear to me that the reason is because "we've been family owned and operated for 25 years," or "it's our superior service," or "we provide exceptional value." But, actually, the truth lies hidden beneath these clichés.

Self disclosure occurs incrementally — the ability to disclose more about yourself increases over time, with familiarity. How many times have you met someone and immediately spilled your guts? Everything about yourself, your hopes and dreams, your passions? It's tough to dig deep when you feel the exchange is potentially threatening or hostile – even when the intention is opposite, it can feel like you against them.

I've learned that one simple fact hinders the uncovery process: most people are not good at self-disclosure. They are happy to talk endlessly about facts, but not emotions. However, answers like "family-owned," "superior service" and "exceptional value" don't generate terribly helpful uncovery information. Don't get me wrong, it's nice information. But it's not the bottom-line food-truth about your business that is going to get your visitors salivating for what you have to offer.

So, we'll often ask "Well what else could it be?" or "Your competitor offers the same thing, is there anything else?"

And here's what happens next: you start to get defensive. "I've been doing this for 20 years, I think I know my business better than you do." And you are absolutely right. In fact, we're counting on that. But the more defensive you get, the more you close up, the less likely I am going to be successful uncovering your critical information.

It's a sensitive process. The experience of uncovery walks a fine line between being encouraging, yet challenging your belief about how others see you or your business.

It is a delicate issue when we suggest to people who are bone honest, that the reality of how and what they are, may not be exactly as they see it. As in all things, truth and honesty are the strongly held private perceptions of the holder him or her self. They are not necessarily 'the truth' and at the same time, they are not 'lies'.[1]

But uncovery is about getting to the truth. So instead of asking questions that can make you uncomfortable — like "What is your value proposition?" — we ask open-ended questions, questions for which there are no right or wrong answers.

Ask your customers to complete these thoughts for you:

- First time visitors to our store tell us........
- One of the most unusual questions we've ever had was.........
- One thing people tell us they are confused about our business is........
- I was especially proud when I helped a customer with........
- We do lots of things that customers never see, if they knew this they would.......
- The biggest error made by first time buyers is........
- When we talk with customers they always tell us.........,(about our business)[2]

The brilliant thing about this technique is that these questions will encourage you to tell me stories. And when you tell a story, you are able to enter the world of emotion. When you tell a story, you unconsciously provide insights into your passions. When you tell a story, you can self-disclose without fear of providing a wrong answer.

The critical information an uncovery can reveal is not necessarily the sort of stuff that makes you drop your jaw in awe. While the way the insights relate may be quite complicated, sometimes the message itself is very straightforward.

Take this job company we are working with. They defined their objectives based on competition for resumes, thus they saw job boards as their primary model (stuff like Monster.com). During a conference call uncovery, together we were able to identify that this company was different because they were gathering resumes for existing jobs for which they were prepared to actually hire. They weren't brokering jobs — unlike job boards, these guys were hiring! And that has made all the difference. It was such a simple little piece of information — but one that had eluded an intelligent, multi-billion dollar company for years. Once the messaging changed to reflect this, results increased immediately by more than 80%, and now a complete redesign of the entire website will reflect this critical perspective.

An uncovery should be managed sensitively, but to get the critical information, the exchange also needs to be challenging. You may know your business, but you may be completely unaware of your message. Don't be afraid to dig deep enough to find that diamond of information.

Will you allow the information your customers need to remain hidden, or will you uncover it so that it persuades them to buy?

---

1 Russell Friedman, The Grief Recovery Institute
2 With gratitude to Steve Rae

Conversion Tips

Web Content Means Writing Links

Web content is different from print content. Yet many websites have simply ported print content onto their websites. Or, they may have written content specifically for the Web, but they wrote it with a print mindset.

How is web content different from print content? A fundamental difference is that web content can have multiple links. In contrast, print content is linear, such that Page 7 is linked to Page 6 and Page 8. A piece of content on the Web can have many links.

Linking is absolutely crucial to successful web content. You should never write a piece of web content without also writing its links. A link is a call to action. It says things like:

- Find out more details
- Get in touch with a sales rep
- Buy now and get a 10 percent discount
- Subscribe to our free newsletter for more great tips

- **Gerry McGovern** has spoken, written and consulted extensively on web content management issues since 1994.

"Principles and rules are intended to provide a thinking man with a frame of reference."
- Carl von Clausewitz

(Wire)Frame Yourself

Wireframing is a simple, non-technical process. It takes its name from the skeletal structure that underlies any type of sculpture. A wireframe is a skeletal rendering of every click-through possibility on your site. It's a text-only action, decision, or experience model.

Wireframing saves a lot of time and money. The entirety of a website and all interactions are designed and evaluated before costly graphic design or programming. You can click hyperlinks and see where they go. You'll "feel" what it will be like to use the website. In doing so, critical feedback is generated early in the development process. Everything is easy to change in this phase. Many iterations can be done quickly. They can even be tested with end users at a very low cost.

People confuse wireframing with storyboarding. Presented with site-design storyboards or mockups, users, clients, and designers alike tend to focus on visual elements of the prototype rather than the proposed function, structure, or content of the page. Hardly surprising. A bias for tangibles over abstracts is very human. Myers-Briggs (a serious study of personality types) demonstrates that over 70 percent of the English-speaking population prefers tangible, concrete concepts over abstractions. We react to what we see. Even if we know it can be changed, we can't ignore our reaction.

Wireframing puts something in front of decision makers not to excite them visually but to elicit a reaction. A wireframe separates a website's look and feel from its function. It presents a stripped-down, simplified version of the page, devoid of distractions. The purpose is to maintain the flow of specific logical and business functions by identifying all entry and exit points or actions users will experience on every page of a website.

The distinction between wireframe and storyboard is critical. Wireframing defines the 'what' of the creative process. Storyboarding tackles the how. Wireframes are more structural design than visual. Visually, they are boring. Good visual designs are not. Maintaining distinct roles for phases of an undertaking is well described by Richard Saul Wurman in "Information Anxiety 2":

There are two parts to solving any problem: What you want to accomplish, and how you want to do it. Even the most creative people attack issues by leaping over what they want to do and going on to how they will do it. There are many "hows" but only one "what".... You must always ask the question, "What is?" before you ask the question, "How to?"

What do wireframe pages contain? Ideally, answers to those critical three questions:

1. What personas (types of visitors) need to be persuaded?
2. What actions do they need to take?
3. What information do they require to take that action?

Marketers tend not to appreciate linear processes. But if you've been involved in a development project that has gone beyond the delivery date, didn't deliver everything it was supposed to, or went over budget, you aren't alone. When 70 percent of development projects fail and 80 percent are over budget, there's a problem. If 70 percent of buildings were built like websites, most of us would live and work in tents.

Einstein defined insanity as "doing the same thing over and over again and expecting different results." Development methodology should take into account the cognitive processes of the development team and the end users, plus focus on meeting business needs and objectives. Most principles of online persuasive architecture trace their origins to established disciplines, such as architecture. Businesses should develop a lingua franca for development so people don't confuse major issues such as wireframing with storyboarding. So projects are done on budget, on time, and on purpose.

The next time you start a design, redesign, or any other project, don't think about this column. Instead, bear in mind another gem from Albert Einstein: "If I were given one hour to save the planet, I would spend 59 minutes defining the problem and one minute resolving it."

"In order to comprehend its own essence tangibly, the spirit of the time chooses a human being as its prototype . . ." - Stefan Zweig, Erasmus of Rotterdam

Now the Plot Thickens

Storyboarding is where we start defining how we accomplish the what.

If you want your project to be completed on budget, on time, and on purpose, you need to proceed through each phase and its component steps as if on a critical path, refusing to move forward until the current step is done. This may be counterintuitive, but it will save you loads of time and money. Here are the five steps involved in completing the storyboard phase.

1. Persuasive Online Copywriting

The process of answering the three questions every persuasive website must answer helps us determine what content and copy the website is going to need. Those questions, once again, are:

1. What action needs to be taken?
2. Who needs to take that action?
3. How do we persuade that person to take the action we desire?

Once we use this process to come up with content and copy, we can get through one of the critical early stages of storyboarding.

Great online copywriting is responsible for grabbing and holding the prospects' attention by answering their unspoken questions. The answers should be relevant, address their needs and beliefs, and propel them to take the action you want them to take.

2. Rough Sketch

The rough sketch should contain a mockup of the visual aspects of the screen. Create a rectangle representing the page, and block out the elements of your design. Since content is the most important element, start with that. Several other elements must be considered: branding, navigation, page titles, header graphics, and footers, which include copyrights and privacy notices. This is often done using Visio; we use a free stencil of prototyping shapes.

After you've identified the elements, you need to assign each element a priority so you will know which elements need the most emphasis. Then you take into consideration the principles of eye tracking so the elements are placed where a user would expect them to be.

3. Graphical Mockup

After you've chosen an appropriate sketch, start laying it out in Photoshop, Illustrator, Freehand, or whatever your preferred tool. This is the first part of the phase in which we start designing for aesthetics. After all, nearly half of all consumers (46.1 percent) in a Stanford Persuasive Technology Lab study assessed the credibility of websites based primarily on the appeal of their overall visual design. Some things to keep in mind while designing for this phase:

- Scanning and skimming. Lay out your text based on how visitors scan your website and skim text.
- The eight-second Grok rule. The Grok is Future Now, Inc.'s Martian mascot. If he arrived from Mars and had never heard of your company or visited your website before, would he know what your website is about in eight seconds (no matter which page he landed on)?
- Focal point design. This may sound obvious, but you can't imagine how many websites want people to take an action, yet make it virtually impossible to see the call to action. If action isn't obvious from six feet away, your prospects may not know what to do. Don't forget to address your prospects' concerns at the point of action (POA).
- KISS. Or, Keep It Simple, Stupid. Keep in mind the words of Nordstrom's CEO, Dan Nordstrom: "You don't get paid for innovation... You get paid for execution." A BMW and a Ford look very different; however, you could get behind the wheel of either model and drive it skillfully. That's usable design.

Be sure you look at the mockup in grayscale so you can assess how the composition of the piece works without the emotional influence of color. If it looks good in black and white, you've probably got a design that can come alive with the judicious use of color. If it doesn't work in black and white, chances are simple color additions won't play well, either. I can't begin to tell you how many times designs have been scrapped by clients because they were shown the design executed in colors that struck a bad chord. Nail down the design, then add the emotionally charged element of color.

4. Color Mockup

This is where we finally focus on the mood and impact color can create. Better use of color means a better web page or website. If you can carry a color scheme from the landing page to the exit page, you'll automatically create a cohesive look and feel for your site. To understand why color has such an effect on us, we must understand the nature of color. To quote Angela Wright:

Many people think that coloor is just a matter of how things look and it is often dismissed as being purely cosmetic. However, the truth is that colour is light — the source of life itself; there is nowhere that colour does not exist and our instinctive, unconscious response to it is a vital element in our survival.

Color is energy, and the fact that it has a physical effect on us has been proven experimentally time and again.

Wright says that because people's response to color is subjective, it's often assumed their reaction is unpredictable. She disagrees, saying that studying color harmony and psychology can allow you to predict reactions with amazing accuracy. One person may perceive red as exciting, friendly, and stimulating, while another sees it as aggressive and demanding, she says. One person might see blue as calm and soothing, and another may view it as cold and unfriendly.

"It is the combination of colours that triggers the response," says Wright.

If you have corporate colors, choose how to use them on the Web carefully. If you are starting from scratch, use even greater care in choosing your palette.

5. HTML Mockup

Once the color mockup is completed, we can now turn this image into an HTML document. The key here is seeing what can be converted to HTML and what must be an image. This process can be quite a challenge, and it's what separates web designers with graphic knowledge from graphic designers with web knowledge. A savvy coder can code almost any design — but if a designer has an understanding of the limitations of HTML, she can produce beautiful designs without sacrificing usability.

Other considerations are download time, compatibility with multiple browsers, use of cascading style sheets for simplicity, laying out of tables with an understanding of how search engines spider a website, and choosing fonts with an eye toward easy screen reading.

"There are a thousand roads, but only one follows reason." - Chinese proverb

Usability – The On-Ramp to Improved Sales

Usability is something you can no longer ignore. It is like the dial tone for a telephone; you will not miss it unless it isn't there. You have to keep it in mind early on in the design process, and you have to pay attention to usability issues throughout your site. Usability was neglected for years, but suddenly people are talking about it like they've just discovered the Holy Grail. Usability is not the end; it's simply a big step in the right direction.

Usability by itself only reduces your customers' frustration level. That's important, of course, but it's still a far cry from guiding and persuading your customers into doing what they want to do and what you want them to do: buy. Try getting usability to say, "May I take your order?", "What colors do you prefer?", or "Would you like to use VISA or MasterCard?"

Getting Your Bearings

For all the "usability this" and "usability that" these days, it isn't actually all that easy to find a definition of usability out there. One of the most commonly found definitions is simple: ease of use. "Connecting Online: Creating a Successful Image on the Internet" offers a more value-laden meaning: "the quality of enabling your users' productivity." For sure, Connecting Online understands the online business world's general confusion when it comes to usability:

Many businesses look at Web site usability like a foreign object that crash-landed from outer space into their backyards. They've poked and prodded at it, trying to figure out just what it is. Most businesses aren't accustomed to adapting their communications to how their audiences interact with them.

A Smooth Road to Nowhere Still Gets You Nowhere

Make your website easy for your visitors to use, and they'll become more proficient users. But if you want them to become customers, you have to think beyond usability.

Think of it as a road trip. Usability gets rid of the obstacles to driving: the potholes, bad signage, dead ends. It makes it easy for your customers to go places comfortably and smoothly, with minimal interruption. But it can't intrinsically tell them where they ought to be going, much less how to get there the quickest, easiest way.

Usability testing usually measures the effectiveness, efficiency, and satisfaction with which specified users can achieve specified goals in a particular environment. Wouldn't you want your goal in e-commerce to be a sale and, eventually, a delighted customer? Just because users can complete a purchase does not mean you delighted them or that they will ever buy from you again.

The On-Ramp to the Highway of More Sales

You don't want your customers to take just any road. You want them focused on a destination: buying. You want them to take the road that leads them to, and through, buying what they want in a way that is not only quick and easy but also comfortable and delightful.

To accomplish this, you not only have to remove the obstacles but also must guide, encourage, persuade, influence, and motivate your customers to go in a specific direction.

Do you want your customers wandering around easily but aimlessly in the Land of Usability, or do you want them shopping purposefully and buying in the Land of Sales? That land lies beyond usability.

"What's the trick to improving Web site usability? Users. A site can't be judged "good" or "bad" in a vacuum — its value can only be determined by looking at how well it helps users get things done."
- Forrester Research, TechStrategy™ Research: Web Sites Continue To Fail The Usability Test

Don't Confuse Your Web Site with Your Tools

Tools are designed to make our tasks easier. Ideally, a tool is intuitive, easy to use and requires a short learning curve on the part of those who will actually use it. Usability has received so much attention because it fits within the framework of the programmer's rules and established order. Commercial Web development today remains tool-oriented, even state-of-the-art stuff. And the most human-centered professionals in the software world – usability and information architects – are still primarily focused on building a better tool.

Take Jared Spool, a renowned usability specialist. who wants you to "Design for the Multiple Personalities of Users," except he's not really talking personality differences; he's talking skill-set differences.[1] He distinguishes between "core competencies" (the stuff we're really good at doing) and "ring competencies" (the stuff that we're not terribly good at doing), and his organizing question is "How do we design an application for both core users and ring users?" Look at the words: competency, application, extension of skill-sets and knowledge. These are all tool words, not personality words.

Building an exceptional software tool is probably sufficient if you are trying to sell products to people who know exactly what they want, and if your products have unique identifiers, such as Amazon.com's straightforward business model of "book title," "author," "subject" or "ISBN"—how many other ways are there of looking for books? If you are lucky enough to be in that kind of business and have the stomach for the inevitable price competition, you should focus more effort on improving the tool.

The tool analogy may apply to certain business models and the back end or other technical applications (we all want checkout systems that are a breeze to use), but you've got to ask: "Is this really what I'm looking for in my Web site?"

Persuasion Is a Dialog, Not Just a Tool

A commercial website is not a tool. The purpose of your website is to attract, engage with and retain prospects, leads and customers – and it accomplishes this in a medium that is difficult to control. Your visitors are more than simply "users" of the "software." None of them are required to be there. They interact with you because they expect to find something relevant to what they seek.

Recognizing that Web commerce is voluntary and participatory is central to understanding the character of "selling" and "buying" on the Internet. Unlike the majority of other marketing media, the Web is a "pull" (not a "push") medium.

Research shows that most visitors get to a website via four channels: they type in the url directly; they locate a link through a search engine; they respond to a link in an email communication; or they follow the advice of a friend. Your visitors make a decision to visit, and in doing so, broadcast their needs, which they look to you to meet.

A persuasive dialog between you and your visitor is the only way to supply the essential motivation. Some of the most abysmal (and amazingly successful) websites are "adult websites" – and even the most inexpert users manage to figure out how to use them. Motivate your visitors and you've accomplished the lion's share of the job.

More than any other medium, commercial websites attract folks who know exactly what they want – a chicken-and-the-egg proposition that reinforces the idea that commercial websites should be designed as tools. But these folks represent the smallest part of your prospect base.

The two other types of traffic – those who know approximately what they are looking for and those who have an interest but may not actively be in a buying mode – constitute almost every commercial website's sweet spot. They are also the folks websites most often neglect. The persistence of the tool metaphor is the principle reason these critical types of traffic remain underserved in commercial websites. It is much harder to apply a tool to fuzzy objectives like persuasion.

So think about the needs of all those folks who would buy from you with a little bit of help on your part. Think skill-sets, to be sure, but dig deeper and think persuasion, personalities, and motivation. Change the metaphor: it's Dialog, not Tool!

---

[1] http://www.uie.com/articles/multiple_personalities/

"Turn all thy thoughts to eyes, Turn all thy hairs to ears, Change all thy friends to spies, And all thy joys to fears." - Thomas Campion, Turn All Thy Thoughts to Eyes

Gazing into Your Visitors' Eyes

Human behavior is not always predictable. Take "eye-tracking" — the way your eyes move as you search for information. You pick up a newspaper — your eyes go to the pictures first. So it should follow that the same thing will happen when you sit in front of a computer screen, right?

Not so fast now! The Stanford-Poynter Project[1] discovered that when folks read news online, their eyes go for text first, particularly captions and summaries, and graphics only later. Sometimes much later! Sometimes not at all! This has made a lot of commercial copywriters happy. It has also heralded a new field of inquiry: How do visitors scan websites for information.

Why is this information critical for you? If you know how people gather information visually from their browser windows, you've got a powerful design tool you can use right now to support your mission of persuading your visitors to take the action you want. So, how do they do it?

When a user lands on your Web page, she gives the window a quick scan that starts at the top left, moves quickly across the center to the right, then returns leftward, again crossing center, as she works her way down. (Note that this is the pattern for Western cultures.) All this happens in seconds, without the user necessarily fixing her gaze until she reaches the center of the display as she's coming back. It also usually happens without her being aware of it.

What's she doing? She's on a preliminary scouting mission, an effort to quickly orient herself within the context of a page, before she makes the conscious effort to engage with the information. She's also trying to get at least a general sense of whether there's any information there that's worth engaging.

Your logo should be one of the first elements the user encounters at the top of the page (so make sure it's one of the first things that loads). This is your identity. Along with the URL, it lets your users know they've landed in the right place.

Global navigation schemes work well here; they provide the preliminary assurance of general organization and can serve as backup. Make sure your unique value proposition (UVP) is clear and prominent.

Jared Spool's User Interface Engineering group has discovered that a user's gaze ultimately fixes in the center of the screen, then moves left, then right, a pattern of visual fixation true of both new and experienced users. A user fixes on areas other than the center only when she is looking for additional information. The team also found that users pretty much ignore the bottom of the screen and seem to interact peripherally with the right area. (Folks use their vertical scroll bar without actually looking at it!).

Clearly, the center area of the screen is prime real estate, the "active window", where you will either succeed or fail in persuading your visitor. This is the first place your visitor makes a conscious effort to engage with you. When her gaze returns across the screen from its preliminary scan, you want to make sure you present content that will capture her interest and motivate her through the conversion process. If anything on the page distracts her or requires her to disconnect from the center area, she is that much less likely to stay, rapt by your powers of persuasion. And if you've learned the Stanford-Poynter lesson, you'll understand that your copy is much more important than your images.

The left side of the screen can function as a "stabilizing window," a place where people look for particular points of reference that can help them locate the items that suit their needs. Comprehensive navigation works well here.

Even when they remain engaged in the central area, users peripherally attend to the right area. This becomes a valuable space to convey confidence through your assurances, guarantees, and testimonials. Calls to action do well here, too. A "subscribe to our newsletter" link is a good example. For another, notice how Amazon.com has its "Add to Shopping Cart" and "1-Click" action block in the top right, and below this is its "Add to Wish List" button. Because the user is peripherally aware of it, she knows it is there if and when she is ready to take that action.

Using your knowledge of eye-tracking, your general order of business is, first, to orient your visitor, then use your active window to keep her attention and persuade her to become a buyer (or subscriber or whatever your goal is). The other screen real estate on your website is no less important to the overall effort, but your users are simply never going to give it the same visual priority.

If you know how folks scan, you have a template for placing things on your Web pages so your visitors will find what they are looking for where they expect to find it and in the way that engages best. You can use this information to meet your customers' needs and thereby increase your conversion rate!

---

[1] http://www.poynter.org/eyetrack2000/index.htm

"The ability to focus attention on important things is a defining characteristic of intelligence."
- Robert J. Shiller, Irrational Exuberance

Focus on the User, Not the Usability

Usability is related to the individual's subjective experience. Usability as a discipline focuses on use, not the user. Many usability professionals have now moved their core philosophy some and appear to focus on "user-centered design" (UCD). Usability as a discipline, however, can trace its roots back to Frederick Winslow Taylor, the father of scientific management and industrial production.

Usability focuses on improving the tools we use and compensated users for participating in studies, thus providing the intrinsic motivation to help management create more efficient systems. Usability experts gather a handful of "average users" and watch as they engage with the tool in question. Hopefully the user research they conduct is statistically significant.

Market conditions determine what software programs we must figure out how to use; tools and equipment we need at work are similar. But when users land on your website, they bring their own needs, wants, perspectives, and motivations. They're volunteers on your website, and they choose whether they'll continue interacting with you If they feel you don't understand them, if they can't figure out what to do, or if you're just not providing the value they want offered, they're one click away from your competitor's website.

Users evaluate the level of empathy you display for their wants, needs, and desires. Usability is based on the physiological and psychological principle that only an individual's perception can explain. If users perceive you as empathetic, they'll continue to navigate your website despite the usability faults they experience. Am I saying we shouldn't remove the faults? Of course not! However, your website being usable can't overcome an inability to meet the motivations and desires of users.

In 1999, software designer and consultant Alan Cooper brilliantly introduced the concept of designing software with personas. Designers themselves in their users' shoes, imagining different personas that might be using the software. Then they design based on different personas' potential mindsets.

This is an excellent example of UCD. Website design has seen quite a bit of interest in the last year or so. Marketing professionals will be instantly familiar with the process of persona development, as it is very similar to what they do in the market definition phase. The main difference between marketing personas and design personas is that the former are based on demographics and distribution channels, whereas the latter are based purely on users. The two are not the same, and don't serve the same purpose. The marketing personas shed light on the sales process, whereas the design personas shed light on the development process.

So many of the UCD companies created design personas to use during their development process. Don't let the medium get in the way of the message. A commercial website (one in which a business needs to meet ROI objectives and have visitors take some sort of desired action) is more a persuasive and interactive dialogue. It's akin to the visitor having a conversation with your website, which acts as a digital salesperson.

Salespeople instinctively adapt their sales presentations to fit customer preferences. Reading the customer's facial expressions and body language and listening beyond the customer's questions to interpret tone of voice, the salesperson "sells" each customer in whatever way that customer prefers to be sold.

A digital salesperson correctly reads the customer's interests, then adapts the website's presentation accordingly. Like its human counterpart, the digital salesperson will adjust and conform the flow of information to suit the needs and preferences of each individual. Each click on a hyperlink or query in a search engine is a question your visitor needs answered. You present the information in a way visitors want.

The digital salesperson is concerned with addressing the marketing persona. Are you designing your website with the sales process or just the development process in mind?

Scenario Design – Setting the Scene

Scenario design helps users achieve their goals. How do you plan scenarios? Well, if you're designing scenarios for a commercial Web site, one that demonstrates return on investment (ROI) by getting sales, leads, or registrants, you design persuasive scenarios by turning the information you have on your users into personas.

"The American Heritage Dictionary" defines "persona" as:

1. A voice or character representing the speaker in a literary work.
2. The characters in a dramatic or literary work.
3. The role that one assumes or displays in public or society; one's public image or personality, as distinguished from the inner self.

Define a Persona in Three Stages

Personas created for a persuasive experience must initially be defined by completely understanding their needs. Their needs lead into character biographies and narratives of the scenarios they are likely to engage in. These represent and convey their worldview, attitude, personality, and behavior. Personas are constructed from research that describes their demographics, psychographics, and topographics related to how they approach the buying decision process for the products or services offered. This provides insight into the language these individuals use.

A medium-sized business owner seeking a search engine marketing (SEM) firm is likely more motivated by words such as "pay for performance" and other assertive terms than the director of Internet marketing for a Global 100 company. The latter is more motivated by words such as "stability," "accountability," and other methodical terms that would get a superior to sign off.

Valued Words: the keywords and trigger words for each of these personas also vary by where they are in the purchase consideration process. We tie keyword research back to our personas.

The principle value of personas developed for the sales process is that they provide an understanding of how to approach the initiation of relationships. They exemplify how they gather information, how they approach the decision-making process, what language they use, and how they prefer to obtain agreement and closure.

We're not concerned with what an interface looks like at this point. We use personas to define how people will arrive at the website and what questions they have and to connect them to the content that helps them buy the way they want to.

How Personas Link to Content

The structure is everything. During persuasion architecture wireframing (not what most people mistakenly think of online wireframing), we define the structure of the interaction and how each page is connected to others. This allows multiple personas to access the same pages but identifies how to address each persona's needs on the page. The goal is to design an experiential model or persuasion scenario in a context that can be viewed by clicking through hypertext (an interactive flowchart on steroids). The wireframe defines the hyperlinked organization of content. It isn't content yet; it's the definition of the content's objectives.

Wireframing Persona Experience

The Web is about links, connections, and the interactivity of information. Hypertext connects related pieces of information with pre-established or user-created links, allowing a user to follow associative trails. If you take the time to properly understand search engine algorithms such as PageRank, HITS, or citation analysis, you'll discover, at their core, hyperlink analysis and keywords surrounding those hyperlinks have the greatest value. Knowing that, wouldn't it make sense to design those hyperlinks? They improve both search engine rankings and persuasion architecture.

Exploding the Myth of the Primary Persona

A primary challenge of traditional user-centered design (UCD) is that after creating diverse and distinct personas, most design efforts focus on the primary persona. That's like building a supermarket for people who are 5ft. 5in. tall, because that's the average height of American females. Supermarkets in fact plan which items are on which shelves based on who will see them. Take a walk down the cereal aisle. The majority of sweet children's cereal is way below your eye level.

Your website has many types of visitors. Very few commercial websites cater to only one type of visitor with one set of demographic, psychographic, and topographic characteristics. Forrester Research principal analyst Harley Manning writes in "The Power of Design Personas":

In theory, satisfying the primary persona will satisfy all users. In practice, sites that need to serve many types of customers, prospects, employees, and partners optimize for some at the expense of others. This tension will lead to a revival of interest in personalization as a way to automatically route visitors to a version of the site that matches their user archetype.

Conversion rates of 2 to 5 percent are explained by the misunderstanding of personas' roles in persuasion. Not every buyer is ready to buy now. Only the primary persona or, worse, an average visitor is addressed. No surprise, then, most websites convert badly. When a mass audience with diverse needs can self-select based on click-through, you can't focus on the needs of only one. Account for the psychographic, emotional, and linguistic needs of your diverse buyer universe.

A mass-market product with advertising designed for tweens cannot sell to the entire market. Similarly flawed are websites that try to market to Hispanic audiences by translating an existing English website. The marketers don't understand the cultural biases, idiosyncrasies, and linguistic nuances required to persuade Hispanic visitors.

Traditional UCD principles inspire, even if they don't answer all our questions. The objective is to understand the market, the content, and the persuasion processes, not to focus on primary personas, tasks, and software interface design. The latter are important only after persuasion architecture structure and messaging are complete.

Before designing a single pixel or writing a single word, get a feel for the experience personas will have navigating the website with the wireframe. Spend time up front planning the hyperlinks and the words around them, to be sure each page the personas visit will be relevant to satisfying their needs and answer their questions, moving them one step further in the buying process.

Here are four hypothetical personas of possible attendees for a search engine marketing conference. In an atypical example, I've purposely named each persona Janet Smith. They're all college-educated, single women, aged 33-36. They have annual incomes of $65,000-$75,000 and work in marketing. They all live on the same block in downtown Manhattan and work in the same building in midtown Manhattan. They've been using the Web for several years and are proficient in all Microsoft Office applications. They use Internet Explorer as their default browser on 17in. monitors set at 1,024 x 768 and use high speed connections.

From a traditional user-centered design (UCD) perspective, these four personas could be regarded as identical. They share the same demographics. And they share the same goal: attending the search engine marketing conference.

Persona #1: Janet Smith

Janet, a 36-year-old marketing director, works for an Internet company that licenses data to manufacturers on a business-to-business (B2B) basis. The company powers comparison channel websites and well-known manufacturer websites. In addition, it powers all the comparison data at popular industry research websites.

Janet makes judgments decisively. She wanted the website to generate more revenue, so she introduced the business-to-consumer (B2C) concept to run the website as a profit center. Results have been great. Revenue for channel and manufacturing websites is about $5 million, with 90 percent of that generated from the B2B channels. But B2C is rising.

Janet's main challenge is search engines' inability to effectively spider the websites. She understands a website requires optimization (SEO) for search engines. But because the channel websites are dynamic, Janet wants help understanding exactly how to get them indexed. She has discretionary money in her budget to attend conferences but must make sure her assistant can reach her while she's gone.

She has a secondary motivation to attend the conference. She wants to meet and socialize with the industry's top experts.

Persona #2: Janet Smith

Janet is 35 years old and runs Internet marketing for a medium-sized click-and-mortar retailer. The company sells products to a niche market and has been in business 10 years. It's been profitable from the beginning. Last year, it finally decided to build an e-commerce website. The website also offers a few exclusive product lines for testing before they're rolled out in stores.

Janet has assembled a team of energetic young people to develop and maintain the website. The website's done reasonably well in search engines, because Janet works with the content and IT people to focus more on the customer and less on the technology. But with growing competition, changes in Google's algorithm, and Yahoo! soon replacing Google in its search engine results pages (SERPs), Janet wants to stay ahead of the curve.

In the past, conferences allowed her to network with and learn from search engine reps, industry experts, marketers, engineers, Webmasters, and business owners. Colleagues who referred her to this company were actually people she met at previous conferences. She'd like to attend the next conference but must convince her boss to allow her to go.

She'd really like to keep up the friendships she's developed from attending past conferences. This time, she hopes to focus more on the conference itself, and go to sessions on organic search in particular. She doesn't want to miss too much valuable information during the morning sessions because of the inevitable late-night parties and time spent with colleagues.

Persona #3: Janet Smith

Janet, 33 years old, is responsible for search engine marketing (SEM) at an interactive agency. She was recently promoted from media planner to SEM because of her methodical presentation of client documentation. She's still unsure about how to get more return on investment (ROI) from her current ad budget. In her previous position, she oversaw trafficking out ads. She has more direct contact with clients now and is certain she could manage their ad budgets more effectively.

One of the company's plans this year is to begin marketing to Hispanics. She's interested in conference sessions that could help.

Persona #4: Janet Smith

Janet is a 34-year-old PR specialist. She partnered with four other PR specialists and developed a business writing and sending out press releases almost guaranteed to be read. She describes her company as the best of the best because of the experience and flair of her company's people.

Although Janet's style ensures her press releases get read, sometimes in SERPs her press releases are buried below negative press about the company or product she's promoting. Janet wants to provide value to her clients and realizes her SEO skills aren't very good. A creative marketer, she's been in the PR industry for nearly 15 years and on the Web since '96. She's become a household name in her industry. She feels almost forced to learn how to optimize her press releases properly for search engines to remain the expert she is.

Personas as a Tool for Competitive Analysis of Websites

If we accept the above as realistic conference attendee personas, how would they influence the experience and content on the website? Make the effort to empathize with each one. Visit conference websites, and compare each persona's experience. A competitive analysis from your visitor's point of view is more valuable than one from your own.

Conversion Tip

Understand the Stages of e-Commerce

Where are you losing purchasers who want to purchase? There are only six places:

1) Finding — the shopper can't find the right area of the site where your product is described.
2) Selecting — You aren't giving the shopper enough information to select the right product for them. They can't tell the difference between your offerings.
3) Deciding — The shopper can't tell if the selected product is going to meet their needs or desires.
4) Carting — The shopper doesn't know how to tell you they are interested in purchasing this product.
5) Checkout — The shopper can't complete the checkout process to place their order.
6) Fulfillment — The shopper doesn't get the product they ordered or decides they want to return it.

Each of these six areas is a target for repair. Of course, you need to know where you're currently losing purchasers. (One common mistake is that everyone seems to focus on checkout, yet it traditionally is only responsible for 13 percent of lost sales. The first three stages — finding, selecting, and deciding — typically represent more than 60 percent of lost sales. Focusing there would be smarter.)

How do you figure out where you are losing purchases? Well, the simplest way is to watch people buy. Sit next to people who really want to buy something and watch them (without helping) as they go through the shopping process. I'm betting, if you do this 3 or 4 times, you'll have a huge list of things you want to change on the site.

- **Jared Spool**, Usability Guru of User Interface Engineering

"Advertising is criticized on the ground that it can manipulate consumers to follow the will of the advertiser. The weight of evidence denies this ability. Instead, evidence supports the position that advertising, to be successful, must understand or anticipate basic human needs and wants and interpret available goods and services in terms of their want-satisfying abilities. This is the very opposite of manipulation." - Charles H. Sandage

Why Success Among the Failures

When asked why Newport News' online sales had surged ahead of other higher profile apparel e-tailers, like Lands' End, J. Crew and Eddie Bauer, management's response was that it was partly because the company took a different approach to presenting its merchandise.

Rather than classifying merchandise entirely by category, Newport News relies heavily on presenting goods within the context of fashion themes and trends. For instance, following one of the trends dictated by the fashion cognoscenti, the website features a Shades of Summer display that includes a wide variety of clothes that have nothing in common but the brightness of their colors.

That approach appeals more to impulse shoppers. The fashion business is an impulse business. People don't just wake up needing a red short-sleeve dress.

For users who know what they want, the website should sell it easily.

Newport News knows how to design for its business, market, and customers quite well. The bottom line is always the bottom line.

In the early days of the new economy, websites didn't work. Website owners didn't spend time fixing business models and marketing plans. They took little time caring about customer relationships or understanding what prospects wanted. They took less time to contemplate and create content and images that were persuasive and instilled desire. They hired designers and programmers and hoped money would trickle in faster than it poured out. When the party was over, they hired usability experts to fix the disasters their techies created and still filed Chapter 11.

Usability experts observe a few people in laboratories (not their normal environment) but turn their noses up at Web analytics that record what large, statistically valid samples actually do. Asking people what they will do is futile; they don't really know (e.g., they say that they want to eat healthy but "supersize" their value meals). Observing people in a lab is less than optimal, since those are not true market conditions. Observing what people do under real market conditions where the real world distracts and interacts with them is a much more powerful method.

For example, based on tests done with real offers and real audiences, we've found that fonts rarely affect conversion rates. However, we've conducted simultaneous, large-sample A/B splits on e-mail and website copy and found significant change in conversion based on font size and/or style. We even found that changing a font style from Arial to Comic Sans in an HTML e-mail increased conversion by almost 30 percent.

Style rarely matters, but increasing font size is more likely to improve conversion. The font style should be congruent with the message. In the example given above, the message tone was conversational and informal. Comic Sans fit the mood we were trying to create.

Here are my keys to success:

- Usability: important
- Good programming: necessary
- Persuasive copy and design: critical
- Business objectives balanced with customer needs: invaluable
- Customer satisfaction and profit: priceless

Great studies come from usability labs, but I look at the same data and reach different conclusions.

"Radio let people see things with their own ears." - *New York Times*

WIIFM: Your Favorite on the Dial

Isn't your favorite station WIIFM — What's In It For Me!? It's everyone else's favorite on their personal radio dial. How can this be when each personality has preferences in how they interact, view the world, and reach decisions?

Since the time of Aristotle, people have determined that each of the millions of different personalities falls into one of four groups by temperament: Competitive, Spontaneous, Humanistic and Methodical.

A major objective of a website is to be able to consistently communicate to each of the four temperaments, so that the prospect can "self-serve" himself or herself the appropriate information that they require to influence their buying decision. To give each personality exactly what they want and need, we have to take a look at the four basic personality types:

The Competitive wants Accomplishment: These assertive individuals have a deep appreciation for challenges. They enjoy being in control, are goal oriented and are looking for methods of completing tasks. They are usually quick to reach a decision. They want to know what your product or service can do for them to solve their problem.

Guided by intuition and thinking, they seek competence in themselves and others, they want to understand and control life. Driven by curiosity, the Competitive is often preoccupied with learning twenty-four hours a day. These individuals have a deep appreciation for challenges.

Attitude: Businesslike, power oriented

Use of Time: Disciplined, fast paced

Question: What can your solution do for me?

Approach: Provide options, probabilities and challenges

Sample Copy(underlining indicates which phrases this personality type will respond to most strongly): Our approach is personalized to meet your objectives. The <u>bottom line</u> is that <u>your results are guaranteed</u>. Explore our methodology to discover how thousands of clients just like you have been delighted.

The Spontaneous wants Acceptance: These individuals appreciate the personal touch. They like things that are non-threatening and friendly. They hate dealing with impersonal details and cold hard facts, and are usually quick to reach a decision. They want to know why your product or service is the best to solve their problem.

Spontaneous people are sensing-perceiving. They are always engaged in a personal quest for their unique identity and live their lives as an expression of it. For them, integrity means the unity of inner self with outer expression. These individuals like personal attention. They like things that are non-threatening and friendly.

Attitude: Personal, activity oriented

Use of Time: Undisciplined, fast paced

Question: Why is your solution best to solve the problem?

Approach: Provide guarantees and assurances, personal solutions, credible opinions rather than options

Sample Copy:

<u>Our approach is personalized to meet your objectives.</u> The bottom line is that your results are guaranteed. Explore our methodology to discover how thousands of clients just like you have been delighted.

The Humanistic wants Applause: These individuals are very creative and entertaining. They enjoy helping others and are particularly fond of socializing. They are usually slow to reach a decision. They want to know who has used your product or service to solve problems.

Humanistics are guided by intuition and feeling. They need to belong. They often feel that they must earn a place by belonging, by being useful, fulfilling responsibilities, being of service, giving to and caring for others instead of receiving from them.

Attitude: Personal, relationship oriented

Use of Time: Undisciplined, slow paced

Question: Who has used your solution to solve my problem?

Approach: Offer testimonials and incentives

Sample Copy:

Our approach is personalized to meet your objectives. The bottom line is that your results are guaranteed. Explore our methodology to discover how <u>thousands of clients just like you have been delighted.</u>

The Methodical wants Accuracy: These individuals appreciate facts and information presented in a logical manner as documentation of truth. Methodicals are sensing-judging and need to feel free to act. For them, "doing" is its own reward. They enjoy organization and completion of detailed tasks. They do not appreciate the "personal touch" or disorganization. They want to know how your product or service can solve the problem.

Attitude: Businesslike, detail oriented

Use of Time: Disciplined, slow paced

Question: How can your solution solve the problem?

Approach: Provide hard evidence and superior service

Sample Copy:

Our approach is personalized to meet your objectives. The bottom line is that your results are guaranteed. Explore our <u>methodology</u> to discover how thousands of clients just like you have been delighted.

Once you understand these profiles, you can create a website that appeals to your visitors' needs and helps persuade them as they most like to be persuaded. Keep in mind that these categories are generalizations. Humans are amazingly complex creatures, and any classification attempt is a simplification of this complexity. On top of that, no one person is all one personality type. We are all delightful mixtures — one type may predominate, but others come into play, often influenced by environmental factors, social factors, even ephemeral moods. So, even though you may know for a fact that 72 percent of your visitors are Methodicals, that doesn't mean you can design a conversion process that appeals only to the Methodical profile! You need to create multiple but interlinking paths in which their visitors can "self-serve" the customer experience they prefer.

Knowing who your visitors are is going to influence everything you do on your website, from how you structure your selling process, how and where you place different categories of information, what calls to action you provide, how you write your copy, all the way through to the colors you choose.

Resonating Tones on WIIFM

Different personality types ask different questions, require different sorts of information to feel comfortable making their decisions and even take different amounts of time in which to make their decisions. Think about how all this works in the "real" world.

Imagine you are an impressionistic, Humanistic type, and you go to a bricks-and-mortar store to purchase a digital camera. All you want is a camera that takes pictures and isn't a big hassle. You just want to enjoy yourself. The salesperson comes on like a know-it-all and rattles on about pixels and resolutions and cabling and any number of other technical considerations you really could care less about. You want to know, and truly only care about, whether the camera is going to fit into your lifestyle. Will it be a good match for your expectations and how you generally use techie gadgets like this? If the salesperson can't communicate the information you need to know, in the way you want to learn it, you're not going to be happy. You are going to start tuning out the salesperson. And you'll probably walk away none-the-wiser, as well as cameraless.

Now, imagine you are a very Methodical sort of person. You've done the research and inherently understand the advantages or disadvantages of each feature. To feel comfortable about a purchase, you need to know you are getting a camera designed to meet your criteria. You want to speak with someone who knows all the facts and can answer all your questions. But you get a different salesperson in our theoretical store, and this one wants to tell you all about how easy the camera is to use and shows you print-out images and explains how her Mom has one and loves it. This is going to strike you as vague and ditsy. You are going to start tuning out the salesperson and may well conclude she doesn't know the first thing about what she's trying to sell.

Good salespeople know whether or not they are saying what the customer needs to hear, the way the customer needs to hear it, in order to make a decision to purchase. And a good salesperson knows how to redirect the presentation quickly if it isn't working. It's one of the most essential components of "the sale."

Acknowledging personality types online is critical — you are conducting business in a self-service medium. You aren't there to modify your persuasion tactics when you notice they're falling on deaf ears. You only notice you've missed the mark when you check out your Web logs.

Online, it's the responsibility of your hyperlinks to establish, maintain and offer alternatives to your "dialog." So how do you do that?

Let's distill the information above to the basics:

- Competitive prefers to focus on WHAT questions.
- Spontaneous prefers to focus on WHY questions.
- Humanistic prefers to focus on WHO questions.
- Methodical prefers to focus on HOW questions.

Average sales people sell to those that they relate to the best – those that resonate with them. On average they will usually sell to 3 out of 10 people they meet. Another 3 out of the 10 won't buy from them no matter what. The last 4 out of 10 are sitting on the fence. It is the great sales person or website that learns to give these 4 the information and assistance they need to reach their buying decision.

Also, the nature of the products or services you offer will influence who your audience is. Pure impulse-buying is going to appeal most to the friendly, impulsive Spontaneous types.

A site selling engineering equipment is going to attract more Methodicals than Humanistics … and even if a Humanistic engineer requires the product, his job requires that he be concerned with a logical, orderly, precise and features-attentive approach. And if you run an online dating service, no matter how Methodical or Competitive your visitor, she is likely to approach this service in a Humanistic state of mind.

Your ultimate goal is to delight each of your visitors, for the delighted customer is the one most likely to complete a purchase, refer your business to others and return to buy again. This personality stuff is the key. And there's no time like the present for getting personable!!

Have you tuned into your customer's favorite station or will you march by the beat of your own drummer? "It's still an emotional sort of place, an unforgettable crossroads for any traveler, where shoppers from suburbia mix with international businessmen, where kids with buckets and spades mingle with passengers for the Orient Express and where city gents carrying brollies step over more colorful travelers carrying guitars. Spend the morning here and you'll see every stereotype on earth."
- Mike Wallington

Stereotypes Have No Place in Personas

If you sell aromatherapy products, are all your visitors nature-loving women who are vegetarians, do yoga, mediate, promote world peace and wear Birkenstocks?

If you sell satellite service for football viewers, are all your customers blue collar, middle-aged, beer swilling, potato chip crunching male couch-spuds of medium to minimal IQ who brag about the size of their TVs?

Careful now . . . you may be slipping into the stereotype trap. It's not hard to do; stereotypes are embedded in our culture. In some ways, they have their value. But when you do business online, you don't undertake transactions with stereotypes any more than you undertake transactions with a single generic composite of your audience.

You might not see their faces out there behind the computer screens and your Web analytics, but you are dealing with real people who have real needs and complicated motivations. Create a persuasive architecture based on stereotypes, and you're going to miss the mark.

The Pros and Cons of Stereotyping

What's a stereotype, you ask? It's both intangible yet as solid as the person sitting next to you:

ster-e-o-type
- A conventional, formulaic, and oversimplified conception, opinion, or image.
- One who is regarded as embodying or conforming to a set image or type.

Because they are largely based in truth, stereotypes make sense. We quickly know and recognize these people. Students at Miami University have assembled a tutorial project on stereotyping:

If I were to tell you that I resemble a hippy woman from the 60's, you would definitely be able to come up with a mental image of me, right! Flowers in my long, flowing hair, a tie-dyed T-shirt, and bell bottom pants. I am a free spirit, and an open minded Liberal.

Perhaps the description helps you get a mental image of myself. By creating such mental pictures and having a preconceived notion of what a hippy looks like, and what characteristics he or she has, you are using the cognitive short cut called stereotyping. We utilize stereotypes in everyday life to reduce the amount of information we need to analyze. Our world is so complex that we need to categorize who and what we come into contact with on a daily basis. People tend to use stereotypes to "fill in" details about a person if they are not a member of their in-group and they do not possess the motivation to get to know them on a more personal basis.[1]

So, if stereotyping is quite normal – even advantageous – then why fuss about it? The critical problem lies in these two words: "oversimplified conception." Stereotypes are, by definition, superficial. They are shortcuts that, for our purposes, can prevent you from doing the important research that allows you to develop a deeper understanding of who your customers really are, what they really want and how you should be communicating with them.

How often is a stereotype's description free of mean-spirited judgment? Do you generally feel stereotypes communicate respect? All too often, stereotypes incorporate prejudice: white trash, red neck, tree-hugger, flaming liberal, fundamentalist, etc. These certainly conjure up stereotypic images that are not necessarily flattering. They don't get you any closer to understanding the interior of an individual who might very well be interested in buying from you.

When you prepare persuasive copy for someone who is coming to your website, you must be able to empathize with that person. But it's hard to empathize with folks you characterize negatively – even though you might not be aware of that negativity. Develop empathy with your website's visitors, and you'll be able to shape copy that communicates empathetically with them.

Other Types of Stereotyping

For decades, marketers have categorized their audiences in terms of demographic information, a variant form of stereotyping. They group folks by income brackets, residential attributes, gender, and then pitch the message to the category. Take soccer moms. These generally are educated, middle-class, caring mothers who combine work and taking care of the family. This demographic group may share certain traits, but they are also widely divergent in their motivations, needs and desires. The demographics alone do not give you any information about how each of these soccer moms approach a decision to buy. From the perspective of persuasion, these demographic caricatures are one dimensional.

Let's say you're selling life insurance to a 65-year old retired man. He's a veteran and has worked for the same accounting firm for 30 years. He's been married to the same woman his whole life. He is very structured, black and white, detail oriented, methodical, collects stamps and builds model airplanes. You could resort to a fairly typical stereotypic image of this fellow based on this information. But suppose you were to find out just a little more about this guy. Beyond collecting stamps and building model airplanes, he takes Tai Kwan Do so he can practice with his grandson, and he maintains his own blog. Does this version give you something more dimensional? More interesting? Do these small details give you a different insight into this man; do they make him seem more human, the sort of person you could actually communicate with meaningfully?

Go for the Full-Rounded Persona

When you create the personas that will form the basis of your online persuasive process, you want to develop comprehensively fleshed-out characters with names, personality attributes, personal concerns, communication styles, and time management qualities. You want to craft profiles that bring each persona to life; include information like a first and last name, job, worries, family, needs, and desires. Compose a description that is three or more paragraphs long; even include faux quotes from the individual written in his or her own "voice." In essence, you want to create someone with whom you can imagine carrying on a substantive, persuasive conversation that answers the questions they would ask of you.

The development of personas appropriate to your business combines an understanding of:

- Demographics: What are the person's attributes?
- Psychographics: What does the person do psychologically as part of their buying decision process?
- Topographics: How do the demographics and psychographics mesh with similar selling processes within the company's own industry?

Creating great personas depends not only on conducting traditional market research, but more importantly, on talking to individuals in your customer service department, retail sales reps and anyone within the company who has a lot of client interaction.

This valuable information guides the critical answers to the questions that should frame the development of your website:

- Who are you trying to persuade?
- What information does that person need in order to be persuaded?
- What language most effectively engages them and motivates them further into the process?

You want to interact online with people, not stereotypes. So be careful not to design your persuasive process and copy for stereotypes. Don't take short cuts. Get to know your visitors on a personal basis. It will help you understand and communicate with them far more effectively.

---

[1] "Primetime Stereotyping: Social Psychological Effects on an Impressionable Culture." Tutorial by Pamela Davis, Lisa Russell, Amber Ruth and Robert Woods. Psybersite. Miami University: 2002. http://www.units.muohio.edu/psybersite/primetime/INDEX.shtml

Conversion Tip

Ask Everyone at Your Company to Describe Your Customers

Everyone in your company is thinking about your customers. Actually, everyone in your company thinks they are thinking about your customers. But they are probably not thinking about your customers in the same way that you do. If you were to look inside the heads of your coworkers, you'd find all sorts of 'customers' to focus on. Some envision themselves as 'the customer.' Lots of people think of 'my mom' as the customer. There are dozens of imaginary customers impacting the design of your store. Want proof? Send an email out asking everyone to describe the most important customer of your store.

To get your colleagues thinking about the same customer in the same ways, consider:

- How you can make available data (market research reports, user studies, demographic profiling reports, etc.) usable and useful to the folks on the front-lines of product-related decision-making. Blow off the dust, and use what you already have.
- Gathering as much of this data about your customers as you can and create personas. Demand that everyone in the company stop talking about 'the user' or 'the customer' and start talking specifically about "Samuel" and "Roberta."
- Using what you know about "Samuel" and "Roberta" to make design decisions based on real data.
- Building an experience that your personas will love.

Then, with everyone on the same page, look for improved conversion results.

- **Tamara Adlin**, Senior Usability Specialist at a major e-tailer and co-author with John Pruitt, The Persona Lifecycle: Keeping People in Mind During Product Design, Morgan Kaufmann Press, summer 2005

"When dealing with people, let us remember we are not dealing with creatures of logic. We are dealing with creatures of emotion, creatures bustling with prejudices and motivated by pride and vanity." - Dale Carnegie

Is Your Home Page Helping or Hindering Sales?

If you want to increase your online sales, you have to begin at the beginning. Your home page is literally 50 percent of the battle; virtually every visitor will come back to your homepage to reorient themselves. If it doesn't do what it should, your visitors won't be able to get deeper into your website — or they simply won't want to.

A weak home page creates a double disaster. First, there's no sale. And that means that the marketing budget, creative effort, and time you invested to get those visitors all go up in smoke. It's better not to drive visitors to your home page at all than to drive them to a page that loses them. They not only will never come back (repeat, never), but statistics have shown that a person who has a bad online shopping experience tells five times as many people about it as someone who has a good experience.

Good news about you travels fast, but bad news travels even faster. You simply can't afford not to do it right.

Eye Candy Is Dandy, But Not Very Nutritious to Your Bottom Line

What must your home page do to prevent this double disaster? First and foremost, at least the text portion of your page should download fast. How fast? Eight to ten seconds is ideal. More than that and your visitors start to bail from impatience. Beyond 30 seconds and you can kiss most of your marketing budget and all of your first time potential impulse buyers goodbye.

Designers, talented though they may be and eager to show off that talent, typically live in a world of T1s and broadband connections. The hard reality of the online sales world is that many customers still surf at 56K or slower.

In concrete terms, this means your entire home page file should be around 35K, 40K max. Most home pages are bigger — a lot bigger. But that's precisely the problem. They take so long to load that the visitor is gone long before the designer's creative talent can even be seen.

If you want to maximize sales, as opposed to having a beautiful design showcase that actually discourages sales, then the designer's challenge is to develop a great look and feel within the constraints of 35-40K.

A fast download time is just the beginning. Equally important is what the visitor sees once the page has loaded. Here are some of the more critical elements:

- Is the look and feel professional?
- Is the navigation obvious, simple and consistent throughout the website?
- Is your unique selling proposition (USP) clearly stated and strong?

- Is your information architecture constructed from the visitor's point of view?
- Does your navigation anticipate and clearly support all reasonable path choices?
- Does the layout reflect knowledge of eye-scanning patterns and "sweet spots"?
- Does the choice of page elements reflect knowledge of how visitors use text versus graphics online as opposed to in print?
- Are the graphics and the text appropriate and well-chosen/written?
- Does the page reflect principles of good usability?
- Does the page utilize expert sales principles that encourage a buying decision?
- Does the page utilize knowledge about consumer psychology and the different personality types?
- Does the page make use of knowledge about online buying behavior?
- Does the page inspire trust and build rapport? (Remember in these times security is more of an emotional issue than a technological one.)
- Is your contact information easy to find?
- Is help available? Is it user-centered (versus tech-centered)?
- How many help channels do you provide? (e.g., email, FAQ, phone, live on the web)
- Are the smallest details, such as fonts and colors, chosen with an understanding and knowledge of what maximizes sales?
- Does the page delight visitors and inspire them to go deeper into the website? Does it actually guide them in doing so?

Can You Apply the "AIDAS" Test?

Here's a tool from the world of offline sales that is just as powerful online — and perhaps even more so. It's known by the acronym "AIDA," or as our company has expanded it, "AIDAS" (attention, interest, desire, action, and satisfaction).

Every successful professional sale incorporates these elements at every step; they drive the process of turning visitors into buyers. So apply the AIDAS test to your home page:

1. Does the page grab visitors' attention — in about eight seconds?
2. Does the page stimulate interest and reinforce the reader's confidence about being in the right place?
3. Does the page inspire the desire to take the action of clicking deeper toward a purchase?
4. Is how to take that action obvious and easy?
5. After they've clicked, does the next page give them satisfaction by providing them with exactly what they wanted exactly how they wanted it?

Once you've tested for AIDAS on your home page, test every other page on your website. When you've implemented AIDAS on the micro-level of the page, step back and test whether AIDAS works for you on a macro-level. Check if your visitors can move comfortably but irresistibly from your home page, through your entire website, to and through the checkout page.

Conversion Tip

Here is a special note for smaller websites. Large, well-known and frequently used websites like Amazon.com seem to break this rule regularly. Amazon.com's homepage loads well in excess of 30 seconds. However, vistors perceive Amazon.com's homepage to load more quickly than it does. Perception is the key point here. User Interface Engineering conducted research on this topic and you can explore further on their website: UIE.com.

- - **Future Now, Inc.**

"Another piece of verbal cleverness" - Significantly Anonymous Soul Whom We Really Should Know But Don't

Beyond the Sacred Portal of the Home Page

For many website owners the home page of their website is a Sacred Portal through which visitors enter the cyber-structure of your business. They treat their website as if all other avenues of entry were blocked, and the process could only start at Square One.

Everyone knows, even those slightly Web-savvy, that the process can start at any page that is readable by a search engine. With pay-per-click advertisements and email campaigns, marketers can directly influence the starting point. It is possible for visitors to arrive and start digging deeper into your conversion process without ever bothering with the home page.

They'll arrive on a landing page — something very much like a focused mini home page — and how successful you are at catching them will depend on what you do with that page. Landing pages are always sales process pages. They always constitute a step in the conversion process of catching pre-qualified traffic and moving it along its way to taking action. That action might be a micro-action, yet another step in the conversion process. Or it could be the macro-action, the ultimate conversion goal you have for your visitors.

A sales process page actively persuades your visitor to accomplish some phase (and sometimes all phases) of the 5-step AIDAS selling process. There aren't hard and fast rules for which pages need to be treated as sales process pages because they are specific to each business and its objectives. For someone selling candles, the About Us page is probably not going to be a sales process page. However, for someone selling consulting services, the About Us page could easily be critical to the sales process.

The same principles that apply to your home page apply broadly to your landing pages. If a landing page is the first interaction a visitor has with your website, it needs to perform the home page functions:

- Identify who you are
- Communicate WIIFM (What's In It For Me?)
- Incorporate AIDAS for Persuasive Momentum

Unlike any old page, your landing pages can and should be constructed to reinforce the reason your visitors landed there. When they come to you through your intentional online marketing strategies, either by pay-per-click or email, your visitors have a significantly higher degree of interest. You have given them a purpose to come. They see a pay-per-click ad with an offer for a specific MP3 player; you'd better make sure the landing page is obviously relevant to that offer. Don't pay to qualify your traffic and then send them to your home page.

In addition to your own marketing strategies, you get traffic from Google, MSN, Yahoo!, each of which suggests different usage characteristics and behavior. The folks who use Google tend to do X, while the folks who use MSN tend to prefer Y.

This raises the question of whether you should design different landing pages to serve the same overall function, but targeted to the different questions and motivations your visitor is likely to have.

With your search engine traffic, conversion starts with a single click that takes place even before a visitor lands on your website. If she gets what she wants, she'll click again. With each click, she's more convinced you have what she wants. Implement the conversation she expects, and she'll be delighted. She wants to buy from you. You make that possible every time you give her exactly what she wants.

Your overall online responsibility to this person is to figure out what she'll ask and where she'll ask it, then optimize your site based on that. Your landing pages must do a special job in motivating visitors who are more often than not specifically pre-qualified.

Just remember. If folks turn right around and leave, they didn't really land and they certainly weren't caught!

Conversion Tip

3 Tips for Increasing Conversion Rates

Tip #1: Make it fast

Conversion rates jump dramatically once your pages load faster than 8-10 seconds (at any bandwidth).

Tip #2: Make it short

Optimize your copy to give them what they want and get out of the way. Give them benefits, not hype.

Tip #3: Make it compelling

Give your users something of value if they convert. Offer a free whitepaper, and make your copy sell.

- **Andy King**, author of *Speed Up Your Site: Web Site Optimization*

"A magician pulls rabbits out of hats. An experimental psychologist pulls habits out of rats."
- Anonymous

Pulling Customers through Your Conversion Funnel

Imagine that you're looking at a group of people from the top — the wide end — of a funnel. As the funnel gets narrower, not everyone can or will even want to get through. Your goal is to get as many through the hole on the bottom as possible. (The number of people you convert into buyers divided by the total size of the initial group is called the conversion rate.)

To get more people through the funnel, you must engage them in the systematic, professional selling process — actually called "a buying funnel" in sales circles.

Regardless of what they may say, typically 30 out of 100 people are "just looking." That means the remaining 70 are hoping to buy, most of them today. With 70 percent of people looking to buy, you have to wonder why the average website closes less than 2 percent of sales. It has been said that sales is a transfer of enthusiasm.

Want to increase your sales volume by 50 percent? If your closing rate is average, then your site has to transfer enthusiasm to just *one* disappointed customer who was hoping to buy! If your website could transfer enthusiasm to two of those unsold visitors, your sales volume would double — with zero spent in extra marketing expenses. Even if your closing rate is above average, the same principle and process apply.

For most websites, half their visitors or more never get past the home page. Can you think of a better way to kill your sales than to drive away half your traffic? Your first goal should be to strengthen your home page so you lose fewer people at the top. Everything else being equal, that means you will automatically have more coming out at the bottom. If you don't funnel your traffic — despite the marketing dollars you pay — you're letting most of them slip away.

Conversion Tip

Display Products Compellingly

I'm always amazed at how poor some product photography really is. Often it's a grainy representation of a quick manufacturer's photo. But I'm convinced that excellent, compelling photographs help sell products in both paper and online catalogs.

While photos may not do the final convincing that copy is required for, they do attract the eye and help make the product desirable. Some products may need several views of the product to display all the features, with captions below each to point out particular selling points. Arrows can be used if needed to direct the eye.

Part of creating desire is the human element. It's no surprise that many new car photos have a pretty girl standing next to the car, implying a benefit that girls will be more interested in a person who owns a car like this. Bottles of herbal supplements don't have much pizzazz. Instead consider a photo of a happy person of the target age group who is obviously healthy and enjoying life — again, implying the supposed benefit.

Good lighting is important. If you're doing your own photos with a digital camera, get a book on photography lighting to see how this is done. If you don't have the needed photo equipment or expertise, get a photographer friend to assist you. If you pay for a professional to take a photo, be sure that you get in writing all rights to use the images, as photographers often retain rights that will cost you additional fees when you use the images later. Be extremely careful in obtaining images from the Web, since you could be subject to lawsuits from photographers who own rights to photos displayed there. It's best to get good royalty-free photos from the manufacturer or take them yourself.

Sometimes pictures that are overexposed or a bit flat can be improved substantially by increasing contrast in the picture or perhaps sharpening focus using a photo program such as PhotoShop or PaintShop Pro.

For high ticket items, use of specialty photo display techniques may substantially increase the conversion rate. Three common techniques are:

- Zooming in to display the detail of clothing texture, etc.
- Rotating the object, such as a new Mustang convertible, 360 degrees, both outside and from within the driver's seat. This helps the shopper begin to "feel" the sensation of the car in his mind.
- 3D imaging of apparel on a personalized model. Landsend.com has spent millions of dollars licensing their My Virtual Model feature. It allows the shopper to build a model according to body shape, size of bust, waist, height, and weight (though I'm told that the flabbier shapes look better than in real life). Then clothing lines that have been specially programmed can clothe the model. Conversion rates of shoppers who have used the model are significantly higher than those who have not.

You may not be able to afford some of the specialized photo display techniques, but you can use thumbnail photos that display a larger photo when clicked on.

My challenge to merchants is to re-do all of the product photos in your online store over a six-month period, beginning with your best sellers and most profitable products. This will increase your conversion rate.

- **Dr. Ralph Wilson** formed Wilson Internet Services (www.wilsonweb.com) at the very beginning of the commercial Internet in 1995 to help small to medium businesses and organizations learn how to use the Internet effectively.

"Logic is an organized way of going wrong with confidence." - Kettering's Law

Layout and Visual Clarity: It's Not a Matter of Taste

A website is an interactive persuasion vehicle, not marketing department eye candy. Design exists for three reasons: to evoke memories and images associated with your brand; to make you look professional; and to assist with the persuasive momentum of your website.

Will every element of every image, graphic and layout help your visitor become confident in your company, product or service? Will it help persuade that visitor?

Designers hate to be constrained. Yet misconceptions about designing for conversion abound. Most of these are promoted as "best practices." Once designers become aware of how effective and non-constraining designing for conversion really is, they embrace it. Here are some of the basic principles that designers should follow.

Lay Off Inconsistent Lay Outs

Many websites have splash pages that supposedly "look good" or are "for branding purposes." But splash pages disorient visitors by offering a look and feel different from the rest of the website. They can kill the mood for visitors who are buying on impulse. They're an obstacle on the way to more relevant content. They're often used incorrectly, asking visitors to choose a path. That's often better handled through information architecture.

Many websites' checkout processes have a look and feel different from the rest of the pages (this happens with many hosted solutions). While it often makes sense to remove extraneous navigation, you can shock a person out of the buying process by changing the design consistency.

Contrast

An image has two options. It can either blend with the page to enhance a feeling or to increase perceived value, or it can be conspicuous and lead prospects in the direction you choose. How do you design to persuade visitors to take your desired action? Contrast! Contrast makes eyes settle where you want them to. It intuitively tells visitors what to do next. Robin Williams, in The Non-Designer's Design Book, writes:

A reader should never have to try to figure out what is happening on a page — the focus, the organization of material, the purpose, the flow of information, all should be recognized instantaneously with a single glance. And along the way, it doesn't hurt to make it beautiful.

Williams lists six contrast categories:

- Size: Big vs. Little
- Weight: Thick vs. Thin
- Structure: Shifting weight with each stroke

- Form: Rectangular vs. Rounded
- Direction: Straight vs. Slanted
- Color: Warm vs. Cold

Calls-to-action generally should be in contrast to the rest of the design. Visitors shouldn't have to work to find what to do next. Can you spot calls-to-action on your web pages from six feet away? And no, I'm not kidding about that.

Eye-tracking

To lead visitors in the direction of your design, you need to understand the way their eyes track through web pages. Knowledge of eye tracking helps you understand how layout and use of screen real estate should take advantage of the way a visitor scans pages for critical information. People have relatively constant eye-tracking patterns when they land on a web page. They start top left and check that they're in the right place. They'll then scan along the top of the page, drop diagonally to the center of the screen, scan left, then cross center again to scan right, then return to center. Use this information to create a template for placement of various types of information.

Fluid vs. Fixed Design

Prospects use different browsers, set at different resolutions. The visitor, not the designer, controls their choice of browser and settings. You must understand and plan for these implications. Don't try to exert so much control. This does a disservice. Decide whether your website will have a fixed or fluid design. Both have their shortfalls. In a fixed design, your website never changes. The problem here is that some of your visitors may be looking at your website from a smaller or larger browser window than you anticipated. This will cause her to see only part of your website, or cause your website to look tiny in a large window. Fluid design will narrow your page to fit each individual window or widen it to fit the window. Your website can begin to look weird when opened too wide or too narrow. Use your discretion, but test your website pages on at least two separate browser windows, and many different size windows.

Remember the Web is a Voluntary Medium

The Web is a participatory, voluntary medium, and your visitors are in control not only of what they see, but even how they see it.

- Your visitors can resize pages and adjust their screen resolutions.
- They can choose how large or small text appears on their screens.
- They can decide whether or not they want to display pictures.
- They can choose whether or not they want to see color (some can even change the color palette).
- They can view your site on a variety of devices: PCs (and Windows appearance differs from Mac appearance), handhelds, WebTV – each of which presents a different visual format environment.

Your goal is to persuade by delivering content and information in a way that meets their needs. The second you ignore those needs, your visitors are gone. In the mechanics of web design, you can get this much needed flexibility with Cascading Style Sheets (CSS), which allow designers to suggest how the web page should appear. Here are some of the flexibility points CSS add:

- With CSS, you don't have to single out one font, which your user may or may not have installed on their computer. You can cover more bases by suggesting a number of fonts.
- You don't need to specify the actual point size of the fonts you use. Instead, you represent them as percentages of the basic text. Headers and subheadings can be proportionally larger; some text can be proportionally smaller. It will then appear on any device in the appropriate size relationships to the base text.
- To make page layout adapt to a user's settings, you can specify margins, indents and other layout features as percentages, or other relative values, of the width of the element which contains them. So when users change the size of their browser windows, the entire page layout adapts to fit.

It is extremely important to make sure the persuasive objectives of your website are conveyed in black and white, and that you do not rely on color alone to communicate your meaning. Consider that color can enhance your message, but should not be, in and of itself, the message.

Think of designing for conversion as challenging not constraining. How your website looks influences what your visitors perceive. And that, as we all know, is the key that gets the persuasive ball rolling.

"You see, but you do not observe." - Sir Arthur Conan Doyle

Skimming and Scanning Effectively

You take the time to write correctly. Your text is persuasive. How do you ensure a reader engages with the text on your Web pages? This goes beyond a copywriting issue. It's a usability issue. Usability professionals use two easy-to-confuse terms to describe how visitors engage with text: skimming and scanning.

If visitors can't scan and skim your Web pages quickly and efficiently as soon as they arrive, they won't stick around to dig deeper. Not good. While skimming and scanning are related, they're distinct experiences in the usability equation and require separate treatment. Lump scanability and skimability together, and chances are you'll miss the lessons to be learned from the serious usability research that's been conducted.

Before considering how to keep visitors merrily scanning and skimming toward taking the action you want, you must first understand the differences between the two activities. "The American Heritage Dictionary" defines the terms as follows:

Scan: To look over quickly and systematically; to look over or leaf through hastily
Skim: To give a quick and superficial reading, scrutiny, or consideration; glance

They are similar but not the same. Both scanning and skimming are information-gathering activities. People perform them quickly, usually without thinking much. But, they don't work the same way, and they don't serve the same purpose.

Think of it this way: You're on the wild Western frontier. Your trusty horse crests the hill. Before you is a vast expanse. You don't know if there's danger out there. You look around, you scan. There is a thicket to the left, a lake in the distance, a tendril of smoke drifting above a small rise, a wooden fence near you on the right. Your "scan" suggests things look pretty safe. So you spur your horse to a trot. Passing the fence, you notice a piece of paper nailed to a post. It's a "Wanted Dead or Alive" poster. You dismount, get closer, and "skim" the text for the most salient facts to help decide if you'll bother with the fine print.

Let's see how this works on a website. A visitor arrives and her eyes immediately begin scoping out the situation to determine if she's in the right place. First, she'll scan the visible screen for prominent elements, determining if they mesh with her mental image of her mission. As she scans, in addition to collecting top-level clues such as headlines, she'll evaluate larger-scale issues, such as legibility, arrangement, and accessibility. This is where more prominent features, including type size, page layout, and color use come into play. You want to help her to minimize the time she spends finding, sorting, and selecting information and to engage her in the conversion process. If she doesn't find top-level clues she's in the right place or if she finds the page hard to deal with, she's back on her horse, galloping to another website.

Skimming is the second, but equally important, activity. It's reading based, a refinement of the information-gathering process. When a visitor has a fairly good idea of the lay of the land, she's going to start engaging with the copy. She's not ready to stop and read anything thoroughly – yet. She's not sure if it's worth her while. She'll start with a superficial skim, looking for highlights and important keywords that help direct further involvement. This is where bold keywords, bullets, short text blocks, strong first and last sentences in each paragraph, legible fonts, and even effective hyperlink use make a difference. This is a critical distinction that should guide you in improving your websites and its persuasive copy.

If They Can't Find It, It Isn't There

Your website's text must be scannable and skimmable. However, remember not all information has equal value. Is information placed where a visitor is most likely to look for it? Are calls-to-action where they're needed on each page? Do you have to scroll up or down to see them? If you sell products, consider "add to cart" buttons in several places, especially at the bottom of a page after scrolling though lots of text.

Follow the Cursor

Here is an interesting problem. At a website where I clicked the call-to-action, on the next page, in the spot where the previous call-to-action appeared, my cursor was resting. But it was now on a link to the privacy policy. This made me curious about the privacy policy. Unintentionally, I was asked to disengage from the shopping process.

Make your website simple to interact with. Guide visitors to accomplish your common goals. They came to do business with you, didn't they? Make your website as intuitive as possible. Every element, text and graphic, on each page must be placed for persuasion. If you're deliberate in design, the success metrics will shine.

"When I read a book I seem to read it with my eyes only, but now and then I come across a passage, perhaps only a phrase, which has a meaning for me, and it becomes part of me."
- W. Somerset Maugham

Help Their Eyes Find It

Every one of your visitors is barraged daily with massive quantities of information. How do we cope? We become remarkably selective in our consumption. Some folks say this is a function of impatience. I figure it's a basic survival skill.

There are a number of strategies available that allow you to streamline the information you present to your visitors: they're your navigation schemes, your qualifying schemes. You can also locate website elements where your visitors expect to find them. Then, there's designing for scanning and skimming.

Evidence suggests that if your readers read online (and Jakob Nielsen says 79% of them don't,)[1] they read "shallow but wide" and pay attention to text before they look at pictures.[2] So how are you going to grab their attention and communicate your message as quickly as possible? Try some of these tactics.

Headings

Headings are extremely important online. They are the points of reference on your web page. They are also creative design elements. Headings create extra white space that allows your visitor to visually organize the information you are presenting. Look to print media for examples you might be able to adapt to your website.[3]

- Keep main headings short enough to fit on one line. Main headings will define the message on your page.
- Use subheadings to continue, expand and visually separate your information. Subheadings also help a visitor more effectively orient herself when scrolling down long pages.
- If headings echo your navigation, make sure the words are exactly the same. This provides clarity and consistency for the visitor.
- Use headings as design features: different colors, different styles or sizes of type will help attract your visitor to the information, as well as help her scan for it.
- Consider indenting text from the left margin of the header. This creates additional white space that helps set off the heading and adds a greater feeling of balance to your page.
- Read just your headings. If they were the only words a visitor read on this page, would they communicate the basic point?

Pull Quotes

Pull quotes can be more than graphic fillers. They help capture a visitor's attention, illuminate your key points and add style to your web page. They also break up large blocks of information to aid scanning.[4]

- To create effective pull quotes, identify the key phrases in your copy and highlight them at various places in your layout.
- If you use several pull quotes, present them in the order of your message, then read them in order to see if they, independent of your text, make your point.

Not everyone thinks pull quotes are brilliant solutions for scanners and skimmers. There is certainly one downside to graphic pull quotes: they generally don't format properly in non-graphical browsers (such as Lynx text-only browser). In text-only incarnations, these graphic slices of text wind up embedded in the regular copy, so they look and read out of place. If you plan on using pull quotes, it's a kindness to provide text-only versions as well.[5]

Highlighting Text

Within the paragraphs of your copy, some words and phrases are more important than others. When your visitor has made the decision to pay more attention to your copy, she'll most likely skim it before truly committing to reading. Highlighting or bolding is a way to distinguish the essence of your message.

- Don't highlight everything; then you're just back to Square One.
- Don't highlight just for emphasis, as in "I really mean don't highlight just for emphasis." Highlight for critical information.
- Once you've highlighted the words, read them as if they were the only text on the page. Do they develop and carry the message?

Embedded Links

Text hyperlinks give your visitors quick access to the content they want without forcing them to figure out your navigation system or requiring them to click through multiple layers of your website. Used well, embedded links not only capture attention, they keep your visitors actively engaged in your conversion process by keeping them within the active window.

- Make the link as short, concise and intuitive as possible.
- It is important to include key words, or trigger words, as part of the link. "Users expect to find 'trigger words' in the links. A trigger word is a word (or phrase) that causes the user to click. When the trigger words match the user's goals, they find those words right away and the links make them more confident that they are going to find their content."[6]
- Make sure you deliver on the implicit promise of the link. If you embed a text link for "methodology" and that delivers the visitor to your page on "services," you lose credibility.

Big Picture Guidelines

Gerry McGovern produced this list of scan reading design guidelines, and they are well worth paying attention to (quoted in entirety):

Maximize familiarity: Structure your website in a way that is familiar and consistent. This will mean that the reader has less to learn and can more easily focus on the core content. For example, most people expect to find the 'Home' link in the top left of the page. Placing it anywhere else makes it more difficult for them to scan.

- Design from shallow to deep: A homepage should contain short text that brings the reader deeper into the website. As they link deeper you can provide more detailed content.
- Classify well: Choosing classification terms that are readily understandable to the reader is crucial.
- Write punchy headings and summaries: If the heading is not descriptive and compelling, the reader will likely leave.
- Be direct: Be short. Get to the point. Explain in precise, simple language exactly what you have to say to the reader.
- Don't waste the reader's time: Remember, the one word that best describes the scan reader is: impatient.[7]

Jakob Nielsen reminds us that online we can communicate our points only if our text content:

- is broken up by headings
- is shaped into lots of punchy, single idea paragraphs
- puts key phrases in bold face
- bullets key points
- avoids jargon and rhetoric
- is straightforward, and
- is short [8]

When it comes to scanning and skimming, as in all matters business-related, keep in mind your mileage may vary. Maybe one of these suggestions won't work for your application. So think of these in the broader sense of principles rather than rules, then reach for your own brand of scannable opportunity!

[1] "How Users Read on the Web." Jakob Nielsen. Alertbox. October 1, 1997. http://www.useit.com/alertbox/9710a.html
[2] Stanford-Poynter Eye-Tracking Study. http://www.poynterextra.org/et/i.htm
[3] Linda Moore. http://www.gr-lakes.com/~lmoore/index.htm
[4] Linda Moore. http://www.gr-lakes.com/~lmoore/index.htm
[5] Adrian Holovaty. http://www.holovaty.com/blog/archive/2002/10/31/1234
[6] "Getting Confidence from Lincoln." UIE tips. Jared Spool. April 25, 2003. http://www.uie.com
[7] "How you can design for the scan reader." Gerry McGovern. April 29, 2002. http://www.gerrymc-govern.com/nt/2002/nt_2002_04_29_scan.htm
[8] "Ever Wondered What Your Users Looked at First?" Sitepoint. http://www.sitepoint.com/article/273/17

Conversion Tip

Online Merchandising

1. Know Your Customer, Your Brand and Your Category and Merchandise to Meet the Customer's Needs

Allocate your home page and category page real estate to accommodate your customer base. Incorporate selling tactics that engage the shopper. Test an array of tactics to meet their needs including top sellers, feature products, sales/ promotions and brand boutiques where appropriate. Devote appropriate space to each and assess the performance adjusting real estate and initiatives based on learning.

2. Incorporate Functioning Onsite Search

Ensure that your site's search quickly drives consumers to their desired products. Merchandise your results screens with the requested information and store merchandising tactics. Keywords and misspelled words and phrases should be accommodated. Consumers should be able to edit or filter return results based on criteria appropriate to your category.

3. Deliver Comprehensive Product Information

All products should contain the requisite information for the customer to make a purchasing decision. Short scanable descriptions are ideal with key facts on the product. Zoom is a standard and alternative views and color change can be a factor in some categories. Remember the layout and look and feel is often as important as the content itself.

- **Lauren Freedman**, President, the e-tailing group

"Is it not in the most absolute simplicity that real genius plies its pinions the most wonderfully?"
- E.T.A.W. Hoffmann.

KISS Your Customers If You Want Them Back

KISS, short for — "Keep it Simple, Stupid" is a message and principle of persuasion on the web. The key to successful website design isn't sophistication, it's simplicity. Designing for simplicity is anything but simple (as if I needed to tell you that). But well-thought-out simplicity is what makes the successful websites successful. Here are some hints for how to "keep it simple."

- Limit page load times. The best websites load in about 10 seconds. The bottom line is that nobody is going to wait more than 30 seconds for your page to appear. Want your website to appeal to most people? Many people still surf at speeds under 56K, have their monitors set for 800 x 600 resolution, and don't even know they can change that, much less how.
- Make clear, strong text immediately available. On the Web, visitors look first for relevant text, not graphics. That will also keep them interested while graphics load. Use graphics only if they help prospects understand what they are looking for or if they convey information that can't be conveyed effectively through text. And keep graphics as simple as possible so they load quickly.
- Offer simple and consistent navigation. Your average prospect will view two to three pages before leaving; so, at best, you're two clicks away from dead in the water unless you help her get where she wants to go quickly.
- Respect conventions. Blue, underlined text means hyperlink, or "Click here," to almost everyone. Don't confuse anyone! Avoid underlining or using blue text for anything else. Place your navigation cues on the top or left of every page, with the same links arrayed at the bottom. Use reasonable categorization schemes (a series of tabs or something similar works well) for multiple elements.
- Avoid scrolling if you possibly can, but if you must use it, use vertical scrolling only, never horizontal, and place the most important information above the scrolling line. Get your most important information to your prospects fast!
- Make everything obvious. First and foremost, help your prospect see the information — white backgrounds are quick to download and help information stand out. Label stuff, and do so clearly — no jargon. Offer concise explanations. Always remember: If your visitor can't find a function, it's not there!
- Never strand your prospect anywhere on your website. Imagine you're lost in the middle of a huge store with no signs. Where's housewares? Where's checkout? Where's the bathroom? How much do you want to buy now? So, on your website, provide clear navigation from anywhere to anywhere, and do it on every page. Keep all your navigational links within your page. Unless you

want to encourage your customers to leave, don't direct them to the Back button on the browser. Any trip to the menu bar is an opportunity for your prospect to kiss you goodbye.

- Make sure your website search gives fast and accurate results. The average shopper doesn't know how to use search and most search functions give bad or no results; so often that shoppers are better off with links. But if you really think you have to use a search function, label it clearly with instructions. Provide a mechanism to make it simple for users to narrow their search. If your search hands over too many irrelevant results, prospects will feel overwhelmed and leave.

- Don't assume the reader is an expert user. Technology is a wonderful thing, but Joe and Josephine Consumer are years behind the tech types. Therefore, your GUI (graphical user interface) should be simple. Also, never make them download plug-ins. Average shoppers don't know how, and even if they do, why take them away from the shopping process and force them to do something else because some designer thought it would be cool? Prospects don't say, "Wow!" — They leave. If you can't design it into your website and still have it load quickly and do all that other important stuff, leave it out. Give your prospects simple, clear instructions and helpful tools to guide them through the buying process.

- Earn respect by attention to detail. Visitors are looking for a reason not to trust you: Check for typos, grammatical errors, screen error messages, images that don't open, browser compatibility problems, functions that don't work — everything. Then have someone else check again. The best websites build their brands by creating a great user experience.

Here's what the top 100 websites have in common — fast download times; few graphics; little, if any, multimedia; no frames; similar navigation systems; high-contrast text with lots of white space; most links in "traditional" blue, underlined text; no background imagery; very few obvious JavaScript tricks; no DHTML; no splash pages; and a solid database-powered back-end. Simple! Now, pucker up and give your prospects a big, delightful KISS.

"Fear of trying causes paralysis. Trying causes only trembling and sweating." - Mason Cooley

Overcoming Analysis Paralysis

Keeping your website visually simple is just part of making sure that your prospects won't be confused or frustrated. This extends too to the navigation.

Many designers and information architects plan their navigation based on George Miller's landmark research on recall tasks. His research concluded that the human memory system has a capacity of 7 plus or minus 2 chunks.

First of all, that research was done almost 50 years ago. Second, while Miller's research has stuck in people's minds, a lot of other research indicates that the number may be as small as 4, not 7. But even more important, designing good navigation for a website has little, if anything, to do with prospects' recall ability. The key, rather, is in how human psychology handles choices.

Where to Go, I Don't Know

Here is an example of how people typically handle choices. It's a Saturday night and you've gotten together with a bunch of friends. You're the first to suggest, "Let's get something to eat!" Another friend pipes up and says, "What are you in the mood for?" How often do you hear those infamous words, "I don't know?" If someone had shouted, "Pizza or Mexican!" everyone would have had an immediate opinion. But when faced with too many choices, our brains seem to freeze. Instead of making a choice, we become paralyzed thinking about which one to choose, and often end up not choosing at all.

The Alternate-Choice Close

Although it seems counterintuitive, the best way to make a sale is to limit the buyer's choices. An alternate-choice close presents the customer with a simple choice; regardless of which choice the customer makes, the sale is closed: "Will that be cash or charge?" "Do you want that in yellow or blue?" "Would delivery tomorrow be OK, or would Friday be better?"

Studies have shown, and experienced salespeople know, that if you ask simple yes/no questions, you're likely to get a "No," but if you offer customers a clear, simple choice, they are very likely to choose one of the options you offer, and you make the sale.

If you recognize that every step in your navigation is a mini-sale, you have to design accordingly.

Navigating to Avoid Paralysis

There are numerous navigation schemes. Hierarchical, global, supplemental, and embedded links are the most common. Hierarchical navigation helps people keep track of how deep into the website they are (e.g., books/subjects/business). Global navigation schemes, such as tabs, help direct and orient the customer to what types of products are available (e.g., Books, Electronics, Music). Supplemental or local navigation allows users to get to related information within a category rather than between categories (e.g., Advertising:

Web, TV, Print, Radio). This is particularly helpful when your visitor has landed on your website via a search engine but hasn't landed on quite the right page.

But from our work with clients, we've discovered that the navigation scheme important to actually closing more sales is the embedded-links scheme. It's very easy to implement. Within the body of your copy, you simply place links to the places you want prospects to go next. Of course, what works best on your website can only be determined by testing. And, naturally, embedded links are only one component of a complete navigation structure.

Done well, embedded links will engage your users effectively as they browse within the "active window" of your website. The active window is the main area of your page, underneath or to the side of your main navigation. It is where you place your body text, display your products, and present your offer. It is also where you want to keep your visitors' eyes focused. If you properly engage them in this area by providing the right choices for them to click on, you persuade them to follow the path you want them to take. This is also why it is very important to keep a consistent look and feel around the active window.

The Power of Blue

Be conventional; it brings results. When designing for the Internet, it's foolish to make your prospects learn quirks of your website design when what you want them to be doing is shopping.

Ask anyone who has logged only a few hours of Internet surfing, "What color are hyperlinks?" They will reply blue. The color blue for links is a very powerful population stereotype. When you break that stereotype by using a different color scheme, you undermine the usability and, ultimately, the "shopability" of your website. You actually hide your links instead of making them easy to find. On the flip side, people get really ticked off when something is blue and underlined yet is not a link

They Want to Buy

Don't make it hard for your prospects to find what they want and buy it. By choosing the right navigation scheme, you not only make the process easy for your customers, you also make it a process that actually influences the closing of more sales.

"Before I go out to take a picture of someone, I just stop at the city desk and say, 'Do you want him gazing out toward the sunset or picking his nose?' " - Calvin Trillin

Image and Website Images

It's the nature of the Web that words are the foundation of the medium. This does not mean images can or should be neglected. One very effective way to boost your conversion rate for retailing, lead generation, and even content and self-service websites is to optimize your images.

Blurred Vision

Have you ever clicked an image (it may say "click for details") only to land on a page displaying a larger image, but no site elements and no way of either buying or leaving? Perhaps the image appeared as a pop-up (that may or may not be blocked) with a huge product picture, but no call-to-action. Click "larger image" here. The only way you can get out of there is to click the browser back button or close the window.

This halts persuasive momentum. An image's objective is to facilitate the buying process, not to make a website look cool or flashy. Every pixel should carry its conversion weight in gold. If a picture doesn't help sell, it could hurt. It wastes valuable real estate. If you use a shopping engine like Froogle, the fight for the click-through starts with an image. How does your product image stand out from your competitors'?

Pictures or Words?

Words work for procedural information, logical conditions and abstract concepts. Images work for details, location, and explaining spatial structures, but does the image convey real value?

Words are symbols. Symbols are powerful conveyors of abstract thought. Usually, images aren't as precise as words. Be careful what your images convey. You may think you're saying one thing, but images may say the opposite.

What Should You Show?

Present the product image first as a thumbnail — a small version of the image that loads quickly and that your prospect can click on to bring up a larger version. The larger version then either reconfigures their entire screen or, even better, appears in a pop-up. Here's where pop-ups do have an advantage: your visitors can view the image while at the same time staying visually in touch with the source page, which helps them remember where they are in the navigation scheme.

Thumbnails are especially useful if you are presenting a series of product pages that include multiple images (possible exception: thumbnails are not necessarily a good thing to include on search results pages — it depends on your product). In general, thumbnails allow you to get product images to your visitors much faster. They allow your visitors to scan your offerings quickly and bypass slow downloads of images for products that don't interest them. Your visitors can decide for themselves what they want to look at more closely, and having done that, are naturally going to be more patient as a larger image loads.

A website owner wanted to use a pop-up to display a larger image of a vitamin bottle. What's the value visitors get from the front of a vitamin bottle? What a visitor should see is a larger image of the back of the bottle. The label is what could be significant. One way to do this would be to have an image of the front and an image of the back of the bottle side by side. Then, link to a page with a larger picture and additional details (features). (After all, they clicked for more details). That way, you display all the calls-to-action. These could include an add-to-cart button or present all the product size and feature options. The persuasive momentum continues.

A pop-up isn't the best option for this situation. They generally slow momentum. The point of the image is to persuade. Many people fail to realize images are used to aid in the persuasion process, not just portray what the product looks like.

An Excuse to Buy

Never overestimate your visitor. Assume she needs more information. TigerDirect is a wonderful example of a website that isn't afraid to explain and explain and explain. It uses images, words, and lots of them. When the page with images loads, you'll see they spent time optimizing and compressing them for low bandwidth.

Lands End uses images and diagrams to provide visitors the information they need. The possibilities are endless for informative and persuasive ways to use images. For example, you might zoom in on an accessory like a wallet to see the grain and stitching (they miss with "enlarge image").

What's the Image Trying to Convey?

There are three things an image can convey:

- Features
- Benefits
- Values

Features

Does the image accurately portray product features? Consider alternate ways to show features. To feature product size, you could place it in the palm of a hand, next to a competitor's product, or sit it by itself so that you cannot address the prospect's questions as to how it compares.

Benefits

Does the image convey the benefits? If you sell cookware, is the image pots and pans, or the food those pots and pans produce? People don't always buy a pan. They may buy an easy way to clean, or slice food. For example, consider how many ways you might portray a simple cheese cutting board. Just look at how these retailers — Williams-Sonoma, Sur La Table and QVC — show this simple item:

WILLIAMS-SONOMA

VIEW BASKET | SIGN IN | SEARCH [keyword or item #] [GO]

SHOP   GIFT IDEAS   RECIPES   ONLINE CATALOG & QUICK SHOP   REGISTRY

Olive Wood Cheese Board & Knives
Internet/Catalog Only

A Mediterranean hardwood prized for its distinctive grain, olive wood lends its beauty to our cheese board and knives. Each knife has a stainless-steel blade designed for a specific type of cheese: vide blade for semihard cheeses like Emmentaler, heart-shaped blade for hard cheeses like Parmigiano-Reggiano, a curved spreader for soft varieties like Brie, and thin blade for semisoft cheeses like Gorgonzola. A serving fork is also included. The pieces are handcrafted in Italy. Board is 8 1/2" sq., 3/4" thick. Knives are 4 3/4" long overall. The knife set includes the four different types of knives plus a serving fork. A Williams-Sonoma exclusive.

Larger View

Board $54.00   Qty: [ ]

Sur La Table

Home
Shopping Bag
Customer Service
My Account

ONLINE CATALOG & QUICK ORDER   CULINARY PROGRAMS   GIFT REGISTRY   STORES & EVENTS   RECIPES

SEARCH keywords or item # [   ] [GO ▶]   Request a CATALOG [GO ▶]   Sign up for our NEWSLETTER [Enter e-mail address] [SUBSCRIBE ▶]

SHOP BY CATEGORY
Appliances
Bakeware
Barware
Coffee & Tea
Cookbooks
Cook's Tools
Cookware
Copperware
Dinnerware
Glassware
Housewares
Knives
Specialty Foods

Cook's Tools > Cutters / Choppers / Slicers / Boards   << Item 33 of 33

Bamboo Cheese Board & Knife

Turn an ordinary block of cheese into something extraordinary by presenting it on this stylish board. The 10" square board fits comfortably on a crowded coffee table. Crafted from bamboo, a naturally replenishing wood, it is harder than maple. Includes 9½ " stainless steel cheese knife. Hand wash.

QVC Homepage   Shopping Cart | My Account | Order Status | Customer Service

QVC   Accessories & Shoes   Apparel   Beauty   Clearance   Cooking & Dining   Electronics   Gifts & Flowers
QUALITY. VALUE.   Home Accents & Furnishings   Home Improvement   Jewelry   Sports & Fitness   Toys, Crafts & Leisure   All Categories
CONVENIENCE.

Search for [   ] in [All of QVC.com ▼] [Go] More Search Options

24-Hour Product Review
Today's Special Value
Item On-Air
Watch QVCTV LIVE
TV Program Guide

Search Results > Cooking & Dining > Product Detail   Previous Next

Item Number H108569
Maple Cheese & Cracker Tray with Tempered Glass Trivet

QVC Price $39.50
Shipping and Handling $4.97
Save! Buy two or more and save on S & H. Click here for details.

Cheese please! Give your parties an extra touch of elegance with this beautiful maple cheese and cracker tray. J.K. Adams is proud to surround Michel Stong's original tempered glass trivets with a lovely tray. There is ample space for crackers on two sides of the 8" glass trivet. The tempered glass can be cut on and is in fact preferred when serving harder cheeses. Measures 13" x 13" x 1-1/4". 1-year LMW. The glass trivet is food and dishwasher safe. Clean board after use with warm water and soap. Wipe dry. Don't soak in water. Occasionally run in a bit of mineral oil to help protect the wood from

You Might Also Consider...

H88322 • $38.50
Polish Stoneware Traditional Sandwich Tray

More Views   Enlarge

1. Quantity: 1 ▼
2. Gift Options ▼

K180940 •

Value

A value image needn't be placed near a product. These images may convey the value of your website as well as the value of a product. Look how ClickTracks, a Web analytics company, uses these images on their website.

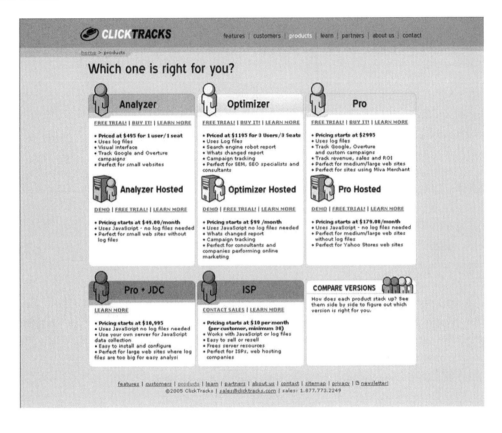

Does the Image Convey Your Image?

Obviously, images must have the same "feel" throughout your website. Image quality, look and feel must be consistent. Images must relate to your website and the value you're trying to portray. If each image looks and "feels" different, you'll lose your website's overall value.

Value is conveyed though the words and images you use. Credibility and value are life and death. A visitor needs a reason to buy a product on your website, not to search for a lower price. The words and images on your website must be consistent with the value you convey.

"I've got the world on a string, sittin' on a rainbow, got the string around my finger." - Ted Koehler

Harness the Power of the Rainbow

Color doesn't simply look nice (or not). It speaks to the subconscious, evokes meanings and feelings and moods, and has an incredible ability to influence buying behavior. There has been lots of research on color and its impact on the subconscious, but here are some basics that should go into planning the use of color on your website, even before you write your first line of html.

Consider that how you use color when you design for e-commerce is very different from how you'd use color if you were designing for a personal home page or pushing the outer edge of the avant-garde. As a business, you have some very real constraints to cope with: credibility, legibility, navigation, persuasion, down-load times, browser compatibility, and more. Ignore these, go wild with a cutting-edge design exercise, and you may delight a few design aficionados but you will probably alienate the vast majority your customers and prospects.

Alex Walker[1] suggests you start the process of color design with words: take a piece of paper and write down adjectives you think describe the ambiance of your business. Think about your style, the feel you want to convey, the characteristics of your target audience, and pick all the words you can think of that apply. Now, from this list, select the Top Five — the best of the best. These are the words that will guide your imagery and selection of colors.

Assemble a collection of nature pictures with subject matter or colors that you feel represent you and what you do. When you've selected an image with a color range that feels most appropriate, scan it into your computer, then, using the eye-dropper tool in your image program, pick out your palette by going for the most prominent colors.

Since we associate colors with moods, qualities and emotions, that's where you want to go next in selecting your colors. What colors come to mind when you visualize your Top Five words? Deep greens? Rich tans? Soft blues? Urgent reds? Pick two or three, absolutely no more than four colors. I've seen super websites that simply rely on monotones! Fewer colors make for a stronger statement and tend not to over-stimulate or tax your viewers. In e-commerce, color is a clear case where less is often more.

Next, don't rely on color as the core of your design. Walker reminds us there are six basic and equally important elements that make up effective design: line, shape, value (lightness, darkness, shading), blank space, texture/pattern and color. An excellent way to see if your layout works well is actually to remove the color. If it looks good in black and white, then you've probably got a good design that can come alive with the judicious use of color.

Color can play other important roles. It can help organize your website visually. It can draw your prospect's eye toward the most important information on a page while it deemphasizes other information. It can help convey the structure of your navigation system. You can use it to code different features you offer or areas of your business. Color can highlight a special offer or a limited-time offer.

Before you take your first step onto the proverbial Yellow Brick Road of e-commerce, you should:

- Define the mood of your business.
- Select a limited palette of evocative colors.
- Make color an integral element in a strong design.
- Make color work for you in organizing your content.

The keys are to use color intelligently and intentionally. It is a powerful influencer.

---

[1] "4 Simple Steps to Coloring your WWWorld!" Alex Walker, SitePoint, 2/25/2001. <http://www.webmasterbase.com/article.php?aid=357&pid=0>.

"An optimist is a person who sees a green light everywhere, while a pessimist sees only the red stop-light. . . The truly wise person is colorblind." - Albert Schweitzer

Color Wheel or Mood Ring?

Color is important – for those of us in e-business, it's an integral part of the way we "speak" to our visitors. And people respond, even at a physiologic level, to colors. The field of research regarding relationships between color and personality is, shall we say, under-plowed. Statistically Significant types hedge about the validity of any instrument that purports to determine hard and fast connections between the two factors.

But there is a lot of anecdotal evidence, and even those who pooh-pooh the entire concept as metaphysical rubbish (colorists and winter people, indeed) find validity in studies that identify human emotional response to colors.

One of the most influential works on the psychology of color comes from Dr. Max Lüscher, a German who created the Lüscher Color Test in 1948 (his work was translated into English and published in a book of the same name in 1969). Lüscher bases his test on eight colors:

Each of the eight colors has been carefully chosen because of its particular psychological and physiological meaning – its "structure". [1]

Let what he has to say about the effects and associations of each color stimulate your thinking about the ways the colors on your website might influence your visitors – through what they suggest about you and what they "say" to them.[2]

Gray

Gray is the color of neutrality, "neither subject nor object, neither inner nor outer, neither tension or relaxation." Gray feels as though it is not colored, not dark, not light – a separation between two distinct entities, a demilitarized zone free from stimulus. Gray communicates an element of non-involvement or concealment. It's a color that remains uncommitted and uninvolved.

Blue

This is the color of calmness, repose and unity, symbolically the color of sky and ocean. Looking at blue relaxes the central nervous system – blood pressure, pulse and respiration rate all go down, which allows regenerative systems in the body to work on healing. When folks are ill, the physiologic need for blue actually increases! The physiologic associations with blue are those of tranquility. The psychological associations are of contentment, gratification and being at peace.

Green

Beyond its symbolic associations with nature and growth, green is the color of "elastic tension" often associated with the desire for improved conditions: the search for better health, a useful life, social reform. It expresses the will in operation, firmness, constancy and persistence. It is a color that a person who possesses – or wishes to possess – high levels of self-esteem responds to strongly. Green is associated with:

…many forms and degrees of "control," not only in the sense of directed drives, but also as detailed accuracy in checking and verifying facts, as precise and accurate memory, as clarity of presentation, critical analysis and logical consistency – all the way up to abstract formalism.

Red

Physiologically, red makes blood pressure, pulse and respirations rates go up – it's an energy-expending color. Red's associations are with vitality, activity, desire, appetite and craving. Symbolically, red is blood, conquest, masculinity, the flame of the human spirit.

It is the impulse towards active doing, towards sport, struggle, competition, eroticism and enterprising productivity. Red is "impact of the will" or "force of will" as distinct from the green "elasticity of the will.

The person who favors red "wants his own activities to bring him intensity of experience and fullness of living."

Yellow

Where red stimulates, yellow suggests. It can elevate body rates as red does, but its effect is less stable. Yellow is primarily the color of happiness, cheerfulness, expansiveness, lack of inhibition. It is the welcome warmth of the sun and the glow of a spiritual halo. While calming and relaxing, the color does suggest a desire for change, that things are never quite at rest – people who favor yellow may be very productive, but that productivity often occurs in fits and starts.

Violet

A combination of red and blue, violet "attempts to unify the impulsive conquest of red and the gentler surrender of blue, becoming representative of 'identification'." Purples are mystical, suggesting sensitive intimacy, union, enchantment, the blurring of thought, desire and reality. Violet represents a longing for wishes to be fulfilled and a desire to charm others.

Violet can mean identification as an intimate, erotic blending, or it can lead to an intuitive and sensitive understanding.

Because it is so strongly associated with the idea of the world as a magical place and the need for wish-fulfillment, a preference for violet can communicate some degree of vulnerability or insecurity, perhaps a need for approval.

Brown

Symbolic of "roots," hearth, home and family security, brown is a darkened mixture of red and yellow, with reduced qualities of these colors. The impulses of brown are not as volatile as red, not as restless as yellow – yet the color has subtler warm, welcoming and sensuous qualities. When brown is favored, it suggests an increased need for "physical ease and sensuous contentment, for release from … discomfort."

Black

Black represents the absolute boundary beyond which life ceases, and so expresses the idea of nothingness, of extinction. Black is the "No" as opposed to the "Yes" of white. … white and black are the two extremes, the Alpha and the Omega, the beginning and the end.

With its strong associations of renunciation, surrender and relinquishment, black is often seen as a negative color. But it can emphasize and enforce the characteristics of the color it surrounds.

The Lüscher Color Test (http://www.colorquiz.com) theorizes that if colors generate emotional responses and associations, then the colors people prefer could say something about their current emotional status. Reflect on how your visitors might be reacting to the colors on your website. Maybe it's time to go check out those paint chip samples?

---

[1] All quotations from: The Lüscher Color Test. Dr. Max Lüscher. Ian Scott, translator and editor. New York: Random House. 1969.

[2] I have simplified the colors into categories. In the spirit of academic propriety, Lüscher's comments are specific to the colors he identifies in the test, which you can see for yourself at ColorQuiz. Lüscher's red is an orange-red rather than a blue-red, his blue is dark rather than light. His green has a tinge of blue.

"There are many methods for predicting the future. For example, you can read horoscopes, tea leaves, tarot cards, or crystal balls. Collectively, these methods are known as 'nutty methods.' Or you can put well-researched facts into sophisticated computer models, more commonly referred to as 'a complete waste of time'." - Scott Adams, The Dilbert Future

Reading the World of Color

Beyond matters of personal preferences and body physics, colors have a cultural context – a color can become symbolic or representative of something that has its own associations of meaning. This symbolism won't be the same for all cultures. So a friendly word of caution to non-American readers: some of these associations are U.S.-centric, but I'll bet you have parallels.

Colors also have a commercial context – colors can encourage folks to tap into particular moods, influence a purchase, affect point of purchase behaviors. And it is through commercial applications that we've acquired a lot of our knowledge about human reactions to color.

The Rainbow

Red is excitement, drama, urgent passion, strength, assertiveness and an appetite stimulant. It's the color of the Valentine's Day heart or the rose of love, the red apple and the fire engine. It's the red of a Coca-Cola™ can that promises excitement and good times. It's also the color of the Devil! Lots of casinos pair red with yellow (so what does that say about McDonalds and Burger King – they're gambles?) and have discovered people are happier to risk their money under red light.

In most commercial applications, it seems folks respond best to red when it is used as an accent or high-light. Strong preferences for red are linked demographically to those who feel most secure – both econom-ically and personally. Men favor yellow-reds; women prefer blue-reds.

Pink makes most people think of baby girls, so you'd think a lot of feminist types wouldn't be too keen on it. But, along with yellow, pinks are considered the warmest and most cheerful of colors . . . and pink is the more popular of the two. Soft pinks generate simple, uncomplicated emotions (hot pink, just like most fluorescent colors, is low in popular appeal). In fact, pink is so successful at eliciting gentler reactions that it is a color often used in prison cells (I can't vouch for this firsthand!).

While orange may suggest fire, vitality, warmth and energy, all lovely associations, it's the color most-detested by Americans (it is more popular in Europe and has particularly strong appeal in Latino and French cultures). Maybe it's the '70s associations. But the research suggests if you're going to use orange, it's best tolerated when you are evoking a natural association. Like carrots. That, or go for a deeper orange that is earthier.

Yellow is the very first color the eye processes. It's bright, sunny (as in "light" as well as "powerful"), welcoming, cheerful, and the color most visible to the human eye. Lots of its associations are positive: deities with glowing halos and golden hair, enlightenment, and precious metals. But it evokes a few nega-tive responses as well in associations with dishonesty, cowardice, egoism, betrayal and caution. When it's paired with black, it suggests warning – think stinging insects, all those traffic caution signs, and labels for hazardous materials.

Green is a mixed bag. It's the color of nature, a sign of growth, the harbinger of Spring and warmer weather. Green represents optimism, good luck, freshness, fertility and suggests that things are getting better or healing. As the color of money (at least boring old American bills), it has strong associations with finance, business, economic stability and entitlement. And then there's hunter green or British racing green – rooted in tradition, classic, affluent. Green is actually the most restful color on the eye, and human eyes can discern more shades of green than any other color.

But green has its downside. Green is linked with envy, sickness, slime and decaying food. Yellow-green chartreuse is the second most-hated color in America! The best favored shades of green across all consumer lines, including gender, are the blue-greens.

One group of people who respond very well to green is the "influencers," those opinion leaders to whom folks go for advice. They also happen to be about the only segment of the American audience that responds well to orange!

Blue creates an optical impression that objects are farther away than they really are. But it's the number one customer favorite regardless of shade – although men favor a darker shade of blue than women. Blue is the preferred color for evoking "a soothing, calming tranquility in a frantically fast, often insecure world." It is no accident that so many corporate color schemes, think IBM's Big Blue image, incorporate blue (which is also the second-most favorite color for business suits).

Blue is also the color of the local policeman's uniform, which suggests power and authority, but also inspires confidence, a sense of safety and trustworthiness. For some cultures, blue is the color that wards off evil spirits, the ultimate color metaphor for protection.

And red, white and blue, together are still the biggest best-selling combo for packaging in the US. Let's hear it for the power of color and national pride (for the Irish is it green, white and orange?). So when you want to make your visitors feel better about how much you're going to charge their credit cards, give them the bad news in blue!

Purple is a complex color, both in terms of its associations and the reactions different people have to it. Interestingly, it's also the hardest color for the human eye to discriminate. It can be magic, or intense and ephemeral like the final glow of a sunset, or brave like a Purple Heart. It can be regal and full of authority, rich and jewel-like.

Purple suggests intelligence and creativity, but it also suggests cruelty, and in some cultures, purple is the color of mourning. If the purple is on the blue side, people tend to associate it with mystical qualities; if it's on the red side, the associations are more sensual. Red-purples grab people's attention more effectively than blue purples. Those between the ages of 18 to 29 are especially partial to this color.

Brown is the earth, roots, giving of life. It is also linked with wealth and a subtle but expensive taste, particularly fur shades. It's a secure color, a home-grown color, a grounded color. However, brown is also associated with things that are dirty and unclean. The enormous appeal of chocolate and coffee has given brown a bit boost in popularity, evoking qualities of comfort and satisfying aroma.

White is the color of the dove of peace, crispness, tidiness, innocence, moral purity and cleanliness – after all, the goal of laundering is whiter whites! It can also connote sterility and blandness. Off-white is a neutral, but pure white is considered a brilliant color (capable of producing optical fatigue) and is highly visible to the human eye.

Pretty much anything goes with black – it sets off specific contrast associations when paired with other colors. Black can be an extremely influential color; along with gray, it's the top choice for your business suit. It's the color of mystery, of things not yet revealed. It is a strong color, unequivocal. Black is a polarizing color that suggests an opposite: empty/full, dark/light, evil/good.

Black also carries positive and negative connotations, and you should consider its use judiciously. On the one hand, black can be sophisticated, elegant and representative of modernism. This is an association especially true for wealthy, achievement-oriented women. On the other hand, it can symbolize corruption, emptiness and depression — for many socio-economic groups and cultures, black is before all else the color of mourning, grief and death.

Movement

This colors-associated-with movement is separate from the other discussion, because it's important to consider color for encouraging appropriate action on your website. Think of traffic signal colors, firmly engrained in your visitor's mind. Red means stop, under no uncertain terms, wait, don't move. Yellow means caution, be on the lookout, be prepared to act quickly (in an ideal world, it's not supposed to mean go faster!). Green means go, you have the right of way, you can advance in good conscience. Does this give you pause to rethink your red call-to-action buttons?

For Setting the Tone

People associate certain qualities or emotional tones with individual colors or groupings of color. Pantone color expert Lee Eiseman elaborates on these associations.

- Traditional: burgundy, teal, navy, hunter green, gold, plum, slate blue, vanilla.
- Nurturing: peach, honey yellows, warm rose, cream, grayed lilac, baby blue, soft green.
- Romantic: pink, rose, sage green, lilac, antique while, cameo blue.
- Tranquil: blue, blue-green, cool lavender, seafoam green, mauve, light gray, natural.
- Contemplative: neutral gray, beige, taupe, off-white with colored accents.
- Whimsical: true red, bright blue, daffodil, kelly green, orange, periwinkle, vibrant pink.
- Sensuous: warm red, mango, plum purple, hot pink, gold, deep blue, chocolate.

Start looking critically at that colorful world around you. There's a reason banks like green in their carpets, while the local burger joint probably wouldn't touch green with a ten-foot pole. When you begin reading the colors around you, you can begin to apply them in meaningful ways to the persuasive dialogue you establish with your visitors.

Selected Resources

1. "All that glitters is not sold." MarketingProfs.com. January 2001.
2. "Results of the Roper/Pantone Consumer Color Preference Study." http://www.pantone.com
3. "ColorScopes: Color Profiles." http://www.pantone.com
4. For pure poetic color fun: Hailstones and Halibut Bones: Adventures in Color. Mary O'Neill and John Wallner. Doubleday. 1990.
5. A wonderful site to explore: Color Matters, http://www.colormatters.com/entercolormatters.html
6. Color Voodoo, http://www.colorvoodoo.com/cvoodoo.html

"Let us become thoroughly sensible of the weakness, blindness, and narrow limits of human reason: Let us duly consider its uncertainty and endless contrarieties, even in subjects of common life and practice." - David Hume

Color and Usability

If the ability to distinguish color is a critical element of your website's persuasion architecture, then your website isn't as user-friendly as it could be. And it won't be persuading some folks as effectively as it could. At least ten percent of your audience has some form of vision impairment that makes it difficult for them to see your website as you intend it to be seen. There's partial color blindness in which the perception of some colors is affected (the most common is red-green). If you want to understand how a color blind person experiences color, visit vischeck.com There's total color blindness (pretty rare). And then there are the folks who are partially sighted and blind.

Those with mild impairments simply live with the limitations. Those with more serious impairments have a range of assistive technologies available that allow them to change how your webpage appears in their browsers – "The better to see you with, my dear."

Basically, we're talking LCD (Lowest Common Denominator). The cool thing about LCD Design, when you do it right, is that nobody loses!

Marta Eleniak, a UK-based usability consultant, offers up a series of color checklists "that will help you design sites that are suitable for the widest range of users possible."[1] Here's a sampling of her ideas that will improve the usability of yourwebsite:

- You need strong contrast between any background color and the over-lying text color.
- Keep the backgrounds behind your text solid and plain – no patterned stuff.
- Make sure that color is not the only way you communicate information the visitor must understand to move forward in your process – indicating a field that needs to be corrected on a form through color alone is not a good idea.
- Employ color-coding very carefully – no more than five different colors and keep them consistent across the website.
- The best combination for readability is black text on a white background.
- If folks will be looking at the page for a long time, or if your specific audience is elderly, use brighter colors.
- So that visitors can easily distinguish your colors, "choose darker shades of blue, red and purple, and paler shades of green, yellow and orange."
- When the difference between adjacent colors is necessary for meaning, don't put red alongside green or blue alongside yellow.
- Don't use grey for text or grayscale for diagrams that convey critical information.

- Because blue-receptors in the eye are least numerous, avoid blue for small text and diagrams with thin lines.
- Some color pairings can create headaches, perceived vibrations, phantom shadows and other optical illusion type situations for your visitors. Avoid pairing color chart opposites (e.g. blue and red) and high chroma colors (e.g. blue and yellow).

One of the more important acceptance tests you can run is to evaluate each of your pages first in grayscale and then in black and white (the most extreme form of contrast in which your website can be rendered by an assistive technology). You want to make sure the persuasion architecture of your website holds under these manipulations.

Color should enhance your website's experience, but because so many people perceive color in so many different ways, color cannot define your website's experience. Bear in mind the words of the influential teacher-artist, Josef Albers:

"If one says "Red" (the name of a color), and there are 50 people listening, it can be expected that there will be 50 reds in their minds. And one can be sure that all these reds will be very different."[2]

1. "Essential Colour Checklists for Web Design." Marta Eleniak. Sitepoint. April 28, 2003. http://www.sitepoint.com/article/1126.
2. Interaction of Color. Josef Albers. New Haven: Yale University Press. 1975.

"It has long been an axiom of mine that the little things are infinitely the most important." - Sir Arthur Conan Doyle

Case Study: Max-Effect Before and After

John Morana knows how to design killer ads for the Yellow Pages. What he can do would knock your socks off. Trouble was, his website wasn't knocking anybody's socks off. Now, John had already made a few changes. And they were good improvements. But not good enough. So he called us. And, together, we got down to brass tacks.

Certain aspects of John's website were well done. In particular, his text was formatted for scanning and skimming: it was blocked nicely; key text was bolded; benefits were bulleted. The text itself made effective use of hyperlinks that appealed to different personality types. His navigation elements were simple and consistent. The phone number was prominent.

But, he was only getting one or two leads a week. Folks just weren't getting past the home page. So we scrutinized that first.

Look & Feel

It didn't take long to find a big problem. As aesthetically pleasing as John's old home page might have been to a designer, it screamed "Don't Bother!" to prospects. The background was black (a somber, sometimes negative color). Various text elements were red, or purple, or teal … sometimes yellow. Most dispiriting for the potential client who landed there, much of the copy was reverse-type grey.

This sort of design creates usability problems. And if you're an ad designer hoping to get prospects to believe your ads are going to get folks to take action, you want to do everything to promote your credibility. How credible do you look when folks aren't even persuaded to get past your home page?

The new home page look and feel is brighter, conveys energy and, most important, highlights the copy that is critical to Joe's conversion process: once you've focused on the central headline, you are quickly drawn to text that is benefit-rich and includes hyperlinks as internal calls to action.

Copy

John's old home page copy was fairly benefits-oriented. It did include a degree of self-congratulation, but the key problem lay elsewhere. The old copy read:

Eliminate Yellow Page Advertising Hassles Forever
… And watch your calls & sales SKYROCKET !
A Custom Designed Yellow Page Ad by MaxEffect Will:
- Maximize your readership, phone calls & sales... 24 / 7 / 365
- Save you money... Using the most cost-effective sizes & colors
- Save you time... Minimizing YP sales rep calls & DIY struggles
- Eliminate Yellow Pages frustration, doubts & deadline worries
- Nullify your competitors... Letting you dominate your classification

Yellow Pages advertising is expensive, time-consuming and fiercely competitive. A new, custom-designed ad by MaxEffect will let you easily conquer your rivals and save you time, money and the aggravating headaches common with Yellow Pages advertising. Study the following Ad Samples, read a few Testimonials or review our Risk Free Guarantee. But whatever you do Place Your Order Now . . . before your competitors !
MaxEffect clients have asked us, even PAID us, to NOT ACCEPT ORDERS from their competitors. They've learned something you absolutely MUST... A custom-designed Yellow Page ad by MaxEffect is your most powerful weapon when doing battle in the Yellow Pages directory. Your new advertisement will reign supreme.
If you're determined to drive your Yellow Pages ROI to the absolute MAX, you need to Order MaxEffect Now.

As you read this rather heavy-handed copy, notice the way the words speak to "pain" and focus heavily on negative associations: eliminate, hassles, minimize, struggles, frustration, doubts, worries, nullify. Then, "Yellow Pages advertising is expensive"! And it doesn't help that the copy suggests John is bribe-able.

Here's the new copy:

Maximize Your Investment!

Place Your Business under the Yellow Page Advertising
Spotlight and Listen to Your Phone and Cash Register Sing!

Dare to stand out within your Yellow Pages category!

Then your potential customers will . . .

- Be drawn to your Yellow Page ad more strongly than anything else on the page.
- Be engaged by your ad so they read it entirely!
- Recognize that you are the solution to what they're searching for.
- Call you, visit you & buy from you!

For just a onetime, low investment you get an express in-depth company evaluation, outstanding graphic design and persuasive creative messaging that will deliver immediate results.

Best of all, your new MaxEffect Yellow Page ad is 100% Guaranteed. Check out some happy clients' ad samples and read about all the business we've generated for businesses like yours.

Contact us now to dramatically increase your sales opportunities!

This shorter revision is more to the point, removes the hard sell, speaks to "the heart of the dog" in a positive light and is more believable. And while Yellow Page advertising may be expensive, this copy eliminates the discussion of money in favor of convincing the prospect of the value (remember, value is rarely about price).

Product Presentation

Think about a Yellow Page ad, any Yellow Page ad. Can you bring one to mind? Kind of unmemorable entities aren't they?

Naturally, John had a whole page of sample ads clustered together on that black background. And they were really great ads, but we figured we could make the product presentation even more persuasive.

Now, instead of 13 samples, you'll find only two. But each is paired, in before- and-after fashion, with the client's former ad — the one that ran before John worked his magic. The juxtaposition highlights John's abilities with startling clarity. Anyone looking at that page who needs an ad is going to be impressed.

With these changes in place, John exceeded his ultimate goal with an over 600% increase in leads per week. In fact, he got more business than he could handle! So he found someone to help.

Recently, John raised his rates, figuring that would discourage some of the visitors to his website and help him catch up with his workload. It didn't.

What a problem to have, huh!

Home | Yellow Page Ad Samples | Contact Us | Yellow Pages Ad Prices

☎ 1-800-726-7006

maxeffect™
yellow page ad design

Maximize Your Investment
▷ **Yellow Page Ad Samples**
Contact MaxEffect
Testimonials
Risk-Free Guarantee
FAQ's
No Nonsense Pricing
Free Ad Evaluation
Design Tips
About MaxEffect

COOL WINTER SPECIALS

Contact MaxEffect Now!

Yellow Page
Ad Samples

Some Yellow Page ads generate a phenomenal response...
Now YOURS can too!

Click thumbnails for larger Yellow Page print ad samples.

Before MaxEffect Yellow Page Ad Design **After** MaxEffect Yellow Page Ad Design

Before MaxEffect Ad Design **After** MaxEffect Ad Design

But first, you must decide! You can keep running the same humdrum Yellow Page ads you've always run and continue hoping for the best or you can **once and for all...**

Seize complete control of your Yellow Page ad investment, **dominate your heading** and listen to your phones sing with a...

Tantalizing, **eyeball-grabbing** Yellow Page ad from MaxEffect. Your new, custom-tailored Yellow Page ad will be meticulously crafted... **to keep your phones and cash register ringing** for the next 12 months! Isn't that why you're spending all that money on Yellow Pages ads in the first place?

Your prospects will be **drawn to your Yellow Page ad** with the gravitational pull of a black hole—leaving your competitors dazed and confused... and wishing **they** had discovered the advertising design prowess of MaxEffect first!

If you're going to be running Yellow Pages ads for the next 365 days, isn't it just plain common sense to have **the most effective ad** you possibly can?

If you agree Click here to contact us or Click here to view more print ad samples.

"Lost in a gloom of uninspired research." - William Wordsworth, The Excursion

Fix Your Navigation and Enjoy Improved Conversion Rates

Broken navigation is the biggest challenge faced by e-commerce websites. Traditional navigation methods contribute to embarrassingly average 2 to 3 percent conversion rates.

The information architecture technique of card-sorting adversely affects navigation and website structure. Traditional card-sorting is flawed. Usability expert Jared Spool agrees. He recently wrote about his own Category Agreement Analysis (CAA) card-sorting technique. In standard card-sort, you put one product per card on index cards without regard to category. Users then group cards into user-defined categories. CAA differs by allowing users to sort items into multiple categories.

According to "Information Architecture for the World Wide Web," card-sorting "can provide insight into users' mental models, illuminating the way that they often tacitly group, sort and label tasks and content within their own heads."

That's all wonderful, but it fails to recognize the difference between usability in a controlled environment and the voluntary nature of an online shopping experience.

People approach categorization by identifying similarities in an upward process. If I say "cat," you think a cat is a feline, which is a mammal, which is a living thing. We intuit from specific to general. This right-brain, holistic approach considers the inter-relationship of things to one another. Once complete, we can potentially look back to see how top-down can illustrate differences, not just similarities.

CAA takes the opposite approach. It sorts products based on top-level category, then requests possible secondary categories. It requires general-to-specific reasoning, which is left brain (more mechanical). No foundation is built by first observing similarity. Instead, it requires differentiation.

CAA also assumes people who perform categorization represent a single, homogeneous type of website traffic, another mistake. Usability experts focus on usability first, persuasion second. Survey solutions suffer the same limitations: Participants are in a lab looking at a website. It can't be assumed they'll look at it the same way under natural conditions.

The technique is deeply flawed, but it's how categorization for 99 percent of e-commerce websites is performed. When Sally looks for a red sweater online, she's successful because she knows exactly what she wants. The clothing website's navigation reflects women's clothes —> tops —> sweaters. The site created a category path she can use to navigate from general to specific to find that elusive red sweater.

Visit your own site as if you knew exactly what you wanted to buy (start with a search engine query, if you like). Start clicking. Ask a colleague to count your clicks. How many does it take to complete your purchase or inquiry? The number is your minimum-clicks-to-buy metric. This works only because of two inherent assumptions: you know precisely what you want (your brain already performed the specific-to-general categorizing) and the retailer implemented that path in top-down categorization.

What about people who shop without knowing precisely what they want? Say Sally's boyfriend Joe wants to buy her something for an upcoming winter trip to Quebec. He starts in "Women's Clothes" but is quickly lost. It doesn't help that 53 percent of CAA card sorters put the red sweater in "Tops." He isn't certain what he's looking for. He may narrow his search using a top-down approach, but he doesn't classify what he seeks that way. Joe's shopping in a right-brain mode. His goal is more emotional than the impersonal "Can she use the gift in Quebec?" His question isn't solely "Will it keep Sally warm?" CAA didn't help Joe accomplish his goal.

Visit your website as if you were browsing. Again, ask a colleague to count the clicks. How many does it take to complete a purchase or inquiry? The number is your target-clicks-to-buy metric. Most shoppers fall into this category. Look at the top keywords on shopping search engines. Notice how imprecise they are.

Persuasion architecture demands you first identify each persona. Then, research the keywords each persona is likely to use. To do this, use services such as Wordtracker, Overture's and Google's keyword suggestion tools, Web logs and internal search queries, and interviews with customers and customer-facing employees (sales and service reps). You'll get lots of clues for labeling categories. Finally, plan each persona's website experience as a persuasion path. Only when that path is complete can you look for commonalities between pages that indicate globally accessible links and other categorization techniques.

Now you can perform any card-sort variants. CAA's statistical, left-brain approach should be applied only over a set of field-test respondents who can be identified as given persona archetypes. Joe and Sally are better served by the results of people like them, who categorize the same way they do.

Fixing Broken Navigation

Having stated what is wrong with how navigation schemes are developed, let's look at how you might fix your navigation and hence improve your conversion rate. First, check if any of these basic navigation types are broken?

Hierarchical — that sideways, tree-like line of text that indicates where the user has been. It reminds me of those little kids in the fairy tale who "left breadcrumbs" so they would know how to get home and often looks like this:

Home Page > Automobiles > Classics > Convertibles

Global — this scheme offers access to all areas of your site, using tabs or a running list. The Future Now, Inc. site shows this. It is the tabs across the top of the page. It is really simple and easy to use. You can access this navigation from any page of the site, too, because the system is consistent over every page.

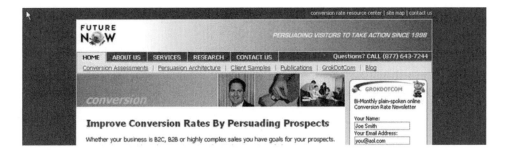

Local — allows users to get to related information within a category, not between categories. This is most helpful when your visitor landed on your website via a search engine, but hasn't landed on quite the right page.

Embedded Links — This is another very easy scheme. You simply place a hyperlink within the body of some text. You just have to be careful how you phrase the link to suggest where it will take the user. (NOTE: the links in the following examples are not real.)

Here is an ineffective use of embedded links: I am <u>writing a novel</u> about a woman who was murdered. Will that link to how to write a novel? Thoughts about writing a novel? The novel itself? It's not terribly clear. Here is a more effective use of embedded links: I am writing a novel about <u>Jack the Ripper</u>. Want to read an <u>excerpt</u>? The user can more easily assume these links will take her to a discussion of Jack the Ripper and a sample of the manuscript.

Site Maps — Most people skip these completely. Typically only 1-3 percent of visitors use a site map. There is too much information for most visitors to bother with, and they do not strike most users as being as creative as some designers would like to think. According to Jupiter Research analyst Eric Peterson, "site maps have a tendency to be used as a Band-Aid on sites that have not placed enough emphasis on the self-service search experience."

You could also argue a site map does have some value as a supplemental navigation tool just in case your customers can't find what they were looking for using your primary navigation. Site maps have search engine marketing (SEM) value. Websites should generally have site maps for that reason alone, but many don't. A site map containing links to all your pages allows search engine spiders to find deeper content within your website. Though all these links may be useful to a spider, they're usually too much for the typical visitor.

Most e-commerce traffic navigates via a combination of persistent global navigation, local supplemental navigation, and contextual embedded links. All work together to drive visitors to their optimum conversion paths. When a specific persona's needs are overlooked in this categorization and labeling exercise, website navigation fails.

Review Basic Human Behavior

To develop useful navigation that helps your customers shop and moves them ever closer to the close, design your website the way your customers think, so your website anticipates the way your customers want to interact with your "store." People search for and gather information in fairly predictable ways. And navigation has a very simple role to play. It orients the customer by letting him know where he is, and it directs by letting him know where he can go as well as how to get back. Here are some pointers for improving navigation:

- To optimize your site, you need to recognize users are task-oriented, or "goal-driven." They pursue what they are looking for rather single-mindedly, and even when they are browsing, they browse within a narrow field.
- Users rarely look at logos, mission statements, slogans, or any other elements they consider fluff.
- If a page does not appear relevant to the user's current goal, then the user will ruthlessly click the Back button after two or three seconds.

- If users don't understand a certain design element, they don't spend time learning it.
- Most users hate distractions, such as flashing gifs, and also hate un-requested intrusions, such as pop-ups.

And, above all remember these three cardinal rules: keep it simple, make it intuitive and be consistent.

Improve Navigation Before They Arrive

Not all visitors will arrive in a predictable manner. You need to plan for those who do not arrive at the correct page. For example, site maps are useful for 404 or other error pages. They help orient the reader. You certainly don't want visitors to get a Windows default message as they do at Ernst & Young, Eddie Bauer, and Macys.com. A custom 404 page, such as CafePress.com uses, is optimal.

Marketers often forget the importance of unique page titles for search engines. They're equally important for people who want to find your website among their bookmarks. It's also useful to have a unique favicon file show up in the browser's address bar. It's saved with a bookmark (if you save Yahoo.com to your favorites, you should see the red Y! icon by the name). Finally, to avoid people typing your URL incorrectly, it's helpful to have simple URLs people won't forget or mistype. These are just a few ways to help your readers navigate your website even before they arrive.

Putting It All Together

Keep these pointers in mind as you create the structure that will enable your readers to successfully and painlessly move throughout your website.

- Use standard icons and conventions whenever possible. For example, people recognize what a shopping cart is for and know that blue-underlined text means hyperlink. Leverage what they already know. Contradict it just to be "original" and you will lose sales.
- Keep it simple and make it intuitive. Ease of use makes for happy customers.
- Keep your scheme consistent from page to page. Your customer should only have to figure it out once.

- Show the basic structure of the navigation system. It helps your visitors feel more confident, and more confidence leads to more sales.
- Stick to clear, concise labels for your navigation elements. This is not the place to get creative or coy.
- Use text for navigation elements; avoid graphics. Graphics take time to load, and also don't always load properly. Some folks even go so far as to have images turned off in their browsers, in which case, all those pictures you created to direct your traffic were a waste of time and money. If you feel you must use pictures, always include accompanying text.
- Don't link everything to everything. Less is more. Anticipate where your customer is likely to go and build that into your scheme. And above all, keep your links within your page; don't require your customers to use their browser's back button. If you do, you hand them a chance to leave your website completely. (On the other hand, never disable their browser's back button. Hijacking their computer is a great way to lose customers forever.)
- Don't overuse embedded links, and make sure they clearly identify what they link to.
- Test! Test! Test! On lots of different users, different browsers, different viewing options.
- Provide help, online and offline.

Again, it's all about designing your information architecture around the searching patterns and psychology of your visitors, not coming up with something that looks cool but sends your visitors clicking off the site. When you make it easy for your visitors to find what they want to buy quickly and intuitively, more of them will buy, and your conversion rates will increase.

"Currente Cal'amo (Latin), Offhand; without premeditation; written off at once, without making a rough copy first." - E. Cobham Brewer, Dictionary of Phrase and Fable

Copy

The next few articles are all about writing. We've consistently said that the words are what count, so it's time to focus on the copy that you bring to the Web.

Web writing is different. We'll show you why, and then provide some help that will enable you to fashion stuff that really resonates with your visitors.

However, just because writing for the Web is different doesn't mean you can abandon everything you've learned elsewhere about good writing. Some of the old rules apply, some don't. We'll make this clear and easy.

We'll also focus on clarity of perspective in your Web writing, and what it takes to make it personal. Tactically, we'll look at word choice, content versus copy, the use of verbs, the reasons why grammar and spelling still count and the ability to appeal to the senses through language.

For those who take joy in being wordsmiths, we've provided two sections especially for you, plus some great examples of good and bad writing including a "before and after" for comparative purposes. Finally, we've included a section for those who look at words not just as language, but as generators of traffic (keywords) and some hints for those who must communicate effectively with a global audience.

We've highlighted the important principles here, but for a more in-depth look at online copywriting, check out our book Persuasive Online Copywriting: How to Take Your Words to the Bank.

Conversion Tip

Customer Focus Calculator — WeWe Monitor

Realize that the words you use and how you use them are telling your visitors where your focus is. Want them to stick around and eventually take the action you want? Talk about them, their needs, their wants, and how they can get those needs and wants satisfied. Use customer-focused language. Otherwise, they're going to feel like you're the self-centered guest at the party. You may not be, but they only have your words to judge you by.

Because there wasn't a tool you could use to evaluate your site with respect to customer focus, we invented one; we created a Web page for it. You can find it at www.futurenowinc.com/wewe.htm . It's not perfect (there are lots of variables, of course). But it has proven to be so useful that it has become one of the most popular pages on our website.

- Future Now, Inc.

"Personal example carries more weight than preaching" - Chinese proverb

The Power of Being More Personal Online

Now that you understand the underlying reasons why copywriting online is different from copywriting for broadcast, print, direct mail and other offline media, and get why perspective is so important, we'll look at the nuts and bolts of how writing to an active audience changes the words, the style and the format of how you write.

As we've said, online audiences are quite different — because people online are connected, vocal and active within the online environment. You can't write 'at' people online. Instead, you have to connect 'with' them.

This shift in approach makes many demands on an online copywriter.

First, if you want to connect with people online, and be genuine about it, you have to 'know' those people a lot better than you do when you write a billboard or print ad. You have to dig deep to find out about the people with whom you want to connect.

How do you get to know them? Listen in to your customer service calls. Read customer service emails and online chat. Lurk in related newsgroups. Study the logs of your website. In short, take the time to find out what makes your audience tick. What's important to them? How do they write? What terms and phrases do they use?

Once you have done that — once you have a close sense of the people to whom you are writing — you'll be in a better position to write copy that truly connects with what's important to them.

Here's a simple starting point when you put pen to paper or keyboard to monitor: make it personal. Copywriting offline is largely impersonal. But online, everything is personal. So you need to change your language.

As an example, here's what the people at Apple are saying on their homepage about the iMac computer:

Four years ago we introduced the first iMac. It changed the way people use computers. It changed the way people look at technology. Some people even said it changed the world. Now, six million iMacs later, we're doing it again.

And here is what a couple of people said about the iMac in their reviews at epinions.com:

My husband had never before turned on a computer, he has within 3 short months come farther than most, because of the ease of use of the Apple architecture. These machines are designed to be user friendly... no endless hours trying to figure out what a .dll file is anyway!

I have hated all things Apple for so long, and so very vocally, that it literally pains me to admit that I like the iMac. Okay, fine, I love the damn thing, stupid circular one-button mouse and all. I have even willingly stood silent as my longtime Mac-loving friends grasped hands to dance the Hubris Horah around me.

Apple's copy is inward-looking and self-serving. "Some people even said it changed the world." Really? Well, maybe Steve Jobs and his family think so.

The Apple copy has a very typical, offline feel to it.

But what if we were to learn a little from what those two people at epinions wrote? Maybe we could come up with something a little more real; something that actually connects with regular buyers.

We admit it. The new G4 iMac looks a little strange. A little like a big shaving mirror with a fat stand. But we think you'll like it! That flat screen gives a beautiful, bright, distortion-free image. And the G4 processor is going to blast you right up into multimedia Heaven.

We could work on that a little more. But you get the general idea. Say good-bye to that self-serving, Madison Avenue 'ad copy'. And say hello to a more personal style that is in tune with what your customers are saying and feeling.

Are You Using the Words Your Customers Are Using?

Let's look a bit more deeply at words, the special words that relate to you and your business. Except I'm not interested in the words you would use to describe yourself, your products or your services. I'm interested in the words your potential visitors would use. And oddly enough, they don't always call stuff what you'd call it. Let's see exactly why you should care about the words your potential visitors use.

Keywords. You aren't trying to find you. You are hoping *they* will find you. Except they type their words — not yours — into a search engine. The search engine then crawls a bazillion sites, looking especially for text and hyperlink matches. The more effectively you populate your copy, headers and tags with the right keywords, the more likely you are to be found. And the better will be your ranking in the results. Face it, it doesn't do you much good to be the 3,647th result in a search! I don't know anybody who wades in that deeply, do you?

Trigger Words. The sort of words that bring your visitors to your website are the same words they are going to be scanning for the second they arrive. Trigger words. The ones that reinforce connection and confidence. The ones that are the backbone of your copy's ability to motivate the next click. So they need to be there, not just somewhere on the website as words the search engine spiders see, but as the words your visitors couldn't possibly miss.

Think of it this way. Suppose you are looking for a BrandX Digital Camera. You follow a lead, and when you land on the page, you see the word "camera." You might feel a bit disappointed — camera is a big category of possibilities. But if you saw "digital camera" you might feel a bit more enthusiastic. And if you saw "brandx digital camera," you'd probably be clicking your heels. Trigger words are not limited to keywords; they are the special words that encourage your visitors to take action. Trigger words trigger a response — and online that response is the click-through. These words constitute the implicit promise that you understand and can meet the felt needs of your visitors. They are the words that should appear prominently in your headlines and hyperlinks.

Diction. Here's a snippet of copy from the website of a professional Web copywriter:

Today's readers and Web browsers demand frankness and verisimilitude, so your written communications require exacting professional integrity with accurate and adequate research. For concrete, colorful and dynamic written material that willfully attracts customers, Bob Tony* will work with you to develop unrivaled written communications for your marketing materials, grants, newsletters, Web site, or other publications and articles. To ensure you're writing tasks with pacesetting presentation and unparalleled, consistent editorial power, give your deadlines to Bob Tony*. (* Name changed to protect the ostentatious and largiloquent.)

Verisimilitude? Willfully attracts? Ensure with pacesetting presentation? Editorial power? What a mouth- and headful of gobbledygook! Bob Tony is definitely not the fellow you want to use as your model for online copywriting!

Where do you look? To your customers! Folks are out there talking. So listen to what they have to say and how they say it, then model your copy to reflect their needs and concerns. If you're going to invest time doing "adequate research," dig in here!

In the Trenches

We've been examining this issue with an extremely gracious client who has been with us for several years. He helps folks solve personal problems. A series of changes to his website had resulted in a delightful increase in sales. But, as we tease ourselves around here, when have you ever made too much money?

So when we started on a website redesign, we hunkered down and took a fine-toothed comb to the copy. The key question in the back of our minds: How would a visitor describe his or her personal problem?

The copy talked about "emotional trauma" (this was also a hyperlinked item). It asked if you were suffering from "limited thoughts" and in search of "spiritual abundance." It was nice copy, except it didn't really use words we would have chosen to characterize our situations. An insider would understand — and possibly use — this sort of language, but if you ask the average Joe or Josephine what they are in need of, you probably won't hear, "Spiritual abundance."

And what exactly is emotional trauma? If you are stressed out to the max and looking for solutions, do you first think of calling your problem emotional trauma? Are those the words you'd type into a browser? Are those the words that would leap off a page, letting you know you are understood and confirming that you have arrived in the Promised Land? Yeah, right. Not!

Once we decided that not many folks would resonate with "emotional trauma" as a description of their circumstance, we turned to figuring out what they would call it.

We got lots of minds to brainstorm the ins and outs of emotional trauma, generating an incredibly useful list full of words that did not appear prominently in the copy, yet were far more likely to be critical keywords for search engines and trigger words for persuasion. Words like abandonment, rejection, abuse, guilt, shame, workaholic, victim. And the ever-popular stress and anxiety.

Of course, it isn't quite that easy. We know some people whom we would label as "martyrs" on the emotional trauma index. However, if any of them were on the trail for help, they'd probably refer to themselves as "caretakers." Your potential visitors — different personalities with different agendas — will embrace the same range of qualitative distinctions as well.

Dr. Duane Lakin identifies several road blocks that inhibit effective sales. One of them, he says, is that all too often, the message does not fit the audience:

People hear and notice what is familiar to them. Words and phrases that look or feel familiar will have more of an impact on people than the unfamiliar. A philosophy professor addressing a group of industrial engineers will have difficulty speaking their language. Ideas may be expressed, but concepts will not be embraced by the audience. Too often, people talk or write the way that makes them feel comfortable and ignore what is necessary to make the audience feel good or be open to the message.[1]

You can't connect if you don't speak the language. So where do you go to "hear" the language your audience uses?

- Drain the brains of everyone who interacts with your customers and hear how they phrase their own needs. This would certainly include your sales staff and any customer service representative.
- Take the time to canvas consumer opinion forums. Read what folks write and post about you, your product, your service and anything related.
- Invest some time in paying attention to the keywords folks type into their browsers. If you have your own in-site search feature, mine those logs. You can also turn to applications like WordTracker.

"Emotional trauma" was an in-the-trenches exercise for us in dealing with the discrepancy between the words you use and the words they use. Such an exercise is critical to helping your visitors not only find you in the first place, but self-identify once they get to you. Figuring out your audience is a core element in the uncovery process and it is indispensable to creating the prototypic persona who represents your visitors. In very human terms, it is a way you market successfully while you welcome with open arms.

What About eMails?

Example 1: Here's a welcome email from SnapNames.com:

Dear (Your First and Last Names),
Welcome to SnapNames, helping to secure your domain.
To make changes or additions to your account please use the following username and password.

They put your name there — but they didn't manage to make their welcome personal.

Example 2: Here's a welcome from Customatix.com. No name, but the copy is infinitely more personal and engaging.

Well, you've done it now. By opening a Customatix account, you've just changed the way you're going to buy athletic shoes forever. Be careful. The surgeon general reports that designing your own cool athletic shoes can be highly addictive.

Do you have to be that casual? No, but you do have to make an effort to write in a way that better makes a personal connection.

So What Does It Mean?

Copywriting online *is* different. You need to get to know your audience better — and you need to write to people in a way that is a whole lot more engaging and one-to-one.

Developing relationships. Connecting with folks. It's what the Internet has always done best, and you can turn it to your advantage if you take the time to understand what your copy needs to do so you can create copy that earns its keep.

[1]The Unfair Advantage: Practical Applications of NLP for Sales and Marketing, Duane Lakin. 2000. p10.

"The content of a thought depends on its external relations; on the way that the thought is related to the world, not on the way that it is related to other thoughts." - Jerry Alan Fodor, The Elm and the Expert

Content, Copy, Language, and Pre-purchase Behavior

The goal of good content is to expose business value and articulate it in a way that matters to the customer. Great copy persuades the reader to take action.

These two website components should work hand in glove. Copy gets much more attention that content, probably because it's more akin to advertising language, the marketer's vernacular.

Let's first take a look at content. You've no doubt heard the maxim, "content is king." Is that always so? Let's take a look.

When Content Isn't King

A while ago, when heavyweights like Forrester Research proclaimed content the single biggest motivation in getting people to log onto the Internet as well as return to a website, folks started jumping on The Content Bandwagon. After the initial rush to pad websites with tons of content, folks are finally starting to examine both the role and the value of content a lot more critically.

Now that we've got some experience and some data, what we know is this: not all content is created equal. There are times when content is at best pointless, at worst actually destructive to conversion rates, and in any case most definitely not King (or even Prince).

According to a UCLA study, the Internet now beats out radio, television and magazines as an information resource (only newspapers — by a tiny margin — and books ranked higher).[1] People do come to the Internet to get content. But don't go thinking just because people go online for content, they want that content from your website or that providing it automatically will help your sales. Think of it as the online equivalent of the old "milk argument," the one that says 90 percent of the people who go shopping buy milk, so if you want to increase sales in, say, your hardware store, all you have to do is add a milk cooler.

There is a difference between searching for content and going shopping. When people want content on the Web, they go to websites that specialize in precisely the content they seek. When they want to buy something online, they want websites that offer a simple, trustworthy and streamlined buying experience (as well as outstanding service and great value), The only content they want is stuff that will directly help them make a more confident buying decision. Anything else only confuses them, or distracts them from buying, or slows the sales process, or bloats your website.

In e-commerce, content provides a lot of what you would get from a real-world salesperson. You gotta have it, and because it occupies a central place in supporting the primary sales goals of your website, you cannot give it secondary consideration in the planning and execution of your website. You must make sure you have the content you need — but only the content you need, and content that is going to earn its keep.

You need content that's clear, concise, vivid, compelling, and strictly related to your product or service or to your expertise. It must motivate the shopper directly toward becoming a buyer. These days, folks are even monitoring the effectiveness of their website's content by tracking which elements prompted the best overall results.[2] When you back-up killer content like this with a website that excels at the 5-step professional selling process — as an expert salesperson in the offline world would do — you will have a website that doesn't just lay there and hope people will buy; you will have a website that sells.

Content is not King when it exists simply for its own sake, or when it attracts unqualified traffic that isn't interested in making a purchase from you, or when it undermines your sales process, or when it adds distracting layers that impede your prospect's momentum toward becoming a buyer. So if you jumped on The Content Bandwagon, consider putting your content on a serious diet. Only then will you find yourself with content that truly rules!

But What About the Copy?

Most advertisers think in terms of 30 or 60 second commercials, generally 120-150 words maximum. But online, prospects want all the information they can get.

Our colleague Gerry McGovern wrote:

Advertisers tend to think in intervals of 30 seconds or less. This has a huge influence on the type of communication. It becomes much more emotional and visual. The Web is a very different world. The Web is a result of an increasingly literate consumer. It is no surprise that the Web started off in universities. The Web works better with facts rather than emotions.

Not Enough Words

I'm reminded of the emperor in "Amadeus" saying he didn't approve of Mozart's composition because it had "too many notes." Linguistics research backs up the premise: it takes around 300 to 500 words to cover a topic. One study proves reading comprehension drops off after 300 words, then not again until 3,000 words.

If you write less than 300 words, it may be nearly impossible to properly explain what you offer over your competitors. Writing copy for a website is about making a point correctly rather than quickly.

Direct marketers often err on the side of the absurd. They employ copy ad nauseam. They write so much copy, I doubt they even bother to read it all. I can just imagine them saying, "Shoot, by now they'll give up and have to buy it."

How Many Words?

Let's try a simple exercise in empathy. A prospect arrives at your website, hungry for information. She looks for all she can before she feels confident enough to purchase. She's curious as to what she's buying. If you don't give her all the information she seeks, she'll find someone who will. She wants relevance.

Perhaps not coincidentally, when search engine companies characterize what's important on webpages, they look for what searchers will find most relevant.

Maybe all those linguistics Ph.D.s at optimization companies read the same studies I do.

Says iProspect research:

Depending on the search engine, between 250-400 words seem to work well. Search engines do two things primarily: they index text and follow links. The more indexable text available, the better job search engines can do in understanding the pages' content.

Understanding your customers keeps you a step ahead in this game. Search engines and people alike look for many of the same things. Specific titles, headlines, and body text that speak directly to customers make them more willing to buy from you and increase search rankings. Make sure to lay content out so it's skimmable and scannable.

Content Must Address Personas

By developing personas, you learn who your customers really are and what they really want from you. This helps you to persuade better. Each persona has different content needs. One may know exactly what she wants. Another may only have a general interest in your product category.

For the first persona, clear, precise navigation is enough. The second requires copy that incorporates the five-step sales process and AIDAS to sell her anything. The more information you provide, the closer she'll come to a sale.

When you focus on a persona's needs, you find the resolution points, which allow you to develop the conversation your prospect seeks. You spend time answering her questions, not dumping everything on one long page.

The elegant beauty this medium provides is the ability to relate pieces of information connected by pre-established or user-created links that allow the user to follow associative trails.

The Right Length

How long should copy be? There's an old advertising expression from the '50s that is hardly politically correct but certainly makes the point. Copy should be as long as a women's skirt: long enough to cover the essentials but short enough to keep it interesting.

It's ironic, the website bearing the name of the king of long-copy ads, Ogilvy.com, links from the home page to "what do we do" with almost no copy. That should have been obvious from the get-go. You can't assume a visitor knows all about your brand, no matter how famous you are. No brand is universal.

We'd like to say there's a healthy debate going on out there about how long the copy for your website and emails should be, except there really isn't. Everywhere we turn, we read admonitions to keep your copy short because folks just can't be bothered to read lengthy copy.

The truth is, your copy should be as long as it needs to be. Not a word more, and not necessarily a word less! David Patterson wrote about the five most important things to consider in email marketing. One of them was "brevity."

"We all know the expression short and sweet. In email marketing, it might be better said, "short is sweet." People want to get through their email quickly. If you send a message many screens long, they're likely to react the same way they would if you were the driver in front of them doing 20 in a 50 MPH zone. Expect to be passed by at the first opportunity and to receive the virtual equivalent of the universal rude gesture."[3]

Do we agree with him? Well, sort of, but not exactly. To explain our reluctance to endorse the "short always" point of view, here's an interesting story about copy length.

A software marketer tested three different sets of copy for an email campaign:

- A tried-and-true version with three brief paragraphs
- A slightly longer version — about three-quarters of a printed page — that expanded on the offer details
- A one-and-a-half-page version with lots more detail on the offer, products, and company.

He mailed all three at the same time in plain text to three equal-sized segments (50,000 names) of his house list. The winner? The page-and-a-halfer! Although it was substantially longer, it produced a 7.5 percent click-through rate and a 4 percent conversion rate. The "slightly longer version" came in second, with a click-through rate of 6 percent and a conversion rate of 3 percent.

Kind of makes you question that Short Copy Rule, eh?

So what really gives? Are we saying we all ought to be writing reams of copy for our emails and websites? Hardly. What we will tell you is this: when folks indulge in lengthy copy, they are often rambling. Copy gets long when you don't get to the point or when you try to say too many things all at one go. This is the sort of length that wastes people's time and makes them head for the hills. We've said it before: copy is always most effective when it says one thing really well.

But we've also stressed the importance of speaking to your visitors' emotional needs, creating mental imagery that puts them center stage, developing relationships based on the unique personality you have chosen to convey. So you have to say what you need to say. And you have to say it engagingly, applying all those wordsmithing techniques we've talked about. Because what Rudyard Kipling said is absolutely true – words are "the most powerful drug used by mankind." They certainly bear the lion's share of your persuasive message.

If you short-change your copy – bleed it of its persuasive power – you can do serious damage to your conversion rates.

All things being equal, short copy is better. We've heard it's possible to make almost any point in 500 words or fewer (and, no, we're not presenting this as a rule!). Therein is the challenge of writing well and working some editorial magic. Because if you can say exactly the same thing in fewer words – accomplishing exactly the same goal – that's a very good thing indeed.

Make Your Copy Usability-Friendly

Understanding human eye-tracking behavior helps you optimize the organization of your copy on your web pages. It also helps to understand how folks scan and skim copy.

Use bulleted points to detail critical information (including your value proposition)

Get important information to your visitor first; elaborate later (think newspaper articles)

Highlight important text by using bolding, color, a highlight feature, or making the critical text a link (as appropriate)

- Use "white" space to separate your points
- Keep your paragraphs concise and small – eyes glaze over when they encounter impenetrable blocks of text

- Use font sizes that don't require magnifying glasses
- Avoid light type against a dark background (reverse type) – stick with contrast combinations that are comfortable on the eye

Win Their Hearts. Their Minds Will Follow

Copy, long or short, must be the right length. Length is based on your personas' needs. Does your website attract visitors who have no interest in your offerings yet visit out of curiosity following aggressive search engine optimization (SEO) efforts? Do you specifically target your customers with language that inflames their minds and opens their hearts to what you offer?

The right content for your website, and all online communications, is smart. It's what your customers seek, what search engines are looking for. It's just the thing for improving conversion rates. And, if done properly, it separates yourwebsite from the competition.

---

[1] "UCLA Report Finds Internet Surpasses Television as Key Information Source." Harlan Lebo. 15 August 2000

[2] "Optimize Content to Maximize the Bottom Line." Charlie Tarzian, ClickZ, 30 March 2000

[3] "The Five Most Important Words in Email Marketing." David Patterson. MarketingProfs.com.

". . . but then most men mistake grammar for style, as they mistake correct spelling for words or schooling for education." - Samuel Butler, The Way of All Flesh

Don't Make Know Mistayque

While we are addressing parts of speech and such, it's not a bad idea to take a look at grammar and spelling in general. Grammatical glitches and spelling screw-ups abound in Web content, and they push our buttons — the wrong ones.

They'll push your customers' wrong buttons too. In your quest to create Killer Copy, you simply MUST pay attention to these details. Look at it from your customers' point of view: if they see you can't be bothered with the most basic grammatical and spelling details, how are they going to trust that you are up to handling all the other details of doing business and not just satisfying but delighting them? If your business is providing content, all the more reason your readers expect you to be letter-perfect.

Think we're too picky? Then look at what happened to Janet Roberts, who publishes Ezine-Tips. A newsletter subscriber decided to unsubscribe because she found it "difficult to put faith in advice about how to publish an email newsletter from folks who frequently make grammatical and spelling errors in their newsletters." The unsubscriber added, "This leads me to think that if you can't even proof your content that you're writing, how can I be sure that you're checking your sources or promoting valid suggestions/advice." Fortunately, Ms. Roberts (who is certainly not grossly negligent when it comes to writing) took the plucky approach and suggested, "Let our embarrassment be your gain." And then she offered this advice:

- Always review your copy thoroughly.
- Then have someone else review it again.
- Keep a handy stable of writing references and use them whenever you aren't 100% certain. Minimum requirements are a dictionary and style manual (Ms. Roberts likes On Writing Well by William Zinsser. We vote for The Transitive Vampire by Karen Elizabeth Gordon. Strunk and White's Elements of Style is the classic bible.)

To these suggestions we would add:

- Spell-check. But don't stop there.
- Grammar-check (intelligently). If your word processor has the option, use it — but be aware it needs a human monitor. If it doesn't, use a human.
- And if you can't be bothered, pay someone to be bothered in your place.

There's more. Keep an eye out for those there/their, your/you're, to/too/two, hear/here, its/it's problems. Remember that a customer doesn't give their address, but rather customers give their addresses, or a customer gives his or her address.

Be painfully vigilant. On the other side of every one of your grammatical or spelling errors is an unnecessarily irritated customer who may very well become an ex-customer, or a potential customer whom your misteaks will push aweigh. To err certainly is human. But basic, careless and avoidable errors will cost you business.

"Every man likes the smell of his own farts." - Icelandic Proverb

Can't Smell It on the Web?

There's a myth that you can't sell on the Web items you need to smell, touch, or taste to appreciate. If you believe it, it's costing you potential sales. People say, "You can't smell it, so you can't sell it," not because it can't be done, but because they can't figure out how to do it. Or, they assume it can't be done and never bother trying to find a solution.

The idea behind selling is to help your customers create a vivid mental image of enjoying the benefits of your product or service. That image creates, in turn, the desire to buy your product or service. The key is to involve them in the process by using active voice, compelling verbs, powerful nouns, and evocative adjectives and adverbs. You make it happen not with pictures but with words.

Mark Twain appreciated the power of words: "A powerful agent is the right word... Whenever we come upon one of these intensely right words in a book or a newspaper the resulting effect is physical as well as spiritual, and electrically prompt." The right copy can sell just about anything.

You've lost yourself in a book or an article, haven't you? One where the author paints a picture of a setting so evocative all your senses are engaged in your imagination? Between the power of the word and your own naturally creative mind, you can easily find yourself in Charles Dickens's grimy London, Frank McCourt's impoverished Ireland, Herman Melville's tense shipboard world, Amy Tan's Chinese enclaves, or John le Carré's underground.

Folks in advertising and direct mail have long known the evocative power of words and have harnessed it to incredible effect, selling every imaginable kind of touchy-feely-tasty stuff (saying "smelly" here might not work the way I intend — and there you have it: the power of words!). Words sell perfume, gourmet food, wine, travel, music, clothing, even art. The list is endless. You've experienced this if you've ever been influenced by ad or catalog copy.

The J. Peterman Company produced one of the most wildly successful catalogs on record. The text is so rich everyone loves to read it. The company continues in the same spirit on its website:

Signature Collection. A record of my discoveries. A fabric I couldn't put down, a hat I absconded, an irresistible aftershave, numerous things that somehow ended up in my trunk, my office, my farmhouse, everywhere. Things I wore. Wore again. Kept finding more reasons to wear. A collection of signature items — things I think you'll agree are distinctive in a world overcrowded with the mundane. Things worthy of the signature.

Do we want some of that Signature stuff? You bet! Caché, lived-in comfort, distinction. We were hooked even before we looked at a specific item.

Yearning for a fruit you can't find in the local produce section? After you read this, we'll bet you don't have to taste or smell sapotes first before deciding you want to buy some from Harry and David:

White Sapotes (Sa-PO-tays). Somewhere between a banana and a papaya — and known to only a few. Scarce and delicious, this dreamy tropical variety seduces fruit-lovers with its creamy, custard-like texture and subtle tropical flavor. Grown in limited quantities and hard to find at markets because they have to be painstakingly pollinated by hand. Delicious in a mixed fruit cup or sorbet, or sliced over ice cream.

Or how about this for perfume from Sephora.com?

Vera Wang has captured desire in a modern, floral bouquet. The first encounter is a flirtation that begins with Bulgarian rose, calla lily, and mandarin flower. The flirtation is followed by a passionate kiss of gardenia, lotus, iris, and white stephanotis. The fragrance is wrapped in a final embrace of sheer musks, white woods, and precious floral nectar.

Good copy not only offers descriptions but also makes connections, creates images, draws on experience (either actual or imagined), and involves the reader. Good copy unifies the product with your prospect's perceived need by exciting her emotions. We should know by now that buying decisions may be rationalized with facts but ultimately are based on emotions. Want to sell something you think has to be seen, tasted, smelled, or touched to be believed? Get a good copywriter. That person can convey the experience of the most sumptuous cashmere coat in words that won't just equal an actual touch but will surpass it by evoking images and emotions.

Why speak to the emotions? It's straight out of Sales 101. When you want to capture your customer's interest and speak to their felt need (the thing that makes them want to buy), you sell the benefits, not the features of your product or service. A classic example? Take the electric drill. Nobody is going to buy one just so they can have an electric drill. They buy one because they want holes. Clean holes, deep holes, accurate holes, fast holes, holes of many sizes, holes in different materials. Most folks don't care what the drill is made from or how the circuitry is toggled — they care that it makes holes. They might also care that the drill is light-weight (but spare them a discussion of the space-age aluminum alloy casing), maneuverable, UL approved, has a super-long cord and comes in its own carrying case. But they only care about those things because they add to performance, convenience or safety — benefits, not features, and they appeal at an emotional level.

Selling on the Web is not just about the images people see; it's also, and perhaps even more so, about the images that exceptional copy creates in customers' minds. Don't assume you can't sell it on the Web. You can. All you need is to find the person who can take your words to the bank!

"Style and Structure are the essence of a book; great ideas are hogwash." - Vladimir Nabokov, Writers at Work

Advanced Wordsmithing: 3 Stylistic Ways to Become Memorable

You're out to create a personality, an identity, distinguish yourself from the crowd and communicate with your email readers or website visitors in language that moves them. In language that helps them remember you. Having talked about larger-scale wordsmithing frameworks to shape the direction of your copy, we're now going to reach into our grab-bag of ideas to help you shape the style of your copy. Because so often, all that is rich and provocative lives in the details.

Show not Tell

Be patient, have faith in your ability to put together a credible reality in your reader's mind. Instead of saying "This car is the fastest sports car in the market today", make the reader experience the feeling of maneuvering it… the cold sensation of the door handle, the whoosh of the leather seats when she jumps in, the roaring of the engine when turned on, the tight turns that satisfy, the way she gets "pushed" against the seat every time her foot touches the accelerator, the tremble of the gear stick in her hand as she prepares for the next shift, the way she attends to the sounds of acceleration, listening for that precise moment when the engine will sing, "Now … take me to the next level." See?

Engage the Senses

To uphold the attention of your readers, use shapes, colors, and names of things to which they can easily relate and create strong, clear mental images. Though distinct to each person, these images do require everyone's active involvement. Mental images are composed of all senses; therefore words like "sweet", "bright", and "smooth" enhance their "visibility". By strengthening your mental images you'll haul your listeners to the places you want them to go… like your checkout page!

Say you adore dark chocolate. You go to a website and read this product description:

Premier imported Belgian Dark Chocolate with a characteristic bitter-sweet edge.

Maybe that works for you if you really know your chocolates, but most people want to "sample" that chocolate before they tap in their card numbers. They want to experience the color, the smell, the mouth-feel, the lingering after-taste of a dark chocolate. Don't make up flowery nonsense — the copy should be honest — but tell them what they need to read so they know this is the stuff they really want!

Smooth, full-bodied, with a bite but not bitter, deep color, individually wrapped in gold foil that enhances the anticipation of the richness waiting within. A chocolate to savor.

That's what our senses tell us we're going to get excited about!

Be Specific

Specifics are more believable than generalities, as the chocolate example suggests. And specifics about your products or services are far superior to generalities (or even specifics) about you. Authors of every genre tend to gain your willing suspension of disbelief by means of details. It takes careful attention to describe accurately things you want people to imagine in a certain way. Make each point very clearly; give your readers the respect they deserve as you captivate them by making powerful, relevant, and specific statements about stuff that matters to them — not you — every opportunity you get.

Dare to be memorable. Dare to think outside the box and color outside the lines. It isn't exactly a traditional corporate style, but you want to win the hearts and minds of people who are actively involved in a dynamic, interactive medium of communication. And you aren't going to do that by being lackluster and boring!

"Translation is the paradigm, the exemplar of all writing.... It is translation that demonstrates most vividly the yearning for transformation that underlies every act involving speech, that supremely human gift." - Harry Mathews, *"The Dialect of the Tribe," Country Cooking and Other Stories*

When Your Copy Must Leap Oceans (Or Even an Inconvenient River or Two)

Today, English happens to be the language used by about 80% of all websites. We did read somewhere it could be Chinese by the year 2007. But for now, the lingua franca is English. So what do you do if your business has a more global reach and you have to make sense to non-native readers of English? You write basic!

Now, we make no bones about it. Do NOT use our stuff as a model, because the last thing we're about is writing basic English. And that's a perfectly acceptable model — you're never going to appeal to all the folks all the time no matter what you do. Sometimes you choose to "target" your writing.

But we know some of you out there need to communicate effectively with those for whom English is a second language. So here's what you do:

- Use short sentences — 15 to 20 words, and 20 words puts you close to the danger zone. Writing concise, direct sentences is most of the battle.
- Use simple sentence constructions — Subject - verb - object (if any), followed by any extra information. You start confusing folks when you insert lots of phrases between the core elements of a sentence.
- Use the active voice — When you use passive verbs, you risk making your meaning ambiguous.
- Avoid "phrasal" and "modal auxiliary" verbs — Phrasal verbs have two or more words, verbs like call up, pull in, pick away at and drop down. Choose a one-word verb that says the same thing. Modal auxiliary verbs include stuff like should, could, can, would, might and may. Example: A representative should contact you within 48 hours. Does that mean he will, he might not, he has a moral obligation to or that it could take longer than 48 hours? Native English readers understand these words based on context. They usually confuse non-native English readers.
- Use pronouns clearly — Notice the last two sentences in the previous section. The "they" in the last sentence refers to a noun in the previous sentence, but which one? Words? Native English "readers"? Or did we make a grammatical mistake and refer in the plural to "context"?
- Use simple, common words with clear meanings
- Use positive language — Stay away from negative constructions (which can be hard to translate) and negative images (which are depressing and can be insulting). "Don't you just hate it when …" is a negative construction (don't) with a negative image (hate). Double negatives (as in "not uncommon") are doubly troublesome.

- Avoid clichés and slang — We wrote "I make no bones about it." Can you imagine what that means to this audience? Nothing.
- Proof very carefully — Writing that is grammatically correct and free of typos is enormously important with this audience! These folks are generally good with English grammar and if you break the rules, you risk confusing them.
- Get some help — If you know people who speak English as a second language, ask them to read your copy for clarity and to help you identify potentially offensive language. This is especially important if you are using humor.

P.S. If you want to study a good model for International English, pick up a copy of the *Herald Tribune*, a newspaper that writes in English for a global audience.

P.P.S. About those flags, animated and otherwise … ditch them. If you offer your website in multiple translations, use the correct name of the language instead of the country's flag for identification. Which flag would you use for English (you can choose from USA, Great Britain, Australia, New Zealand, Canada and Singapore)? And which of four languages would you be indicating by using the Swiss flag?

"Your audience gives you everything you need. They tell you. There is no director who can direct you like an audience." - Fanny Brice, The Fabulous Fanny

Keywords, Search and Conversion: Do You Write for Readers or the Engines?

Somewhere, someone is online looking for your product or service. They have a specific need to fill. Do you know what that need is? The answer lies in the keywords they use.

When we consult with clients, their keywords are among the first things we look for. Keywords are mental images linked to what lies in the heart of your customer. Your customer searches for a specific need they want filled. They come up with a keyword or phrase that to them best describes a product or service that will satisfy the need. The key is to find the keywords your prospects use and feed them back. When you do that, two things happen: You know what they want; and you know how to tell them you have it.

To produce and optimize a website without understanding what your customer wants is like opening a steak house for vegetarians. With keywords you can set up your website to create the persuasive buying momentum needed for each visitor.

Keywords Build Confidence

None of your visitors will be persuaded to buy unless your presentation elicits an emotional reaction. Keywords comprise the language that elicits emotions. The most important emotion your visitor is looking for is the feeling of confidence that they are finding what's relevant to their needs.

Consultant/researcher Kelly Mooney expressed it this way: "Online shoppers do not conduct the linear purchases that many retailers envision. Rather they browse a catalog, talk to friends, go online to research a product, visit the store to experience it, go back to the Web to comparison shop, then make the purchase either online or offline."

"Retailers think of shopping as a funnel," Mooney continued, "but it's non-linear, sporadic and [unpredictable]. Under the old model, the purchase was the end result; under the new model, confidence is the end result. It used to be that consumers would make the purchase and hope they made the right decision. Now, they can say they know they made the right decision."

When your website uses your visitors' language, they see you have the solution they seek. If your points of resolution include the keyword they thought to enter into a search engine, they'll conclude your website is the one they searched for. When points of resolution include a hyperlink to the information expected, they know they're on the trail and, like a bloodhound, they salivate before the reward. You can't use keywords to drive just any traffic. They must be used to drive the right traffic.

Because keywords are much more than a way to build traffic, prioritize each one.

To do so, categorize your traffic using these four criteria:

- Traffic potential
- Prospect's intent
- Stage in the buying process
- Likelihood to convert

This helps determine the importance of each keyword. More specifically, it tells you who your customers are, and who they should be.

Calculate a Baseline Conversion Rate

Once you have all your keywords, strip out any that are bringing traffic that doesn't convert. Top search result rankings that bring traffic but no action dilute the overall conversion rate. Be careful not to strip out terms with latent conversions. Understand that this latency is usually related to what stage in the buying process a prospect is in, and whether it's an impulse, a simple-considered purchase or a complex-considered purchase. A website that sells sugar gliders tracked people from when they clicked on a PPC ad to when they purchased. We observed the following behavior:

Search Term	Latency to Conversion
Sugar Glider	14 days
Sugar Glider Supplies	6 days
Sugar Glider Food	2 days
ZooKeeper's Secret (food brand)	1 day

When prospects have confidence and know they made the right decision, they convert. Which of these terms would you think has the greatest likelihood to convert? ZooKeeper's Secret, of course. Visitors searching on a product name declare their intent to purchase. There's no reason why a term like this shouldn't convert at 90 percent and better. This is no fantasy or bold assertion; it holds true for several of our clients' sites.

Keywords as Triggers

Many websites, tools and databases can help locate keywords. Find them, test them, use them to your advantage. Remember to consider plurals, synonyms and misspellings. Brainstorm keywords into pairs and select the best ones to create key phrases.

Keywords often broadcast online shopper intent. Trigger words talk to specific personas based on the keywords they use. For "stylish overcoats" a website might tell a humanistic persona, "so many people find our stylish coats perfect for…" and link to a page where testimonials to your style appear, before the next point of resolution. For the competitive persona you might write, "Our stylish coats are made from the highest-quality…" These people tend to care more about the prestige of the best coat, not the most stylish. Keywords paired with the correct trigger words are the most powerful asset a website can have to persuade visitors to buy.

Use keywords and trigger words to attract visitors. Include the keywords at the point of resolution. Anticipate and answer your prospects' questions as expressed through their search terms. Do these simple things well and your bottom line will feel the impact.

"Search every acre in the high-grown field, And bring him to our eye." - William Shakespeare, The Tragedy of King Lear

In-Site Search Engines

When we're asked to evaluate a website, among the first things we do is analyze the effectiveness of that website's internal search engines. It's an obvious place to start. Visitors who search reveal a great deal about their intent.

We observe that about 50 percent of all website searches end in results that don't meet visitor expectations. Website analytics often reveals that search results are one of the main visitor exit points. Sadly, the searched-for product is often sitting in the client's warehouse.

Search expectations are high. Visitors expect search results to be accurate and relevant. After all, if Google can index 6 billion pages and return relevant, accurate results, why can't a website with a much more limited set and scale do the same?

Sadly, the research does not have many kind things to say about in-site search. Here's what two authoritative research reports tell us about the status of in-site search applications:

Jupiter Research

- 33% of customers look first to website search instead of navigation — this means the majority (67%) are looking to your navigation and qualification schemes before they even consider website search options.
- 50% will turn to website search if the navigation and qualification schemes do not help them find what they are looking for.
- 45% say they find paging through results too time-consuming.
- 44% are uncertain exactly what to enter in the search field so they can get the information they want.
- 39% are irritated that website search works differently on different websites.
- 39% are irritated that website searches don't cope well with misspellings.
- 38% found the search results irrelevant.
- 21% are irritated that they can't enter sentences when typing in a query.
- 13% don't know what to do without help.

37 Signals

These folks provided a thorough and informative report highlighting in-site search experiences on 25 top websites. The good news, Jason Fried tells us, is that if you enter a perfect, error-free, specific search, 92% of the evaluated sites produce accurate and relevant results. But there's some bad news, too:

- 72% of the websites could not match misspellings with the appropriate product.
- 68% did not allow the user to filter or sort search results.
- 64% were unable to provide valid results for mixed specification searches.
- 56% couldn't handle synonyms and related terms.
- 56% provided little or no help if the search concluded with "no results."

Want to see what you can do to make the right choices regarding in-site search engines? We'll help you by providing our ideas through a series of questions and answers. Then, ask these same questions about your own website, and take the steps you believe will make a difference.

Does Your Site Really Need a Search Engine?

Do not just assume that your website needs an in-site search engine. Based on research conducted by us, and the people at UIE.com, visitors who navigate your website via standard navigation convert more often and spend more money.

One in five visitors use search on a website to find products or other content. However, numerous studies show that a purchased item from search is approximately 35 percent less expensive than an average item found through traditional navigation through the website.

More often than not, in-site search engines are just another way to bog down your customer with technology that ultimately interferes with shopping instead of helping it, no matter how good your intentions were. And not just in my humble opinion. Research proves it. So here it is in a nutshell: Don't do it. Instead, let the design of your website be your most effective searching tool. And if you absolutely must include a searching function, then do it right.

Don't take our word for it. Listen to what others have to say. As Larry Constantine, Director of Research & Development at Constantine & Lockwood, Ltd., says,

Indeed, the research on searching is both clear and consistent. If a visitor uses a site-based search engine, their chances of finding what they are seeking, even given that it is on the site, are drastically reduced. Jared Spool has found that using the search box can cut a visitor's chance of success in half. In other words, if, instead of searching, visitors stay with browsing and follow links, they are twice as likely to find what they seek. The implications of this for the design of e-business sites are enormous.

Here's another commentary from Jupiter reported in internetretailer.com: "By itself, full-text site search merely provides a technical solution to a technical problem," says Jupiter analyst Matt Berk. …The solution is for site operators to move beyond the traditional search/find-keyword/result model toward experience-enhancing functionality. Such a "discover and dialogue" model would, for example, better coordinate site search and information architecture, as well as negotiate linguistic differences between users and site operators. "Technology alone can't manage the dialogue," Jupiter says.

There are alternatives to internal search. One of our clients asked us to evaluate their website. It had fewer than 25 pages, but they had implemented an internal search engine anyway. We showed them that navigation could be improved by simply categorizing products correctly.

So, we killed the search engine and recategorized the products. Conversion increased over 140 percent. Our client's average order also increased by 22 percent. Our suspicion is that this happened because visitors were upsold on those category pages.

OK. You're still not sold. You just know that your visitors need the help. Before you put in the search engine and walk away from it, test its functionality, and make sure you get the right answers to the following questions. You'll be glad you did.

What Happens if a Visitor Misspells a Search Term?

If you go to WalMart.com and type "faberware" into the search box, you'll see a result for "Farberware." Notice Wal-Mart doesn't assume visitors know how to spell (or type). How many times have you misspelled a keyword on Google only to see, "Did you mean: [corrected keyword]?"

Try the same search on Macys.com. You'll get "Your search on 'faberware' produced 0 items." Is this because Macy's doesn't have any? Nope! Type the word correctly, and you'll get results.

Companies such as Macy's should mine their Web analytics data to find all those failed terms. Then they can take remedies to correct them. Our client MagMall.com sells magazines. It's spent several hours a week (over the last four years) looking for all those failed terms and matching them to relevant magazines. This ensures it returns accurate results for visitors. It's part of the reason it's continuously improved conversions, year after year.

Can a Visitor Sort Results by Price, Brand, and Availability?

Cruise over to JR.com, and type in "digital camera." You'll get a couple hundred results thoughtfully presented in a way that's easy to sort. "Top Sellers" display first, but you can click on a link above the results to sort by brand, title, and price. J&R knows people compare its offerings to results on comparison shopping search engines, such as Shopping.com.

If you search for a digital camera under $100 on sharperimage.com, you'll still get results, but not for digital cameras. The retailer doesn't have digital cameras in that price range.

How Well Can Your Engine Handle Related Words and Common Synonyms?

If you, like us, are a summer softball enthusiast, you might have an interest in picking up one of those clicker thingies baseball umpires use to keep track of balls, strikes, and outs. We tried to find one using "clicker," "counter," "score keeper," and a variety of other possibilities on about a dozen websites. We know that they are not called "umpire clickers", but that's about as good as it gets for us. We can never remember the exact term. If you go to Amber Sporting Goods, you get a relevant result. However, if you go to Fogdog Sports, it tells you, "We are having trouble locating a match for your search: umpire clicker." It doesn't offer a way to refine the results. Who do you think is more likely to make the sale?

Can a Visitor Search Using Mixed Specifications?

When we speak about mixed specifications, we're talking about things like gender, color, etc. (as in "red wool men's sweater")?

Is It Possible for a Visitor to Get No Results At All? (And are tips and help readily at hand?)

Just for the fun of it, we searched online jewelry retailers for "purple diamonds." It's not likely we'd find any real results, but what shows up is interesting. Try this search on Diamond.com and you get:

The item that you are looking for may not be featured on our site at this time. We may simply be waiting to receive the item into inventory. If we don't currently carry it, we may be able to find it through one of our suppliers. We'd be happy to help you locate the item you're looking for. Please contact us at our toll-free number (1-888-DIAMOND) or via our special request page.

ICE.com returns, "This site does not carry 'purple diamonds', but we thought you would like to see the items below." It proceeds to show you some category of items and additional search options.

JCPenney shows you bedding options instead of colored diamond jewelry.

For a similar example with a real search term, go to SmartBargains.com, which offers great deals on a variety items. Type in "Mephisto" (as in the comfortable walking shoes). Even though the retailer doesn't have any, it fails to show any related shoe brands. It does carry ECCO, which competes directly, and Rockport, which is a down-market alternative. Don't you think offering an alternative is better than offering nothing at all?

The absolute most important thing to do, especially if the search comes up void, is to provide your visitor ways to get right back into the shopping experience on your website. Re-integrating links need to be in the active window. Options need to be logical. The natural tendency on a failed search is to leave the website. What can you do to keep them there?

Also, pay attention to Qualification. Remember, no matter how successful your in-site search application may be, the majority of your visitors will not make it their first port of call. Probably not even their second. They will turn to it only when all other options have failed them.

You Need an Advanced Search Option?

When a simple search produces nothing, maybe it's time to make the customer perform another click and load up yet another page. (We're kidding, right?) What that amounts to is an illogical form of punishment. Remember, anytime you involve your visitor in the "system," that visitor is not shopping! And for the average shopper advanced search options are hard to understand – and they generate bad results, too. What you get is a shopper who is confused and frustrated and maybe even feeling stupid that they somehow don't know what they're doing — definitely not the right feeling for a satisfying customer experience.

Most of your visitors don't arrive at your website thinking, "Boy, I really hope there's a search box on the home page for me!" In fact, most of your visitors only turn to a searching feature when all else fails them. And when that fails them, too, you've lost them.

What You Should Do Next

Invest time searching your website and those of your competitors. Search for some of your best-selling products, as well as for products you'd like to sell more of. If you can't find them easily, what makes you think your visitors will?

Carefully consider if there is any way you can avoid putting in an internal search engine. If it just can't be avoided, then do it right:

- Structure the searching function to your information. Don't use generic applications. It is worth the time and trouble to tailor-make your engine?
- Understand human psychology to the extent you can anticipate the nature of their queries and include every possibility in your engine.

- Allow users to qualify or constrain their searches with additional check boxes or drop-downs (default the most likely selection).
- Incorporate the use of synonyms and equivalents, and for very large websites, it helps to "establish an internal glossary of terms and a thesaurus that maps equivalents."

In short, make it work. Make it work for you *and* your visitors.

"Great men wait for the right moment to abandon caution. The rest of us abandon it when impatience becomes too much for us. " - Mason Cooley, City Aphorisms

Shopping Cart Abandonment May Not Be the Real Problem

Many prospective e-tail marketers are too often focused on how many visitors abandon their shopping carts. While this is not a trivial issue, it may not be the most important. On a site converting at three percent, improving the abandonment rate may boost it up to 3.3 percent. Not bad, but let's look deeper.

The more time a visitor spends on your site, the more likely she is to buy. Most e-tail sites experience their greatest visitor drop-off in the first two or three pages visitors see. From then on, drop-off is relatively minor. If you focus on providing relevant and persuasive content based on understanding visitor intent, easily inferred from Keywords (or ad copy, or the e-mail they arrived from), you'll have a much higher overall conversion rate.

Visitors who are thoroughly persuaded are often uncannily motivated to navigate even the worst checkout process.

E-tailers are better served doing these three things:

- Improving their home and landing pages.
- Improving their persuasion scenarios.
- Ensuring that the persuasion scenarios aren't interrupted.

As you've been reading, you've seen many ways to increase your site's performance; how to qualify visitors; how to improve your overall planning and structure and better define micro-actions in persuasion scenarios; and how to use persuasion architecture to help improve home and landing pages. So now with all of this behind you, it is time to look at the shopping cart.

Persuasion Occurs One Step at a Time

The goal of each website page is to persuade. All pages should link together, in a step-by step-fashion, to guide visitors through the process of buying from you. Lead them though, one page at a time, and constantly anticipate their every move. Make them feel comfortable and in control.

Website visitors often compensate for a lack of information. A study by User Interface Engineering, "Are the Product Lists on Your Site Reducing Sales" confirmed this:

> ...shoppers could not ascertain enough information from the product list, so they clicked back and forth between the list and multiple individual product pages... Pogo-sticking is the name we gave to this comparison-shopping technique... It's an indication that you are losing sales.

Is a visitor searching for a product, or for information? If she wants information, she's not yet persuaded to buy. It's important to give her enough information to make a decision, and supply it in the right place. At the point where she wants more content, supply it. Make sure it answers all possible questions.

Aside from not allowing the visitor to enter the persuasion process, pogo-sticking leads to a generally unpleasant shopping experience. If a visitor must navigate back and forth, she can become frustrated. Remember, she's always one click away from goodbye. Harness everything in your power to make the shopping experience enjoyable.

Plan for this; don't hope it will happen. Create a decision tree for each page. This helps you understand the possible decisions she may go through, allowing you to create pages based on what the visitor wants. She feels in control, and you are also able to influence and persuade her. When a website speaks her language and anticipates what she's about to ask, it reinforces confidence in her own decision making ability.

Nobody wants to feel out of control. That's why people feel awkward in face-to-face sales situations. A website is the introvert's favorite salesperson. It answers questions without her having to speak with someone she doesn't know. We all have both extroverted and introverted qualities. Online shopping appeals most to the introverted right brain.

Navigation Must Just Feel Right

Persuasion works most effectively if all pages on a site have the same look & feel. Design affects how visitors relate to a Web site on both a conscious and unconscious level. Visitors expect things to look a certain way and be located in certain areas. They expect to find familiar navigation at all times.

Many navigation schemes exist. Yours should apply to the entire site; otherwise visitors can become disoriented and lose confidence. The goal of good navigation is to orient and direct customers to and through a purchase, subscription, phone call or whatever action you want them to take as part of the persuasion process.

Think holistically. Each page should contain all the information a visitor needs at that point in the persuasion process, or at least link to it. Answer visitors' concerns and questions rather than allow trivialities to act against them. Scenarios should be designed so visitors spend time only in the persuasion process, not on anything extraneous. That's the only way to build confidence in the product or service to which the self-service persuasion path leads.

Metrics are wonderful management tools, but they sometimes allow managers to myopically focus on the wrong issues. Forget your shopping cart problems. Focus on the bigger picture. Many more people leave your website from the first and second page. It's the nature of the medium that shopping carts will be abandoned. The final steps in the persuasion process are the hardest to implement and produce the smallest return on investment (ROI).

If people come to your website voluntarily, why do so many leave within the first three pages? Do they think you don't have what they want? Perhaps you haven't persuaded them it's worth the effort to find out.

Refurbishing Your Shopping Cart Is a Matter of Priorities

Even when you've covered every base imaginable, humans will still leave for reasons you can't control. There is no 100% conversion rate because this is not a perfect world. Because fewer folks bail out of your shopping cart compared to the number who bail out before they even get to checkout, keeping more visitors in your conversion process from the get go helps you increase your conversion rate by multiples.

Metrics Can Help You Decide If Your Shopping Cart Is the Problem

If you are on top of your Web analytics, you'll know where your biggest problems are. These are the key metrics that will help you decide where you should be directing your energies.

Single Page Accesses. This is a percentage of the number of people who landed on a particular page – it might be your home page or it could just as easily be a landing page – and made it their first and last page. In other words, they came, they saw, they bailed. You really want to consider these pages before anything else. What is wrong and how can you remedy it? These visitors weren't even inspired to look a single page further into your site!

Scenario Analysis. Ideally, you want to follow your visitor's path through your website. Is he clicking where you want him to click? Is he following the breadcrumb trail you have so painstakingly crafted for him, only to jump ship on the fourth page? If they don't get to the shopping cart, you certainly don't need to worry about them abandoning it. Look at the pages they reject and evaluate how to improve things.

Shopping Cart Abandonment. This isn't simply how many people don't complete the process. A checkout process can be a number of steps, and each step is its own little mini-conversion. You really want to know where in the shopping cart folks get frustrated enough to say goodbye, because that's the point where the cart's conversion process is failing.

So, check your metrics and if you've got a tidy little cybershop and still want to improve your shopping cart abandonment rates, then we'll give you some ideas for how to fix your cart.

Conversion Tip

Avoid Scary-Looking Forms

People don't like to type, deal with pull-down menus or give out phone numbers. People are suspicious when you ask for their email, age, and/or income. If you don't need it, don't ask.

Some ways to shorten forms:
- Get the zip code, then thereís no need to type in city and state.
- If you ask for phone number, give a very nice reason in small type next to the box.

If they do have to make an effort (answering lots of questions):
- You'd better have a big fat picture of the enticing item they'll get, for doing all this work, next to the questions. (ie. Not just copy . . . but a real-looking discount coupon.)
- Never ever stick a button next to the "submit" button that says "clear form" or anything of that nature. If they hit this button, and clear their work, they leave and are not coming back.

- **Anne Holland,** Publisher of MarketingSherpa

"I like to think of sales as the ability to gracefully persuade, not manipulate, a person or persons into a win-win situation." - Bo Bennett

20 Tips for Lowering Shopping Cart Abandonment

Shopping cart abandonment is a significant problem. In some market verticals between 65 and 75% percent of shoppers abandon their online shopping carts before completing the checkout process. Here are 20-tips to help you reduce the number of shoppers on your site that abandon their online shopping carts.

1. Check how many steps are in your checkout process.

This is usually a prime "knee jerk" target for results, but we have found that whether you have 1 step or 7 steps in the checkout process is not all that critical. We had one client with whom we were able to bring their checkout process from 6 steps down to 1, but there was no correlation in reduction of the abandonment rate to the number of steps. Once people found what they came for, they found a way and the time to checkout no matter how many steps were involved. Should you change the number of steps? No! It may not be worth the time, effort and expense of trying to reduce the steps in the checkout process. Try some of these other ideas first.

2. Include a "Progress Indicator" (e.g., "Step 2 of 5") on each checkout page.

No matter how many steps you have in your checkout process keep shoppers oriented by letting them know exactly where they are in the checkout process by step number. Be sure to clearly label the task to be completed at each step. Always give them an opportunity to review what they did in the previous steps and a way to return to their current step if they do go back.

3. Provide a link back to the product.

When an item is placed in the shopping cart, include a link back to the product page, so shoppers can easily jump back to make sure they have selected the right item. Your own experience probably parallels ours. Recently, shopping for a CD/DVD printer, we wanted to know how many and what color cartridges come with the printer. It wasn't obvious where we should click to review what came with the printer so we had to navigate using our back button till we were able to get our questions answered. Not all consumers are willing to take on this navigational challenge and choose to abandon their carts.

4. Add Pictures inside the basket.

Just as adding a link back to the product details page inside the checkout process reduces abandonment, placing a thumbnail image of the product inside the basket can increase conversions by as much as 10%.

5. Provide shipping costs as early in the process as possible.

If possible, provide an estimated cost while they browse. Your visitors want to buy; they just want the answers to all their questions when they want it; and total cost is one of those critical questions. Also, if the shipping information is the same as the billing information, include a box that shoppers can check to automatically fill in the same information. Don't waste their time while testing their keyboard skills.

6. Show stock availability on the product page.

Shoppers should not have to wait until checkout to find out that a product is out of stock. One thing that we also like to see, is "Estimated Delivery Date" or "this product usually ships in x days." Deal with the "I want it now!" mentality, and let them know when they should expect to get their product.

7. Make it obvious what to click next.

Include a prominent "Next Step" or "Continue with Checkout" button on each checkout page. If possible give the shopper a visual cue as to where they are in the process. Make the button you want them to click next the most obvious. One top 50 e-tailer mistakenly placed visually similar "remove from cart" and "checkout" buttons right next to each other. As you can imagine 'many people' click before they read. At this site they ended up clearing their cart, and when they went to checkout found nothing in their shopping cart and immediately abandoned the site in frustration.

8. Make it easy for the shopper to edit their shopping cart.

If a product comes in multiple sizes or colors, make it easy to select or change values in the shopping cart. How many times have you bought a pair of slacks online and wanted the same pants in two different colors? Make it easy for your consumers to add to and edit the contents of their shopping carts. It should be simple to change quantities or options, or delete an item from the shopping cart.

9. Make it your fault.

If information is missing or filled out incorrectly during checkout, give a meaningful error message that is distinctly visible. It should clearly tell your visitor what needs to be corrected. The tone should intimate that the system was unable to understand what they entered, not that they made a foolish mistake.

10. Make shoppers aware that you are a real entity.

Checkout is the time when people's concerns start to flare up. Let them know you are a real company by giving full contact info during the checkout process.

11. Give the visitor the option to call.

If visitors have a problem during checkout or just feel uncomfortable using their credit card online, give them a phone number to call. Use a separate telephone number that is different from the one you use for the rest of your site. This will help you track, evaluate and understand shoppers' needs and behaviors. While you are at it, give them a fax-order form so they can complete their order by fax if they prefer.

12. Make it always about your new customer.

Make the focus of the checkout process easier for your new visitor with whom you do not yet have a relationship than for your registered customer. It is much harder to acquire a new customer than to keep selling to loyal customers. Registered customers will find a way to sign in (if they don't already have a cookie), but don't make the registration and log-on a barrier in the way of new visitors finding their way to check out.

13. Add 3rd party reinforcement messages.

Verisign, BBB, or logos of credit cards have either greatly boosted conversions rate or kept them neutral. In other words they never hurt. Hacker Safe <http://www.scanalert.com> certification seems to be helping clients all across the board especially in sites with larger average order sizes. They claim a 15.7% average increase in orders — directly attributable to earning the HACKER SAFE certification.

14. Present coupon codes carefully.

Be careful how you handle these, you don't want to decrease your conversion rate. You might want to think carefully about where you present this option and how you label it. Coupons should add to the experience not create doubt for those who may not be shopping with a coupon.

15. Deal with pricing issues head-on.

If you sell name brand products and your store is price competitive or truly provides better value, why not try a 'Lowest Price Match' Guarantee.

16. GTC: Get the cash.

Offer more payment options and add other ways to collect the cash. You can offer visitors to option to pay by check, PayPal or any other means you can to get the cash.

17. Offer point of action reassurance.

Check how often information critical to your customer's buying decision gets buried in tiny type at the bottom of the page or in some place where it is not immediately visible when the need to know is foremost in the customer's mind. If you walk into a store, it's fairly easy to find out product warranty information. One can read the box at hand or chat with a salesperson.

Online, give your customer this same option, at the Point of Action (P.O.A.), when he'd figuratively be examining that box. Link right there to product warranties, your company's specific policies, testimonials, even optional extended service plans. Right there! Maybe you take them to the information or perhaps give it to the shopper in a pop-up.

At the exact point when your customer has to start filling in a form with personal information, reassure the customer that privacy is sacred to you. At the point the customer might be curious about your company's shipping costs, make them concretely available. Just when the customer is wondering whether or not it is possible to return the item, if it doesn't suit, make it clear that you have a no-questions-asked return policy. Make the best use of your assurances at the right time and place.

18. Track your mistakes.

Develop a system that keeps you notified of errors during your checkout process. One client noticed a portion of their visitors had cookies turned off. He developed a Cookie-less checkout option and his conversion rate and sales jumped.

19. Save it for them.

We know customers often leave a shopping cart with items in it, but they do return sometimes. Don't be overly concerned if visitors leave items behind. Just plan on doing your best to give them a reason and reminder to return and complete the sale. You may have the ability to save the cart for them or email them that they left items in their cart and can complete their order when they are ready. This can be done online at your website or through the telephone with IVR (Interactive Voice Response). Remember, if they've gotten to the shopping cart, they are most likely considering the purchase.

20. When all else fails, survey.

Try an Exit survey (think of it as an 'objectionator') if people abandon your checkout. Try offering them an incentive to complete your survey or even save their cart. They may just tell you why they didn't complete their order.

These 20 tips can help you reduce your shopping cart abandonment. Of course, every site is different and has its own environment and issues. Don't overly obsess about abandonment rates, since many people simply use the shopping cart as a placeholder for considering purchases or interest to them. These tips help you focus on those whose intent it is to check out and purchase, but may have questions, doubts or obstacles holding them back. Some of these tips will result in dramatic improvements and others might not do much. The only way to find out is to test each.

Remember, the only way to improve your conversion rate is one step at a time.

"Let no one say that taking action is hard. Action is aided by courage, by the moment, by impulse, and the hardest thing in the world is making a decision." - Franz Grillparzer, Libussa, Act 3

The Tips in Action: How CafePress.com Lowered Its Shopping Cart Abandonment Rate

Retailers who put the 20 tips to the test have seen lower shopping cart abandonment rates and improved sales. Here is an example of how CafePress.com, a site that offers independently-run shops as well as syndicated and corporate stores put the tips in action. Cafepress.com manages every aspect of doing business online, including storefront development, site hosting, order management, fulfillment, secure payment processing, and customer service. It is possible for anyone to open a free shop with no upfront costs and no inventory to manage. Here is their success story.

Challenge: Although more than a million companies and brands from Dilbert to the ASPCA run their own CafePress.com stores online to offer everything from branded t-shirts to posters, the old 80/20 rule is in effect.

Just 20% of the stores make the lions' share of sales. This is always a problem when you rely on partners to do the marketing work. Some are fabulous, and others never quite get past the starting point.

In Fall of 2003, VP Sales & Marketing Maheesh Jain considered what he could do to make holiday season sales rock. He knew that pushing, prodding, and encouraging store owners would only go so far.

He decided to tweak one key area of CafePress.com's shops where he had control: the checkout process.

Reviewing his metrics reports, he discovered that 25-30% of shoppers who placed items in their carts and actively began the checkout process never made it all the way through.

A 25% checkout abandonment rate is not all that shocking or bad. Most e-retailers we've spoken with have reported similar figures anecdotally. However, Jain figured with a little focus he could do better. Even an increase of a percentage point or two would make a significant difference to the bottom line for everyone.

Campaign: With help from Future Now, Inc., Jain very carefully began the process of redesigning the checkout. The process had five stages:

- Stage 1. Build mock-ups for evaluation within the redesign team.
- Stage 2. Program the new pages and carry out formal testing for functionality internally.
- Stage 3. Post working samples of the redesign online and ask store owners to pound on them looking for any bugs the internal team didn't catch.
- Stage 4. Launch the new checkout process live to the general public, with a large yellow note on the first page letting people know the system had changed, and asking for feedback.
- Stage 5. After 30 days, reduce the feedback request in size, but still leave it live.

Jain knew his store owners had a variety of different configurations and that the new checkout process would involve some pretty complicated coding. So Cafepress.com decided to provide an outlet for customers to tell them: "Hey! This is not working on my system."

In total, Jain and his team made five major design changes to the checkout process, using 4 of the 20 tips for lowering shopping cart abandonment. Their fifth design change is shared with you as a bonus.

Change #1. Made it about new customers by not requiring registration for check out.

Shoppers no longer have to create an account or login to progress with the order; they can place the order as a guest (and have the opportunity to set up an account later). See the screenshots Change #1 Before and Change #1 After for how this was implemented.

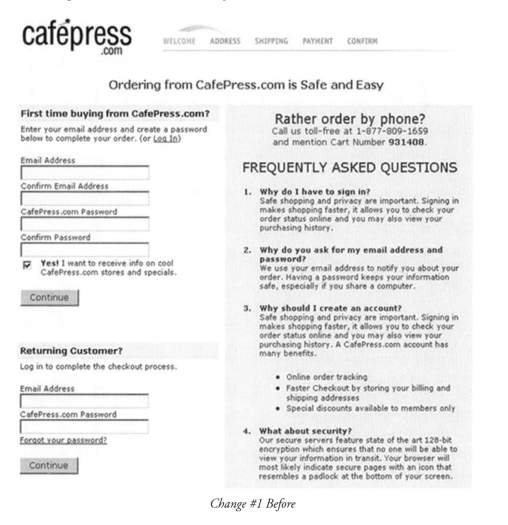

Change #1 Before

Change #1 After

Jain explains, "If you do a survey and ask, 'Does it matter if you have to register or not?', they'll say 'no.' But when they're buying, their actions are very different. A lot of people just do not want to commit to registering up front when they haven't completed the transaction yet."

He continues, "Let them get into the cart as a guest. Let them get through the transaction and at that point ask them to become a member. We're just integrating the registration into the process of buying so that while you're buying you're actually at the same time registering."

Change #2. Streamlined the checkout process after checking the steps in the checkout process.

Every time you make someone click to move to another page so they can complete a process, you're going to lose a percent of the audience. Jain says, "The more steps they have to go through gives them other chances to leave and . . . another chance to get confused."

Plus, the longer a form, the higher the intimidation, "this looks like work," factor.

So Jain and his team boiled down the three separate pages the old cart used respectively for shipping address, shipping method/gift message, and billing details, into a single, sleek, java-driven page.

For example, if users check the box in the new cart saying their shipping address is different from billing, then (and only then) are they presented with a shipping address form to fill out; otherwise, they move smoothly along to the next question.

Similarly, the gift message field appears dynamically only when the customer ticks a "check if this is a gift order" box. See the screenshots Change #2 Before Shipping Address, Change #2 Before Gift Message and Change #2 After Shipping & Gifts for how this was implemented.

 WELCOME ADDRESS SHIPPING PAYMENT CONFIRM

Shipping Address

Please specify your shipping address below. Most items can be shipped anywhere in the United States and internationally. Required fields are designated with an asterisk (*).

> **Get your order faster!** Ship your order to work so UPS won't have to visit your home multiple times.

Shipping Address

Shipping Location *	○ Residential ○ Business
Recipient Name *	
Address Line 1 *	
Address Line 2	
City *	
State/Province *	[▼]
Other (non-US/Canada)	
Zip/Postal Code *	
Country *	UNITED STATES ▼
	☑ Add to Address Book

Please note: CafePress.com is not responsible for import duties and taxes. Click here for more information.

🔒 Your Order is Private and Secure: All your information is safe and secure. The entire transaction will take place on a secure server using SSL technology. Learn More.

30-day Money Back Guarantee!

Questions?
Call toll-free in US
1-877-809-1659
Monday-Friday, 8am-5pm PST or contact Customer Service.

[Continue >>]

© Copyright 1999-2003 CafePress.com. All rights reserved.

Change #2 Before Shipping Address

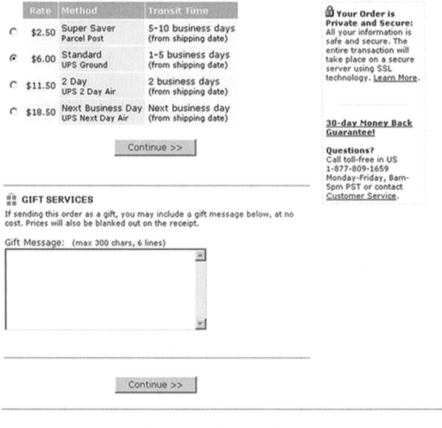

cafépress
.com

WELCOME   ADDRESS   SHIPPING   PAYMENT   CONFIRM

Shipping Method

Please select your desired shipping method. In stock items will ship within 2-3 business days with standard shipping. 2 Day and Next Day orders will ship the NEXT BUSINESS day. Remember, business days exclude weekends and holidays.

	Rate	Method	Transit Time
○	$2.50	Super Saver Parcel Post	5-10 business days (from shipping date)
◉	$6.00	Standard UPS Ground	1-5 business days (from shipping date)
○	$11.50	2 Day UPS 2 Day Air	2 business days (from shipping date)
○	$18.50	Next Business Day UPS Next Day Air	Next business day (from shipping date)

Continue >>

🔒 **Your Order is Private and Secure:** All your information is safe and secure. The entire transaction will take place on a secure server using SSL technology. Learn More.

30-day Money Back Guarantee!

Questions?
Call toll-free in US 1-877-809-1659 Monday-Friday, 8am-5pm PST or contact Customer Service.

GIFT SERVICES

If sending this order as a gift, you may include a gift message below, at no cost. Prices will also be blanked out on the receipt.

Gift Message: (max 300 chars, 6 lines)

Continue >>

© Copyright 1999-2003 CafePress.com. All rights reserved.

Change #2 Before Gift Message

Change #2 After Shipping & Gift

Change #3. Offered Point of Action reassurances.

To make shoppers feel safe, the old CafePress.com checkout had a box at the side of the checkout form with info about privacy, security, shipping, etc.

But, Jain's team thought, why not split up the content in the box, and really integrate it into the form so that the reassuring copy and links appear right next to the part of the checkout process they specifically apply to?

Example: The "Secure Shopping Guarantee" is placed next to the part of the form where the customer enters credit card details.

Example: A "We value your privacy" link is placed directly under the email address field. Compare both Change #2 Before screenshots with Change #2 After Shipping & Gifts to see how this was implemented.

Change #4. Gave the visitor the option to call by offering the telephone option throughout.

Offering an order-by-phone option is nothing new, but CafePress.com stresses this option throughout the checkout process. If a customer becomes uncomfortable with the online process — at any time in this process — the customer can abandon the cart but still complete the order.

However, with over four million SKUs available, many customers were unable to adequately describe what it was they were trying to buy, especially if they had to go offline to make the phone call in the first place. If the customer wasn't savvy enough to write down product numbers, it was, says Jain, "a nightmare."

So CafePress.com now assigns a unique identifier number to each cart, which is highlighted next to the phone ordering information.

Rather order by phone? Call toll-free in US 1-877-809-1659, 8am-5pm PST and reference Cart Number 2054805.

This number gives the operator immediate access to the customer's cart contents. The before and after screenshots for Change #4 show how this was implemented.

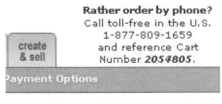

Change #4 After

cafépress
.com

WELCOME   ADDRESS   SHIPPING   PAYMENT   CONFIRM

Payment Options

Coupon Code
Enter your code below and click "Apply" to apply it to this order.

[   ]   [Apply]

Payment Option

Please enter the billing address for this order. Your billing address needs to be **exactly as it appears** on your credit card statement or as imprinted on your check. Required fields are designated with an asterisk (*).

Billing Name *   [_____]

Billing Address *   [_____]

Address Line 2   [_____]

City *   [_____]

State/Province *   [_____ ▾]

Other (non-US/Canada)   [_____]

Zip/Postal Code *   [_____]

Country *   [UNITED STATES ▾]

Please provide us with a phone number in case we need to contact you regarding your order.

Billing Phone *   [_____]

Payment Method

How would you like to pay for this order?

⦿ Pay by **credit card**

VISA [ ] **AMEX** [ ]

If you provide a credit card, the billing address MUST match the credit card billing address.

🔒 Your Order is Safe and Secure

Credit Card Number
[_____]

Expiration Date
[06 (June) ▾] [2004 ▾]

○ Pay by **check/money order**   Not applicable outside the US.

☑ Save this Payment Option

Your credit card will not be charged at this time.

[Continue >>]

Order Summary

Subtotal	$14.99
Shipping and Handling	$2.50
Sales Tax Tax for California shipping destinations only	$0.00
TOTAL	$17.49

🔒 **Your Order is Private and Secure:**
All your information is safe and secure. The entire transaction will take place on a secure server using SSL technology. Learn More.

30-day Money Back Guarantee!

Questions?
Call toll-free in US
1-877-809-1659
Monday-Friday, 8am-5pm PST or contact
Customer Service.

Received a coupon?
Enter it below.

Change #4 Before

Change #5. (The bonus innovation) Tested a viral element at the end.

Inspired by Amazon's "Share the Love" viral marketing offer on the post-checkout page, Jain decided to test something similar.

In this case, his order receipt page invited customers to send up to five friends a $5 coupon via email. Plus, the customer would also get a $5 coupon.

The coupons included purchasing suggestions that Jain decided to swap out once a month. He chose items to promote based on what was most popular, and also what was most unusual. That way he could get easy sales from bestsellers while showcasing CafePress.com's incredible inventory diversity.

To comply with CAN-SPAM 2004, Jain arranged for the system to automatically suppress the coupons that would have been sent to anyone on CafePress.com's Do Not Email opt-out file. Refer to the screenshots Change #5 Before, Change #5 After with Offer and Change #5 After with Order Confirmation & Receipt to see how this was implemented.

Change #5 After with Offer

Please Review & Place Your Order

Please check all the information below to be sure it's correct. Your order is not complete until you click the "Place My Order" button. **This form is SSL Secure.**

[Place My Order]

Shipping Information (Edit)

Shipping Method (Edit)

Super Saver ($2.50)

Payment Information (Edit)

Payment Option (Edit)

Credit Card
4254........1014
5/2005

Gift Message (Edit)

[No Gift Message Entered]

Qty.	Item Description	Price	Discount	Total
1	Large Mug (grokdotcom)(210264)	$11.99	$0.00	$11.99
			Subtotal	$11.99
			Shipping and Handling	$2.50
		Sales Tax Tax for California shipping destinations only		$0.00
			TOTAL	$14.49

PLEASE NOTE: This store is powered by CafePress.com.
Your credit card statement will reflect a payment to CafePress.com.

[Place My Order]

© Copyright 1999-2003 CafePress.com. All rights reserved.

Change #5 Before

cafépress.com

Rather order by phone?
Call toll-free in the U.S.
1-877-809-1659
and reference Cart
Number 0.

welcome | shop all products | shop books | shop music | shop posters | create & buy | create & sell

› Order Status   › Shipping Information   › Satisfaction Guarantee   › Payment Options

Order Confirmation & Receipt

Thanks for taking the time to participate in our Friends program! An e-mail was just sent to the friends you selected for a $5 off coupon.

Thank You.

Your order has been processed successfully. We have just sent you an email to confirm the details of this transaction. For a printable receipt, click on the order number below.

Order Number:

We will notify you via email once your order has been shipped.

If you have any questions or concerns about your order, please contact us.

Send us an email

Phone:
1-877-809-1659

Outside of US:
1-510-877-1570

About Us | Help | User Agreement | Privacy | Intellectual Property Rights

Copyright © 1999-2004 CafePress.com. All rights reserved.

Change #5 After with Confirmation and Receipt

Results: The 5 changes revamping the checkout process yielded a stunning 10-point lift. This figure jumped to 85% with the redesign. "It's been really successful — we've been very happy," says Jain.

Phone orders have held steady at roughly 10-15% of total orders (Jain notes, this slice of the pie stays the same no matter how much the total pie itself grows.) About 85% of the people who call in have their unique cart identifier on hand, either because they're looking at it on their screen or they've written it down prior to cutting their dial-up connection.

The yellow request for feedback promoted a spate of notes, but very few were about bugs in the cart. Jain says these days he gets a handful of feedback notes a week, and all are about things other than cart functionality. (Generally they are product questions.)

The viral program was also a winner. Jain notes, "It worked out really well — we get a fair conversion of new people trying out our service."

The CafePress.com experience shows that by focusing on satisfying the customer's concerns at each phase of the checkout process, a few changes can yield very large results.

Putting the Tips into Action on Your Site: It's All about Testing and Metrics

The Butterfly Effect, familiar from Chaos Theory, grants the power to cause a hurricane in China to a butterfly flapping its wings in New Mexico. If the butterfly had not flapped its wings at just the right point in space/time, the hurricane would not have happened. This theory should be familiar ground for Internet marketers for as the CafePress.com and other cases have shown, small changes can lead to drastic changes in results. It is often the very small variations, infinitesimally minute, possibly unobserved, like the butterfly flapping its wings, that can have extraordinary impact on the final outcome.

Make no assumptions that any of the basic elements of your shopping cart, such as buttons, background colors or a couple of words, are unimportant. Many marketers treat these as incidental design decisions, but they actually can't be ignored as they are all part of your persuasive architecture.

How do you know what elements are important. Test everything! And then keep testing some more (sometimes what made a dramatic impact one week can fizzle out the next). The process we advocate is an ongoing system-wide process of measuring, testing and optimizing for conversion. This will provide those little victories that lead to the winning edge. "The Winning Edge" is what makes a winner a winner whether the winner is your web site or an athletic team. The winning edge is what will determine if your site is a winner or a loser, whether it engages your traffic to take the action you want (converts, or not). Remember no detail is too small. Everything on your site and every element of your shopping cart either adds to or detracts from its ability to convert your traffic.

What Should Be Measured?

There are just ten business metrics, operating measurement, an e-tailer must track to measure performance: visitors, conversion rate, sales, average sale, gross revenue, margin, gross profit, overhead, net profit and growth.

Of these ten metrics that you need to track, only these five are key metrics:

- Visitors
- Conversion rate
- Average sale
- Margin
- Overhead

Why these five the key metrics and not the other five? Simply because the key metrics are the only ones you can do anything about. You have absolutely no control over the other five metrics. They are simply the mathematical results of the key metrics. By exercising control over the key metrics, you can improve your business. The starting point is to make the decision and then put someone in charge. Then, establish and use a "system" for measuring, testing and optimizing your website. Using a system can help you:

- Get more and better qualified visitors
- Learn what visitors really want
- Present better and increase your conversion rate
- Price more accurately
- Increase the effectiveness of your merchandizing
- Understand your errors and learn from your mistakes
- Train others

It makes good business sense to use such a system. Did you know there are still many businesses that measure their key metrics offline but don't do the same online? There are still businesses that do not know how many visitors their website gets in a given month and have no idea how many visitors made a purchase. Without this information, they have no idea if it is the persuasive architecture — the sales — of their website or the marketing that is working or not working. This information is far more important than the forensic data of revenue and net profit that come after the results.

"I am not so foolish as to declaim against forms. Forms are as essential as bodies; but to exalt particular forms, to adhere to one form a moment after it is outgrown, is unreasonable, and it is alien to the spirit . . ." - Ralph Waldo Emerson, The Lord's Supper

What about Your Web Forms?

Most sites have used some kind of form since the Web's earliest days which most of us really don't like filling out, especially online. Most forms are daunting and complicated and require users to exert more effort than they want to. It doesn't matter if we're talking about an e-commerce site's order form, a lead-generation form, or a sign-up form; all require the same crucial but tedious elements, and all must motivate users to complete the task.

Forms face the "microwave" challenge: We want things instantaneously. If we feel something will take too much time, we won't complete it. As you sit reading a form, don't you get the feeling it's going to take a long time to fill out? Peripherally, your eyes scan for the scrollbar that will tell you that the page is long. But, if you really look at it carefully, there isn't that much for you to fill out; perhaps just your billing and shipping addresses and payment information, then a click to confirm your order. What hurts is the perception of the time it will take to complete. But initial impressions count.

One constant we've seen with forms is people don't like to scroll to finish. There's a direct correlation between forms that fit above the fold on the screen and conversion rates. For a really bad form, visit Bloomingdales.com and add something to your shopping bag. Click "checkout — ship to one address." Scroll down to "checkout unregistered." What's the first natural action you see as you complete the form? "Reset form"! Is that really what they want people to do? I don't think so.

The actions it wants people to take, "back one step" or "save and continue," are visually separated from the rest of the form by a horizontal line. If I might offer some free and unsolicited advice, I'd urge Bloomingdale's to lose the reset button.

Wanting to review additional forms that require multiple steps, we searched on Google for "renters insurance," and checked quotes from NetQuote, State Farm, and Allstate. NetQuote starts the form really well, straight from the home page. It asks for my Zip Code and quote type, then I click "Start." On the second page, it's asking for my name and my Zip Code again (it's pre-filled from the home page, though). I fill out that information and go to the next page, where I'm asked a bunch more questions.

At the end of the form, I see a button that says, "I'm Done With This Section." How many more sections are there? I abandon the form. NetQuote did a good job at keeping the form pages pretty short, but a progress indicator to show how many more steps are involved would've been nice.

netQuote®

Residence Insurance Quotes
Homeowners, Renters, Condo/Townhome

Property Location and Type

Address of the property to be quoted:	Address 2 or Apt. Number:
City/Township:	County/Parish: Kings
State: NY	ZIP Code: 11235

Please select the property type: --Select--

Do you currently own (or are you in the process of purchasing) this property? ○ Yes ○ No

Do you now reside, or plan on residing at this property within the next 12 months? ○ Yes ○ No

I'm Done With This Section

Click here to view the NetQuote® Privacy Policy
© 2004 NetQuote, Inc. All Rights Reserved.

powered by **netQuote®**

At State Farm, I use a pull-down menu to enter my state. The next screen asks for my first name and address. The form looks easy. I complete that section; it verifies which New York county I'm in, then I proceed to the next page.

It asks about coverage information. I must fill out contents amount, deductible, personal liability, and so on. State Farm provides a calculator and hyperlinks the terms, in case I don't understand them. Again, I'm frozen. I might fiddle around a bit, but I have questions that are unanswered.

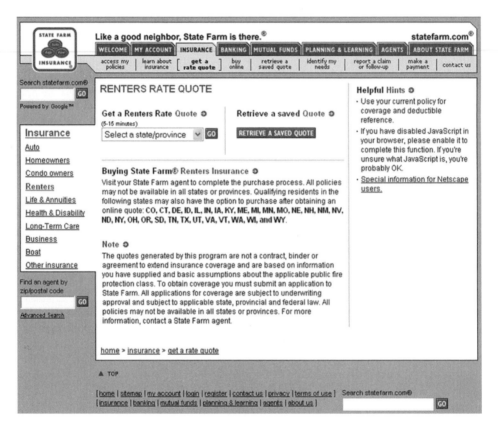

Maybe we'll be in good hands with Allstate. We arrive at Allstate's home page where it easily gets me started on my quote. It asks for type of insurance and my state. Easy enough, so I hit "Go." The next page asks for my Zip Code and another simple question. I continue.

The next page asks for personal information, but it's optional. I like that. It even tells me with a progress indicator that this is step one of two. On the next page, it asks five other short questions. I click "Get Your Quick Insurance Quote Now" and am provided with an estimate quote and offered ways to contact Allstate.

Guess who I'm finally calling? What did NetQuote and State Farm gain by requesting personal information? Could they provide an estimated quote as Allstate did with less information? Could they provide an estimated quote, then ask if I would like a more precise quote should I provide personal information or contact an agent? Seems so.

Do your Web forms show good form? Web forms create an exchange of information and value. If people must spend any amount of time filling out a Web form, you must offer something in return. Narrow

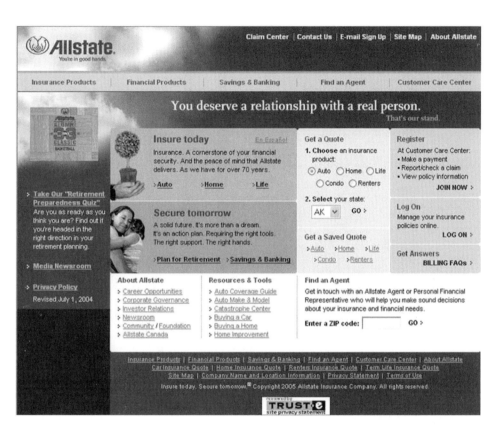

the form fields to only what's absolutely required. Many marketers just love data, so they ask more questions than are truly needed.

Ask for What You Need Only When You Need It

Separate needed from conditional information. RoofSmith.com, used to ask respondents what type of roofing material they need when they chose a new roof. That question was on the first page of the form. It was easily saved for the second page and only displayed if a prospect fills out the new roofing option.

The same can be done on an e-commerce site. Ask a respondent for her billing address. Offer to ship her order elsewhere or send it as a gift. Provide the shipping address fields on the next page only if she checks that option.

Add Benefits along the Way

Web forms often don't include benefits or make them explicit if they're there. This is critical. E-commerce sites should display cart details throughout checkout but not get in the way of each step. For a good example of benefits listed on a lead-generation form, check out the Allegis Group's Thingamajob.

thingamajob.com®
We're Hiring! Are you Ready to Work?

>>We have 12182 jobs waiting to be filled!

> Create An Account
> Post Your Resume
> Member Login
> Browse Our Jobs
> Job Search
> Need Help?

powered by:

AEROTEK
www.aerotek.com

MENTOR 4.
www.mentor4inc.com

TEK systems
www.teksystems.com

ScanAlert™
HACKER SAFE
TESTED 15-FEB

Your Thingamajob Account

Why sign up for your free Thingamajob account?

- We're hiring. Create an account and you can apply for some of the most desirable employment opportunities in the country.
- You can post your online resume within our secure database.
- You can create job alerts designed to meet your specific criteria.
- Only the Allegis Group family of Recruiter's will have access to your resume.
- Our Recruiters will search for a job for you.
- Your information will be kept confidential.

You must create an account in order to submit your resume or create job alerts. Please Complete the Questions Below.

Bold Fields are Required

Enter Your Email Address:

Password must be 6 to 9 characters.

Enter A Password: **Retype Password:**

First Name: **Last Name:**

Address Line1:   **Address Line2:**

City: **State/Province:**
                                         Select a State...

Zip/Postal Code:

Phone: (xxx)xxx-xxxx

Are you eligible to work in the U.S.?   What is your desired rate?
☐ Yes ☐ No   ☐ Year ☐ Hour

Geographic Preference:

⦿ I Already Have a Resume and Would Like to Cut/Paste It

○ I Need Help Building a Resume and Would Like to Build One

○ I will add my Resume at a later time

Click to Create Your Account!

Copyright © 1999-2004 Allegis Group, Inc. EOE

Live Chat
chat is available »

Search for: Accounting Jobs, Administrative Jobs, Automotive Jobs, Aviation Jobs, Business Operations Jobs, Call Center Jobs, Clerical Jobs, Clinical Jobs, Construction Management Jobs, Customer Service Jobs, Energy Jobs, Engineering Jobs, Environmental Jobs, Finance Jobs, General Labor Jobs, Information Technology Jobs, Light Technical Jobs, Manufacturing Jobs, Other Jobs, Professional Jobs, Recruiting Jobs, Sales Jobs, Scientific Jobs, Telecommunications Jobs, Trades Jobs

Set Expectations

If you're collecting information for a lead-generation program, let visitors know what you're going to do with that information. Remind them at the point of action that their privacy is valued, and let them know when and how you'll respond to the lead. Here is how Volvo Construction lets prospects know a dealer will contact them within 24 hours.

Too many companies appear to believe they have no competition. Of the business-to-business (B2B) sites we've looked at, the majority take longer than 24 hours to respond to leads. Leads go cold the moment they're left unattended.

Provide Options

RaDirect promises a "Two-hour guaranteed response time (Monday - Friday, 8 am - 5 pm EST) for North American inquiries only." Notice RaDirect also reminds people they can contact the company via a toll-free number or live chat.

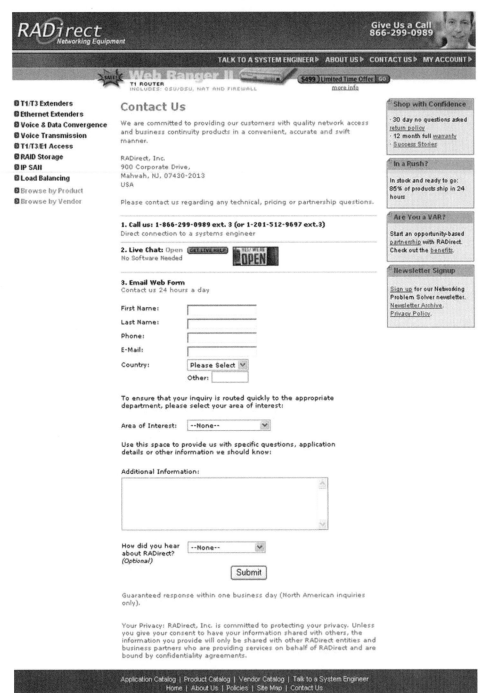

Set Standards

After reviewing all kinds of forms online you will find that it has become some sort of de-facto Web standard to mark required fields with an asterisk (*). Yet offline forms generally only use asterisks when there's some kind of note or exception to the field in question. It's assumed if a question's there, you'll answer it unless it's marked optional.

Shorter Is Not Always Better

Often, people try to optimize a form by getting rid of extra fields. A recent client split-tested a form. Version A requested an e-mail address, version B didn't. Although version B had a slightly higher completion rate, associated sales were dramatically lower. The critical function autoresponders and follow-up e-mail play can't be neglected. Too many people don't spend the time focusing on e-mail communications. Those who do will get those sales.

Error Handling Is Yet Another Dimension

Error handling involves not just the visitor but also the website's response to the visitor's input. Developers are often tasked with writing code to handle errors. Many times, their instructions are little more than "go write some code" to process such errors. They're not given guidelines as to precisely what should happen. Without that information, the result is often error-handling done the techie way: concise, accurate, minimal, and thoroughly unintelligible to the average visitor.

You've seen this before: You submit a form and get an ugly, unrelated screen that says you've made an error. No additional information is provided. Perhaps you actually made two errors. Once you correct the first one, the error message comes back. The website wasn't capable of providing information on all errors at once. It wants to handle them one by one, and gosh darn if it isn't going to force you to handle them one by one, too.

What Error Handling Is Required?

Error handling falls into two categories: error handling for requirements and error handling for type or format validation. The first category deals with required information, whatever the company determined must be completed on a form, such as the address field in a pamphlet request form. You can't send a pamphlet if the customer doesn't provide a mailing address, right?

The second category deals with ensuring that the information provided is of the right type. The mailing address field has an address in it, not a phone number.

When designing Web forms, you must determine not only the required information, but also the format of all collected information, required or not. Perhaps a visitor's phone number is optional. But if she does provide one, your site should be able to determine it is, in fact, a phone number.

Developers tend to bring their binary experience with technology to their handling of Web form errors. They fall into two camps: One favors client-side form error handling; the other likes server-side form error handling. In other words, should the Web form itself contain code that checks required fields and data format before it's submitted or after?

This may seem like six of one, a half dozen of the other to you, but techies passionately argue over which approach is "better." Client-side validation is perceived as faster (a euphemism for "the Web acts more like a familiar desktop GUI application"), but it's typically implemented in JavaScript. JavaScript is highly dependent on the visitor's browser, browser version, and computer platform.

Server-side validation allows great control over the algorithms that operate on the data and bypasses the browser-compatibility issue. But it does require a round trip to the Web server and holds off on error messages until after the user hits "submit."

Developers often miss the point: What's right is whatever satisfies the visitor's needs and creates the tiniest possible speed bump to successful form submission with accurate, intentional data. Developers should use both techniques to better serve business needs, even at the expense of increased complication for those maintaining code.

Provide a base level of client-side error handling. It's a very effective way to deal with required fields and validation routines. Use one of many cross-platform compatible standard libraries for JavaScript form validation, such as qForms, and provide redundant error handling on the server side. This way, no matter what version of what browser a visitor has, you can help provide the information.

Presenting Error Messages

Web sites should strive to present error messages to visitors in a way that makes absolutely clear what must be corrected. A good example is Banana Republic. Follow the "Access Your Info" link on the bottom of the page, and submit an improperly formatted e-mail address. The form returns with red text to tell you what the error is and how to fix it.

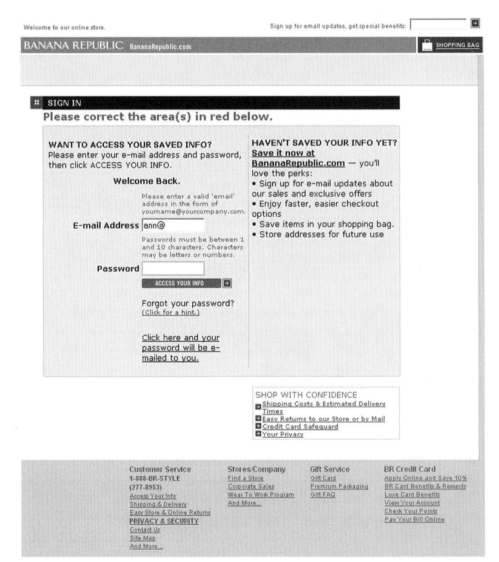

It's helpful to have error page copy written to imply the error is in no way the visitor's fault (even when it is!). Go ahead and blame the Web server: "We're sorry; our server wasn't able to understand your Zip Code." Believe me; you won't hurt the server's feelings.

When performing format validation, don't make users jump through hoops to use a format you prefer but they may not, especially if you can extract the desired format from the provided data. The telephone validation field is one example, such as on Nordstrom.com. The form requires you to enter a phone number with no spaces, dashes, periods, or parentheses. Why? I am the human. The computer running the site is here to serve my needs. It should accept my phone number in any of the several common formats. A skilled developer can certainly write code to handle such situations and still determine if the data provided is a telephone number or my pet's name. Finally, bear in mind this strange but true irony: Customers who do experience problems that are handled well by a company often rank their experience with that company higher than customers who don't encounter any problems at all! Make the necessary changes. They'll maximize your return on investment (ROI) and conversion.

"My definition of an educated man is the fellow who knows the right thing to do at the time it has to be done." - Charles F. Kettering (as quoted by T A Boyd)

Email Strategy — Saying the Right Thing at the Right Time

Is email the killer app marketers yearn for? How about if we just agree that it's a wickedly powerful tool? Like any powerful tool, it has a tremendous capacity to help if used correctly — or to do irreparable damage if used incorrectly.

Rather than wade into the details, let's discuss the overall strategy of email communications. For those of you who remember Objectives, Strategy, and Tactics from school, here's a place where you get to apply the process.

The first thing you need to have is a clear understanding of how your prospective customer arrives at a buying decision. Below is a very simplified process flow of a buying decision:

- Problem/need recognition
- Information search
- Evaluation of alternatives
- Purchase decision
- Purchase
- Post-purchase evaluation

With a clear understanding of how prospective customers buy, you must now consider how to sell to them. Sales is not a pushing exercise, it's a pulling exercise where the outcome needs to be a win-win scenario. If you solve your prospect's problems, they will buy your products or services. So let's take a look at the sales process, with a clear goal in mind: matching the buying and selling processes through email.

Below are the phases your potential customers go through in a complex, multistep B2B sales process (not to be confused with the five-step selling process we apply to designing website flows):

- Suspects — the entire universe of potential buyers for your product or service.
- Prospects — those suspects who have expressed an active interest in your product or service.
- Leads — those prospects in which a decision maker is actively engaged in the buying decision for your product or service.
- Buyers — those leads who are in negotiation with you and have made a commitment to buy in principle but have not yet purchased your product or service.
- Customers — those who have paid for your product or service.

Your email messages must propel potential customers through the five phases. To do so, they must communicate not just information but also energy — energy that will provide the momentum necessary to move potential customers along. This needs to happen at every step, both within an individual email (the micro level) and across an entire campaign (the macro level).

Now, consider these three questions to determine your objectives every time you communicate with a prospective customer, whether via your Web site, email, or any other medium you utilize.

- What actions do prospective customers need to take that will lead to them a buying decision?
- Who has to be persuaded to take action?
- How do we persuade them to take action?

Below are the general objectives for each of the five phases (notice how they parallel AIDAS):

- Suspects — Get their attention so you can qualify potential customers.
- Prospects — Gain their interest so you can further qualify and identify the key players (decision makers and influencers), ascertain their needs, and start to analyze your strengths, weaknesses, opportunities, and threats (SWOT).
- Leads — Stimulate their desire so you can strengthen your past analysis and start understanding their negotiating style, needs, and key issues.
- Buyers — Get them to take action so you can verify your past analysis, correct any missteps, and handle any surprises in the way of closing the sale.
- Customers — Ensure satisfaction so they truly become customers that you can upsell, cross-sell, and resell.

Having a clear understanding of where your prospective clients are in the sales process allows you to design appropriate and effective messages that communicate to their level of interest. Too much detail early on can kill a sale; not enough information later in the process can kill it just as surely.

Truly powerful communication always addresses the recipient's question, "What is in it for me?" If not, then you will never break pre-occupation and get her attention (she's thinking about lunch now, not about your product or service).

Always be answering the question, "Why should I buy from you?," but be sure that you are addressing her at her level of interest and in the language that best suits her dominant personality style. Information that works to convince a potential customer deciding whether to consider you as a possible supplier is very different from the information that convinces her to write a check.

A critical element is to understand that there is a huge difference between informing and persuading. Persuasion is designed to move the reader to action, to get results. To persuade effectively you must always take the customer's point of view, be intentionally short of detail so that you deliberately prompt their questions, and seek out their objections in such a way that the response leads them naturally to the next step in the buying process.

So break pre-occupation, use action verbs and "energetic" words, optimize design and layout, maintain momentum, and actively lead your prospective client through your buying process.

Talk to the right person, say the right thing, say it in the right way, and say it at the right time, and B2B email communications can, indeed, be your killer app. But if you get any of these components wrong, what will get killed is your sale.

Conversion Tip

Targeting Email Marketing Based on Online Customer Abandonment Behavior

Tip #1: Clearly define abandonment

Shopping cart abandonment? Department or category abandonment? Product or item abandonment? Your definition of abandonment will dictate the segmentation and targeting approach that you implement. Select a definition based on overall campaign goals, email creative, and the promotional offer, if applicable. For example, target shopping cart abandoners with offers that motivate them to return to your site and purchase, regardless of product or product category, such as a discounted or free shipping promotion with a price hurdle. Target abandoners of a specific product or product category with offers for popular cross-sells, accessories, and complementary products or services. If you are launching a sale on an individual item or category, you can fuel the launch with a targeted email to your opt-in email subscribers that you know have expressed interest in that item or category by observing and storing their clickstream behavior.

It works very well. Coremetrics' clients, such as Newport News, have realized as high as a 2100% sales increase for targeted emails versus the standard email "blast" to all opt-in subscribers that most eCommerce sites use.

Tip #2: Segment your messaging, but don't "over-segment"

The more sophisticated and specific your segmentation and targeting approach is, the smaller your resulting target population becomes. Be careful to avoid over-segmenting as this will reduce population size and potentially cause positive campaign results to be viewed with suspicion. It is also much more costly (and therefore more likely not to be continued long-term) for your creative group to create such micro messages to deliver to small segments. The most sustainable segmentation approach will yield impressive results even as the target population scales in size.

Targeting abandoners of a new or low awareness product is a common mistake. Instead, target abandoners of related high awareness products or abandoners of the product's category or department and include a cross-sell or bundled purchase offer.

Work with your email vendor to get their input on the right segmentation strategy. And make sure that your analytics vendor, the foundation of your clickstream data, works with them. Coremetrics has partnered with 8 of the leading email marketing vendors to create dynamically targeted campaigns based on Coremetrics LIVE Profile data. You can get a complete list on our website at www.coremetrics.com.

Tip #3: Avoid the Big Brother approach

Abandonment is inherently a negative consumer action. It is a conscious decision not to buy, for whatever reason. When targeting this behavior, avoid invasive messaging that will raise privacy concerns and, quite possibly, turn the potential customer away from your site and brand on principle alone. For example, never call out the abandonment action in email copy or creative. Instead, announce the promotion in a non-obtrusive way (i.e. "As a valuable customer, we thought you may be interested to know that this weekend only product X is on sale for 50% off — our best sale ever").

Tip #4: Don't program customers to abandon!

As tempting as it may sound, carefully evaluate whether automated campaigns triggered by specific abandonment actions are the best way to go. In addition, design and rotate offers for abandonment actions to avoid programming your customers to elicit an offer through deliberate abandonment. By managing the frequency and content of your offers and the design of your targeting strategy, you will keep customers on their toes, hopeful for a compelling offer but not in control of it. In other words, the "black box" targeting approach employed in the past by personalization vendors is highly suspect because every algorithm can be gamed — and that isn't the point.

- **Brett Hurt**, Founder of Coremetrics

"Email got a bad reputation. Email was too often misused for customer acquisition. While it may still have its place in customer acquisition, it is a vital tool in your conversion retention strategies. If you want a simple way to increase your bottom line, rewrite your follow-up, thank-you, order confirmation, shipping confirmation, download confirmation, registration confirmation and any other email that is automatically generated by your systems; as if you were personally writing to your most important customer." - Future Now, Inc.

Content or Audience Targeting – Where Should Your Emphasis Be?

After working through your email strategy, you've prepared a message that you think meets all the requirements necessary to propel your desired audience from the "suspect" to "customer" phase. Your finger is poised on the "Send" button.

You feel satisfied that your message is poised to accomplish its goal, but a voice from within asks, "Will we make any money from this?" To help answer that question, make sure you're thinking of your emails not as letters, but as advertisements.

You send one of four message types in an email communication to your list: a message that drives action (buy now), a message that builds relationships (builds identity, or "brand"), a message that simply provides information, or a message that is sucked into the black hole of cyberspace (the "Deleted" folder).

We'll ignore the last two because they don't help your business results. Buy-now messages are immediate, direct response-type messages by nature, while build-identity messages are aimed at meeting deeper, more long-term goals. We would argue that, whatever your main purpose, some emails can do both. Either way, what we are really trying to do is get people's "share of mind."

To maximize our efforts at capturing mind share, we should understand some physiological processes working in peoples' brains. Short-term memory is electrical; long-term memory is chemical. Most of what we keep in electrical memory is lost during the night; sleep causes the information to fade.

We can only do three things to increase the transfer of our messages from electrical memory to chemical memory: increase the relevancy of the message, increase the frequency of its repetition, or both. Branding is accomplished only when you have a relevant message that is repeated with enough frequency to become stored in chemical memory.

The email marketplace appears to be populated largely with short-term, "buy-now" messages. Even Amazon.com does it. The company delivers relevant messages. But notice how it hedges its bets, including an "add to wish list" option, knowing that people might not act immediately upon the delivery of the message.

If e-commerce companies wanted to be more successful, they could add long-term, brand-building messages into their mix. You can find a good example of a long-term branding newsletter at Thane. The company's newsletter is devoid of pitches, and you can find only two links — one at the top, and one at the bottom. Both lead directly to the Thane site. The company provides high-value content, such as the following from its Weight Loss newsletter, which (hopefully) helps it establish itself as a high-value brand:

Fat burning describes a form of energy supply by the body. Here free fatty acids (FFA), which are created during the breakdown of fat deposits, are "burned without flame," i.e., oxidized. This process is, in comparison to energy extraction from glucose, quite complicated and cumbersome, but it sets free much more energy for the same amount of "fuel." Fat burning takes place all over the body, all of the time. Fat reduction describes a long-lasting process of body weight reduction through the reduction of the body fat component. Fat reduction and fat burning have to initially be viewed as independent of each other. While fat burning takes place constantly and all over the body, a fat reduction will only take place if the body receives less energy than it needs over a longer period of time. In this relation we talk about a negative energy balance.

Which Takes Priority: Right Audience or Right Content?

All of this reaches to the heart of the global advertising debate: reaching the right people versus saying the right thing. Some analytical marketing person once said, "The secret to more effective advertising is to reach the right people." It sounded like it made sense then, and it sounds like it makes sense today.

The only problem is that it isn't true. Attempting to reach the right people has led to more mistakes, frustration, and failures than any other myth in the history of commerce.

Attempting to reach the right people usually leads to overtargeting and a false sense of confidence. It begins when the marketing person says, "I've got the right people." Since you believe this is what matters most, you buy into what he is selling.

When the campaign fails, you don't consider the fact that your ad was not persuasive or that it was not given enough repetition. You simply say, "He didn't have the right people after all." You blame the radio station for having the wrong type of listener, the direct mail company for having a bad list, and the website for having the wrong traffic.

Business owners are frustrated with their advertising because they keep trying to make it a science. It's not a science. Although there are many principles to follow, there are no written-in-stone, scientific rules. The assumption that any one advertising vehicle can provide you with exclusive access to, and attention from, a particular group of people is simply ridiculous. Every American is reached by multiple vehicles of advertising on a daily basis. Just think how many messages are deleted from your inbox each day.

Having the right message is what matters. It's not who you reach, it's what you say. Are you spending most of your time and money trying to reach the right person, or are you focused on making sure you're saying the right things?

". . . when I'm racing, I put winning before everything else. I don't stop until the world gets gray and fuzzy around the edges." - Candi Clark, WomenSports Magazine

Don't Slow Her Down

On your website, a visitor may have a question about what she just read or saw. When this happens, it halts progress and must be addressed. Don't allow anything to slow a visitor down or compel her to rethink in order to continue.

Maintain persuasive momentum. Find potential "speed bumps", that is, points where resolution is needed. Craft answers appropriate for the person reading the copy, and provide subtle calls-to-action with links to needed information. Provide them with the confidence to continue on.

Removing barriers to user action is a critical part of Persuasion Architecture, which takes into account questions asked by theoretical persona. When you've identified different visitor persona and anticipated their questions, provide answers. They'll be delighted. Just don't supply answers to questions they don't have. That's frustrating and could cause them to leave.

And remember to answer their questions, not yours. A common mistake website owners make is to answer the questions they themselves would ask, not what visitors want to know.

Highway to Frustration

Got that smug, he-can't-mean-me attitude? Well, here's a company whose usually brilliant marketing department should know better. A guy in our office wanted to learn about running shoes. Figuring Nike was a good choice for research, he pointed his browser to Nike.com.

Steps he had to take to get what he was looking for:

Typed: nike.com
Page displayed: Amusing Flash
Clicked: nikerunning.com
Page displayed: Interesting Flash
Clicked: Gear
Page displayed: Menu popped up, not what he was looking for.
Clicked: Footwear
Page displayed: Menu popped up again. He's no longer amused.
Clicked: Men's
Page displayed: Flash, returned him to previous page.
Clicked: Trail
Page displayed: Flash appeared. (as did smoke from his ears).
Clicked: Air Divide

Page displayed: Left: blurb about Air Divide shoe.

Right: Picture of Air Divide shoe with orange squares on it. Not what he's after, but he's determined.

Clicked: Orange square

Page displayed: Technical language about Air Divide sole, miniscule amount of useful information.

At that point he was too frustrated to continue.

Nike should provide better information. Our friend has a right to ask why Nike shoes are better and to expect the company will satisfy him. If a Methodical person wonders why celebrities wear Nike, Nike must answer that question. Granted, people look to the brand for style and youth. That's no excuse for a website lacking substance and function.

J.M. Carroll wrote in The Adventure Of Getting To Know A Computer,

When people play in an arcade or on their computers, they are transported to another world where they may get lost or encounter surprises. They usually find this exploration exciting. In contrast, when users get lost in a business application, they become frustrated.

Nike likely views its website as an ad, product or game. On the contrary, a commercial website isn't a product. It's a sales tool. It can be a stylish sales tool, but it must be responsive to different personality types and their different questions. Don't send them screaming in frustration to the competition.

Persuasion -- A Matter of Intention

Nike provides many options, but doesn't satisfy website visitors. When deciding how a website will be structured, make navigation as easy and as simple as possible. Construct the storyboard copy and graphics deliberately and carefully. Make it easy to find points of resolution. Map and anticipate the direction each persona will take. Then create the appropriate Web page.

Understand who your customers are. Walk a mile in their shoes -- through your own web site. Don't slow them down. They are on their way to the cash register.

"If the oarsmen of a fast-moving ship suddenly cease to row, the suspension of the driving force of the oars doesn't prevent the vessel from continuing to move on its course. And with a speech it is much the same. After he has finished reciting the document, the speaker will still be able to maintain the same tone without a break, borrowing its momentum and impulse from the passage he has just read out." - Marcus Tullius Cicero, On the Orator

Momentum

The elements motivating visitors to go from one page to the next and eventually take an action on your site are "momentum." To build persuasive momentum, use AIDAS, the 5-step sales process, create the desire that drives action and make sure there are calls to action on each page. To improve persuasive momentum, focus on how to get people to take the actions required for keeping the sales process moving toward, rather than away from successful conclusion.

Momentum is more than usability improvement. It's about anticipating what your visitor needs to see where, and when. It's about balance, being neither early nor late in providing the information necessary to move the action. Momentum is also about presenting enough choices to keep the visitor engaged, but not so many as to cause overload or "analysis paralysis." Momentum is positive movement, which you enable.

We'll break this chapter into some logical units. First we'll deal with the mechanics, focusing on helping visitors know whether or not they've come to the right place (qualification), and once there finding what they are looking for via information architecture and aids in navigation. Then, we'll look at some specific components of the sales process, and how they provide a link between logic and the emotions. Next, we'll complete the move from the "rational" to the all-important emotional components of momentum, and provide you some detailed guidance in how to apply sales-oriented "emotional intelligence." We'll dwell on one aspect of the emotional domain, buyer confidence, and the things we can do to increase their sense of security and well-being. And we'll focus on some tactical things that will help you ring the cash register. After all, that's why you are here.

As a bonus, we'll conclude the chapter with some thoughts on the complex sale environment. B2B, and large-ticket B2C sales are becoming an ever more important part of the online marketplace. So we thought you might appreciate some very specific advice that focuses on these very special customers.

"Strange to know nothing, never to be sure, Of what is true or right or real, but forced to qualify or so I feel...." - Philip Larkin, Ignorance

Qualifying Your Visitors

There's a knock at your door. It's a friend, and she's really thirsty. You invite her in and proceed to find out what she'd like to drink. You can go about this in several ways.

Option 1: You can ask, "What can I get you to drink?" She runs through a list of drinks she'd be glad to have, and you shake your head every time she identifies something that isn't in your fridge. Gradually, you'll narrow in on the drink, if your friend is persistent.

Option 2: You can ask, "What can I get you to drink? I've got chilled water, milk, orange juice, diet soda, or I'd be happy to make you a cup of tea or coffee." Now you've told her up front what you have, and she can make her selection.

You have just helped your friend "qualify" her choice, making it so much easier for her to get her needs graciously fulfilled by her charming host. More than that, you have treated your friend with respect and removed any chance she'll feel awkward requesting something you haven't got. You haven't wasted anybody's time. Nobody winds up feeling disappointed in the exchange.

This is not just the nice stuff you do in polite society; it's what you have to do on your website. Help them qualify easily, and you'll draw many, many more folks deeper into your conversion process.

Qualifying is one of the five steps in the sales process (prospect, rapport, qualify, present, and close). It goes hand in hand with presenting: by presenting schemes of the products or services you offer, you help your visitors qualify their needs and quickly get to the stuff that interests them. Presenting and qualifying are iterative; you go back and forth between the two as you narrow the field of choices.

Where and when do you start presenting and qualifying? Right up front! On your home page! Smack dab in your active window, which is, after all, your prime conversion real estate.

Does Your Home Page Enable Qualification?

So maybe you're groaning "another thing my home page has to do?" Let's be clear about what needs to happen on the home page:

- You have to let your visitors know they are in the right place.
- You have to communicate your Value Proposition.
- You have to engage your visitors and get them moving deeper into your site.

Your home page cannot and should not be a complete snapshot of everything you are as a business. That would be information overload, which very quickly sends your visitor into Paralysis of Analysis. And many of your visitors will find a lot of that information irrelevant to their needs when they first arrive.

What your home page must do is present qualification schemes, center stage, which lets your visitor figure out if you've got the stuff he wants. Keep your visitor focused on what's important. Don't expect your visitor to check out all the side-bar or top-of-the-page navigation (top-nav) stuff. And please don't require him to use your onsite search engine — this is the online equivalent of Option 1 above! Any qualification tactics requiring your visitor to disengage from the active window work against you. Give him relevant information exactly where his eyes are going to look for it first.

How Do You Qualify?

First, recognize that different visitors have different ways of categorizing information. This is one of the big disadvantages of onsite search engines. Unless your stuff has unique identifiers (think books with titles, CDs with artist names) or unless your search engine is monumentally sophisticated, what you call your stuff may not be what your visitor calls your stuff. And sometimes, the search engine doesn't retrieve what the visitor is looking for.

For example, consider a visitor arriving at the Lands End website searching for a pair of twill trousers. With paper catalog in hand (Lands End is a very effective direct marketer), the visitor identifies what she wants, and enters the item's name in the search box. She gets a screen full of results, but none was the exact item that she was looking for. Only when she entered the catalog product number did the item show up. It was on the website, it just wasn't identified in the standard search using the words the visitor would use in describing the desired item.

Here's the point. Don't depend on in-site search to carry the burden of presenting and qualifying. Folks will tolerate only so much disappointment and frustration using inefficient website search tools. Don't make your visitors responsible for figuring out what you offer! That's your job.

Think about top-level categorization, sub-categorization and all your cross-reference categories. By brand, by room, by function, by gender, by age, by best-selling status — nobody knows your stuff better than you.

Determine how your visitors shop your website by examining your Web logs for navigation path activity, keeping in mind that personality types will influence how your visitors use your website. Pages that experience significant drop-off rates mean you have problems, some of which may be because you've dropped the qualification ball.

Understand your visitors. Figure out the questions they are going to ask about your business and your stuff, then find ways to communicate the answers through your qualification scheme. Your resources for this information could include customer service representatives, sales and buying staff, feedback letters and online user or opinion groups.

Translate your thoughts and your data into sensible, multiple schemes that appear on your home page and help folks qualify their needs from the moment they land on your site. Carry these qualification themes through your sub-category pages.

Also, Don't Forget the 4 Types of Traffic

There are basically four types of traffic that come to your website:

1. The to-die-for perfect visitors, the ones who know exactly what they want and come to you looking for features, brands, and model numbers. Get them quickly to where they want to go without making them jump through unnecessary hoops!

2. The sort-of-know-what-they-want visitors, those who have identified a strongly felt need, but they're still in the process of narrowing down their search criteria. Help them quickly get to the relevant information they need to complete the decision process.

3. The window shoppers, who aren't sure they want anything, but might buy if they saw something that interested them. They have no strongly felt need in mind, but one could be suggested to them. Provide a comprehensive, benefit-oriented overview of what you offer.

4. The lost, who aren't really prospects. They are there by mistake. Quickly let them know they are in the wrong place, and be happy when they go away.

Effectively qualifying ensures you are far better prepared to meet the needs of each group, which does very nice things for your conversion rates.

Are There Any Best Practice Examples?

It's always a little dangerous to single out "best practice" or "best in class" examples in a fast-changing market. What may be world-class today, may be also-ran tomorrow. But at the risk of dating this book, we'd like to point out some firms that really do a pretty good job today.

Check out Dell Computers. Right on their home page they present a two-category scheme: qualify by product category (5 options) or qualify by how you are going to use the product (7 options). Follow an option and see how they continue working through presenting and qualifying.

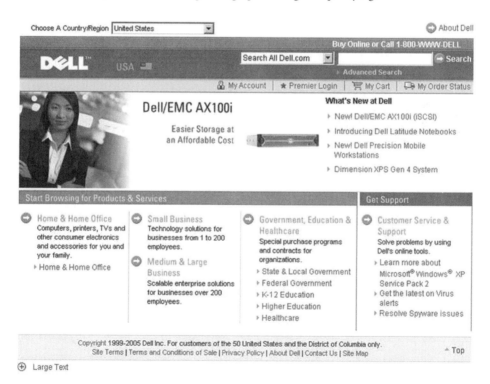

Do we think Dell presents a perfect example of qualifying? Not necessarily. Lots of people out there don't think about computers based on where they use them; they think in terms of the applications they put on their computers. So which computer is best for them if they are looking for something that will turn their living room into a recording studio? Or gives them an awesome platform from which to pursue their gaming obsession?

Stepping away from products for a moment, we invite you to look at the way the American Cancer Society helps qualify needs so visitors can get the information and support that satisfies them — as the tag comfortingly and very humanely promises, "No matter who you are, we can help." This qualification scheme takes into account the nature of the visitor's relationship to the topic and offers links based on the questions these visitors are most likely to ask. Is it graphically sophisticated? Nope. But it does a very nice job of categorizing top-level needs up front.

What about the visitor who arrives on an internal landing page? Maybe this visitor arrives on a product page, but it isn't exactly the product she wants. This is when your supplemental navigation schemes come in, allowing back-door visitors entry to the wealth of your site, drawing them into the splendid way in which you help folks find just the thing they were looking for!

Qualifying is a mandatory component of your website's conversion process, and you have to attend to it in prime conversion real estate. When you intentionally plan for qualifying, you increase the relevance of your website to your visitors, you help them feel more confident using your online service, and you help motivate them further into your conversion system. And the further in they get, the less likely they are to "drop-off."

Help your visitor take the right first steps. Make qualification easy.

"What affects men sharply about a foreign nation is not so much finding or not finding familiar things; it is rather not finding them in the familiar place." - Gilbert Keith Chesterton, Generally Speaking

How Will They Buy It If They Can't Find It?

Most websites have miserable information architectures that mirror the way the company internally thinks about the content and not the way users think about the content. Predictably, users ignore such unhelpful structure." It's been several years since design guru Jakob Nielsen wrote that assessment, and not much has changed since.

Typically, people "ignore such unhelpful structure" by leaving your website without having reached their goals, and they never come back. Want to help your customers shop and move them ever closer to converting into buyers? Then design your navigation to support the way your customers think, so your website anticipates the way your customers want to interact with it. Remember the three cardinal rules of navigation design: Keep it simple, make it intuitive, and be consistent.

Studies demonstrate that people search for and gather information in fairly predictable ways. Navigation has two basic roles to play. It orients the customer by letting him know where he is; and it directs, showing him where he can go and how he can get back to where he was before.

Let me summarize some basic truths about navigation:

- If your visitors can't find what they want quickly and easily, they will leave.
- Website visitors are task-oriented, or goal-driven. The vast majority of the time, they pursue what they are looking for single-mindedly, and even when they are browsing they browse within a narrow field.
- Visitors rarely look at logos, mission statements, slogans, or any other elements they consider fluff.
- If a page does not appear relevant to the visitor's current goal after just two or three seconds, she will click the "Back" button.
- If visitors don't understand a certain design element, they won't spend time learning or thinking about it.
- Most visitors hate distractions, such as flashing GIFs, and intrusions, such as pop-ups and pop-unders.

Many different types of navigation schemes exist out there. Ideally, you should combine elements to create a scheme that works best for your business and your customers. The goal is to orient and direct your customers to and through the conversion step of your persuasion process, whether that conversion is a purchase, subscription, phone call, or whatever other action you want your visitors to take. Let's talk about some of these schemes:

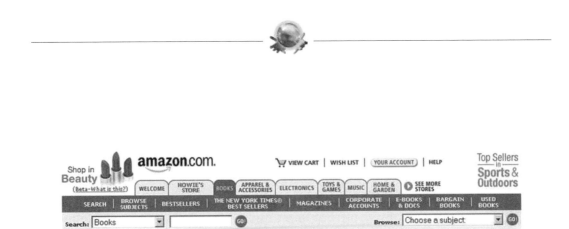

Books > Subjects > Business & Investing > Marketing & Sales

Hierarchical: it's that sideways, tree-like line of text and arrows that indicates where the user is and where he has been. It reminds me of those little kids in the fairy tale who drop breadcrumbs so they would know how to get home. It often looks like this: Home Page > Automobiles > Classics > Convertibles.

Global: this scheme offers access to all areas of your site using tabs or a running list. Take a look at our own site, Future Now, Inc. The tabs across the top are simple to use, plus they are consistent throughout the site.

HOME	ABOUT US	SERVICES	RESEARCH	CONTACT US		Questions? CALL (877) 643-7244
Conversion Assessments	Persuasion Architecture	Client Samples	Publications	GrokDotCom	Blog

Local: this scheme allows users to get to related information within a category but not between categories. This is most helpful when your visitor has landed on your site via a search engine but hasn't landed on quite the right page. We use that on our site as well.

Brew the Best Beer Anywhere

You might find beer that's better than the beer you'll make with The Beer Machine, but you won't find it in a store. The ingredients, the freshness, and the small batch brew method insure unsurpassed flavor. It's what makes great beer great.

You, my Friend are the Brewmeister.

Yes, even you can enjoy creating world-class premium tasting beers on your own with The Beer Machine. And the part that'll have you smiling all the way to the fridge is that it does it in a third of the time of traditional homebrewing and at about one third the cost of store bought beers . Great beer, fast, simple and easy! Now that's the joy of homebrewing.

Craft-Brewed Beer For Pennies

Great beer doesn't have to cost ten dollars a six-pack. In fact every beer you imbibe from The Beer Machine costs just pennies. Yes, pennies. It's just one of the advantages of homebrewing. Brewing at home is easy and inexpensive. If it sounds like a miracle, that's because it is. You must be asking yourself, how does The Beer Machine work?

Embedded links: this scheme is simple but very powerful. Simply place a relevant hyperlink within the body of some text. The most effective way to use this technique is to combine an imperative verb with a benefit: New Superstuff will remove your toughest stains, fast. Register here for a free sample.

Site maps: many websites persist in using these, but this is the least effective form of navigation, and, in fact, most folks skip them completely. They do have some value, particularly for search engines, but don't put too much emphasis on them.

Site-search engines: many websites like to give in-site search engines a lot of importance. According to the latest research, the best websites actually worked hard to prevent people from having to use the search engines. When researchers examined users' clickstreams, they discovered that website visitors were far more successful finding content when they navigated by using categories than by using a search engine. In fact, visitors who didn't use the website's search facilities were far more likely to find their target content than those who did.

The right blend of schemes depends on the type of product or service you offer and, in turn, the nature of your visitor. Keep these pointers in mind as you create the structure for successful and painless movement throughout your website, and you'll be on the right track:

- Use standard icons and conventions whenever possible. For example, people understand the purpose of a shopping cart, and they know that blue underlined text means a hyperlink. Leverage what they already know. Contradict it just to be "original," and you will lose opportunities to convert.
- Keep it simple and make it intuitive. Ease of use makes for happy customers.
- Keep your scheme consistent from page to page. Your customers should only have to figure it out once, if they have to figure it out at all. Frustrate them and they're gone.
- Always illustrate the basic structure of the navigation system. It helps your visitors feel more confident, and more confidence leads to more sales.
- Stick to clear, concise labels for your navigation elements. This is not the place to get creative or coy. Confuse them and you lose them. Check your logs for the terms your visitors are using to search your website.
- Use text for navigation elements; avoid graphics. Graphics take time to load and don't always load properly. Some of your prospects even go so far as to have images turned off in their browsers, in which case all those pictures you created to direct your traffic were a waste of time and money. If you feel you must use pictures, always include accompanying text.
- Don't link everything to everything. Less is more.
- Anticipate where your customer is likely to go, and build that into your scheme.
- Don't overuse embedded links, and make sure it's clear where people are going when they click on the link.
- Test! Test! Test! Use lots of different users, different browsers, and different viewing options.
- Provide help, online and offline.

Above all, keep your links within your page. Don't require your customer to use her browser's "Back" button. If you do, you hand her the chance to leave your website completely. (On the other hand, don't disable her browser's "Back" button. Hijacking someone's computer is a great way to lose that customer forever.)

Again, it's all about designing your information architecture around the searching patterns and psychology of your visitors — not coming up with something that looks cool but sends your visitors clicking for the hills. When you make it easy and intuitive for your visitors to quickly find what they want to buy, more of them will convert. And that's the point, isn't it?

"To this double nature of the visible and invisible world—to the profound longing for the latter, coupled with the feeling of the sweet necessity for the former, we owe all sound and logical systems of philosophy, truly based on the immutable principles of our nature, just as from the same source arise the most senseless enthusiasms." - Karl Wilhelm Von Humboldt, The Limits of State Action

From Logic to Emotions via Benefits

So you're the biggest, the best, the fastest, the first? So what! Big deal! How do you know if any of that answers the question your customer is asking, "What's in it for me?" (WIIFM)

"Features versus benefits" is Marketing 101. But as we look around the Web, we wonder if anybody heard that through their college-day hangovers. Very few people even talk about benefits, much less make the effort to get really good at translating features into benefits. Yet power-packed words describing benefits are what trigger the emotions that motivate us to spend our money, time, or energy. People (including you and me) buy because of the positive emotions associated with the benefits.

"The 2005 model has a 220-horsepower, V8 engine, antilock brakes, traction control, automatic safety restraint system, and both front- and side-impact airbags." This statement may excite some of you out there, but the average consumer (and by "average consumer" I also mean "most of them") is lost after the word "model." Speak to consumers in their language: "This car has a very powerful engine, so it won't need to work as hard as one with a smaller engine. You'll find it a pleasure to own, especially when you want to merge or pass. The extra power will also help you avoid obstacles and quickly get you and your family out of harm's way, while the extra safety features ensure you're all safe and secure. And it's great fun to drive!"

Here's another example: "This ring features a 1.4 carat, pear-shaped cut white diamond with an SI1 clarity grade and an H color rating." Huh? Unless you're a gemologist or you understand the four Cs (cut, color, clarity, and carat weight), that's just gibberish. Here is what might sell diamonds better: "Imagine that special evening when you gently slip this on her finger and stare intensely into her eyes. She peers at this symbol of your devotion, the promise of your future together, and tears begin to glisten. An adoring smile spreads across her face, and at that moment your love is sealed forever."

Would it be indelicate to ask that gentleman if he cared about the four Cs the next morning?

Focus on emotions, not intellect. Emotions are the gateway to making a buying decision. Zig Ziglar, a world-renowned sales trainer, explains, "People usually buy on emotion and then they justify it with logic." Therefore, appeal to their emotions first and foremost. Benefits are the language of emotion. Features are the language of logic. Even people who insist they buy logically or based on features do so because that's what makes them feel better.

One of the common problems companies have translating their product or service features into benefits is that they are "looking at the label from the inside of the bottle," in the words of best-selling author and ad guru Roy H. Williams. In other words, because they know too much about their businesses, they often assume that others, too, not only want to know them but also should know them.

These companies spend time (and money) "assuming" and "should-ing" all over themselves.

How does one get out of this thought trap? We thought you'd never ask. Here is a process to use to identify benefits.

Products' attributes usually have four principal levels:

- Features — what products have. For example, "This application is able to handle multiple users concurrently."
- Advantages — what features do. For example, "This application provides essential information in real time."
- Benefits — what features mean. For example, "This information will allow your managers to keep their fingers on the company's financial pulse at all times."
- Motives — what features satisfy. For example, "This feature will provide cost-savings, control, and efficiency."

List all of the features of your product or service, including standard, technical, supportive, and abstract features. For each feature, develop a subsequent list of relative advantages, then list benefits, and finally motives.

Let's close this section with a simple question: Would you prefer to read an article that will provide you with data on sales, marketing, usability, consumer psychology, and website design, or one that can actually show you how to increase online sales? See? You and your website visitors are really quite alike.

"The emotional appeal of those yells grew upon me steadily . . ." - H.G. Wells, *The Island of Doctor Moreau*

Bringing Emotional Appeal to Your Website

People often ask us what we mean when we say it's important to appeal to the emotional needs of the folks who come to your website. Like, is it really about writing extravagantly, in a fashion that suggests the emotions of the copy's author are stirred up, and yours are about to be next? Should we be in search of flamboyant prose?

It's then we realize people don't really have a handle on what it means to appeal to emotion. For example, if a construction engineer is looking to acquire a large piece of earthmoving equipment like, say, an excavator, how meaningful or appropriate is effusive, flowery language? Will over-the-top prose seal the deal? Probably not!

And yet, however much they may rationalize the result, every single person who sets out to acquire an excavator will base his or her decision on emotions.

Studies have demonstrated that when a person can't connect emotionally with whatever task he is undertaking — even if it is something as simple as scheduling a doctor's appointment — he will not be able to make a decision.

Take scheduling that doctor's appointment. You'll only schedule that appointment when it feels right, when you know the value of getting a checkup, when you have been able to imagine the benefits you will enjoy, when you can actually see yourself doing it, or when you are afraid that not doing it would be worse. You put yourself in the picture and weigh the emotional options.

When you appeal to those options, you help your visitors make their decisions. And the most significant driver for the decision is their perception of . . . yes, you got it right . . . benefits.

Benefits and Features

Earlier we pointed out the importance of features, advantages, benefits and motives. All are important, but as you might surmise by now, the easiest path to making an emotional connection is by focusing on the benefits, not the features, of your product or service.

Certainly features imply benefits. But if you only list features — if you don't spell out the benefits for your visitors — then you are hoping they'll take the time to translate each of your specified features. And that means they have to think on the fly. And, if you make them have to think, you might as well wave goodbye.

I'm looking at the packaging for a Korg Orchestral Tuner. It lists about six features, one of which is: It has a built-in microphone.

Sure enough, if I go looking on the Web, I can find any number of websites that include this feature as part of the product description. But nobody tells me the benefit of this feature. A built-in microphone is not a benefit. But it sure is beneficial to have one, because that means the tuner can hear your instrument, and you haven't got to mess with long cords that always get tangled and a separate microphone that you have to carry around and fidget with. A built-in microphone makes you very portable. It's a pick-up-and-go sort of thing.

Now I'm starting to get to some of the benefits of a tuner with a built-in microphone: I can easily take it anywhere; it's much easier to figure out how to use it; it streamlines my equipment needs; it can tell me if my instrument is in tune (so I haven't got to guess, if I tend to hear things a bit on the sharp side).

If it's a feature, there's a benefit. And when you sell the benefits, you appeal to the emotions. And when you appeal to the emotions, you stand a much better chance of persuading your visitor. So take all those feature lists and start translating them into benefits. Then get that benefit-focused copy up on your website.

Should you ignore the specifications? I wouldn't . . . but you don't need them to be occupying primo screen real estate. The sorts of people who emotionally need to see those specs are going to find them.

Finally, how do you best convey this stuff on your site? Words? Pictures? Our evidence shows that the best way is to create truly great copy. (True — a great picture can help, but it can't do the job alone, ever. And it better not be so big it slows the download, right? Right!) So look at your copy. Are you selling features or benefits? Are you talking about what the product or service is, or how it can make your prospect's life better? If you find you're focusing on features, rewrite your copy to reflect how great that item is going to make your customer feel. Even price matters only when put in the right context. Consider the value of the product or service to your customer's life, then, write killer copy that sells that!

Different Personality Types Have Different Emotional Needs (for You To Satisfy)

You know well that you sell to some very different types of people. Chances are excellent that each one probably fits into one of the personality "types" described below. This is important, because appealing to the emotional needs of the various types requires a somewhat different approach. The key to success is making sure that each "type" can find something that resonates on your site.

Take a Methodical individual. She values order, neatness, facts, attention to detail, accuracy in reporting, credibility, data, truth. She'll be interested in comparisons with similar products or services. She'll appreciate seeing all the tables and product specs, but she'll skip over the testimonials because she doesn't really trust somebody else's opinion.

This person truly doesn't need flowery, evocative language to appeal to her emotions — in fact, that sort of language would turn her off. She needs to feel that you have understood and met each of the qualities she values: facts, order, analysis, information, detail, truth. She likes this stuff — it's what helps her feel the cosmos is in balance.

For the other three dominant personality types, I've assembled a list of qualities that suggest the emotional needs that define their cosmos.

Humanistic: belonging, cooperation, giving, caring, service to others, creative, entertaining, acceptance, freedom, big picture.

Competitive: competence, understanding, control, curious, appreciate challenge, goal-oriented, motivated, success-oriented, accomplishment, future success, direct, to-the-point.

Spontaneous: enjoyment, adventure, authentic, internal integrity, honesty, values, opinions, big picture, personal detail.

Construct your site in a way that it has something that resonates with each type that you anticipate visiting your site. You may have research that shows one or more types making up the majority of your audience, in which case the task becomes simpler. Do your research, then communicate the benefits of your product or service and meet the emotional needs of your visitors — that's the best way to create a human-centric persuasive process that speaks to emotion.

We hope that what we've had to say has provided you with a compelling perspective on why you ALWAYS have to appeal to emotions. It's why you have to sell benefits over features and decide when you're going to promote style or substance. It's the imperative for writing persuasive copy that creates powerful, evocative mental imagery in your prospects' minds — the sort of imagery that allows them to put themselves center. It's why you have to let your visitors know "what's in it for them" and why they should buy from you. It's why you have to woo the dominant personality types of your visitors, employ a selling process that honors their felt needs, and offer assistance and assurances.

"And what about the cash, my existence's jewel?" - Charles Dickens, Nicholas Nickleby

The ABCs of GTC (and By the Way, POA)

You step up to the counter of your favorite store. The cashier smiles at you warmly and asks politely, "Will that be cash or charge today?"

In sales parlance that's called an alternate-choice close. Whichever alternative you choose, you complete the purchase, and the merchant accomplishes GTC — a well-established sales axiom: get the cash.

In the dot-com world, the meaning of GTC can be expanded. If you're doing business on the Web, you can still think of it as get the cash, or you can think of it as get the customer, or you can think of it as get the click. But, however you think of it, definitely think GTC!

The Ka-Ching of Cashing In

GTC may be a nice abbreviation, but what do you do with it? Paint it on your monitor, embed it in your mind, and use it as a guiding principle whenever you are trying to get a prospect to take action.

Let's say you have an e-commerce website and your customer is ready to check out. To maximize GTC, you would offer all of the following, prominently and clearly:

- Alternative ways to pay (credit card, check, COD, money order, etc.)
- Acceptance of as many different credit cards as possible
- Multiple payment channels (secure server, fax, mail, phone)
- Third-party payment services —Yahoo, PayPal, AOL Payment Services, and so on — if you determine they offer benefits to your business
- Security assurances
- Guarantees
- Return policy
- Privacy policy

But notice what you just did. You didn't just do the right things. You did them at the right time, at the right place. If you want to maximize the sales impact of what you do, you have to do it at the corresponding point of action (POA). And that's where we are going next.

Get Them While They're Hot... or Not

You do provide reassuring policies on privacy, returns, guarantees, credit card security, shipping, and so on, don't you? Great! Now also make sure you provide them at the POA.

The key to gaining the confidence of potential customers lies not just in providing assurances but in providing the right assurances, phrased in the right way, and presented when they matter most to your customers as they move through your sales process.

Take a look at Nordstrom.com. With regard to POA, the site does a pretty good job of taking the brick-and-mortar customer experience and transferring some of the fundamentals online. At the bottom of most pages you'll see a section called "Shop With Confidence." As soon as you get to the shopping bag or checkout pages, that same message is not just repeated, it's moved up the screen and displayed more prominently.

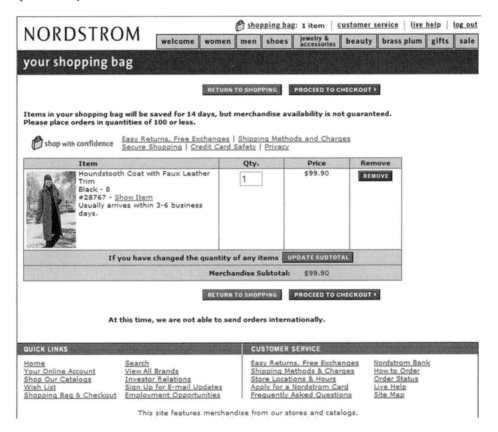

Here is some of the language used in their links:

- Easy Returns, Free Exchanges
- Secure Shopping
- Credit Card Safety
- Privacy

As you move through the (unfortunately way too many) steps of its checkout process, the "Shop With Confidence" message keeps following you.

Don't you want your own customers to shop with confidence, too?

Amazon.com also has a fine example of using GTC and POA. Its "Add to Shopping Cart" button uses both simultaneously. The Amazon.com folks knew it is difficult to get someone to put something into his or her cart. What did they do? Right underneath the "Add to Shopping Cart" text they included "you can always remove it later." Amazing how seemingly little messages presented at exactly the right time can slip in subliminally and affect buying.

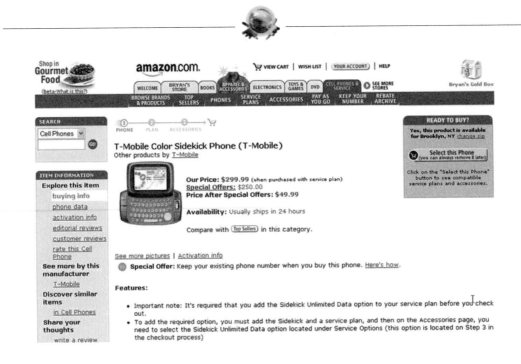

Another Confidence-Builder for Your Visitor – POA Assurance

It's understandable that we all get a bit nervous about taking certain actions. And lots of folks are especially nervous about taking an action online. So, help them along. At the exact point where they can take action, give them the online equivalent of a reassuring smile.

Let's take a minute to consider the Point of Action Assurance. It's an important issue on every one of your Web pages (they all have clickable places, right, or they wouldn't be there in the first place), and the tactic is big-time under-utilized.

Where should POA Assurances show up on your site? Wherever you have a Call to Action on your Web page, you have a Point of Action that potentially raises a question in your visitors' minds.

- "Add to Shopping Cart." Yeah, but what if I decide later that I don't want it?
- "Subscribe." Okay, but what are you going to do with my name and email? I don't want any old Joe to have it.
- "Choose your Shipping Option." And suppose I find out it costs more than I want to pay? Can I change it later?
- "Enter your Credit Card Number (no dashes)." So my roommate hollers not to put anything more on the Visa … it's maxed out … use the MasterCard. Do I get to review and edit my information?

Any action that requires a form of commitment generates concern for important stuff like safety, getting taken advantage of, messing things up. And everywhere you can offer a ray of light, you need to do so. It makes folks feel much happier and more confident and keeps the momentum.

Think about it; the only physical action your visitors can take is to click. They click to enlarge, they click to go somewhere else, they click to search, they click to select stuff and they click to fill in forms. What else is there for them to do? Your job is to make it easy for them to click. And when you answer their unspoken concerns, you pave the way to that pot of gold (yours and theirs).

So examine every one of your Web pages for every click-through possibility you offer. Ask yourself: Is this a place that might raise a question in my visitors' minds? Now, what can you say, right at this point that will encourage them to click? Provide a gentle, confidence-building POA Assurance. Make it easy to say yes (click).

Making a Point of Point of Action

So often we neglect to use POA on our websites. Include a reassuring statement that you value your client's privacy right next to the "subscribe" or "submit" button, and it will increase response dramatically. Display a toll-free number prominently at all times, and if shoppers have a problem, they'll be more likely to call you than just click off to another site.

What do you do to assure your visitors that you are invested in their satisfaction, even if what they order doesn't fit, work the way they expected or delight in every way? How do you let them know you are ready to stand by what you sell, even to the point of taking it back? Are there any good examples of return policies and guarantees?

Here are some examples, both good and not so great, that we've found in 2004 within the online apparel business:

Land's End - this direct-marketing giant has an enviable website; they've figured out how to do lots of things right. So you go to Land's End looking for a pair of slacks, land on the product page and read the benefits, spend just a few minutes filling in measurements, read a discussion of the product qualities, check shipping information. They offer to store your measurements! Next you click on a link below the benefit copy for "More information." Not a word tells you about exchanges or refunds if the item doesn't fit. But there is a link to talk to a live person if you have a question.

You decide to order a pair even without the reassurance, which sends you through a series of secure pages. You log onto your personal account, select style and color and enter your (be honest now) measurements. Along the way, you make a few errors, so you have to reenter the measurements several times. Next, you have to confirm your entries. Then you get to the "add to shopping cart" page, and it is *here* you finally find "Guaranteed Period. If you're not satisfied with any item, return it at any time for an exchange or refund of its purchase price."

The assurance did show up at *a* point of action. But, this item required a lot of energy to put in your shopping cart . . . some assurance earlier in the game would have been nice.

LLBean - Here is another giant outfitter and haberdasher that offers no general "shop with confidence" message when you land on the home page. If you scrutinize the left navigation bar, there is a link to a guarantee. This isn't what most folks are looking for when they hit the home page . . . they might not even know yet if they are going to buy anything. It's too early in the process, so you don't mess with the nav bar guarantee.

You see a shirt you like and click through to the product page. There's no assurance at the point where you are asked to add this shirt to your shopping bag, but you add it anyway. And on the shopping bag page, there is still no confidence statement.

LLBean has a total-confidence guarantee:

> Our products are guaranteed to give 100% satisfaction in every way. Return anything purchased from us at any time if it proves otherwise. We will replace it, refund your purchase price or credit your credit card. We do not want you to have anything from LLBean that is not completely satisfactory.

But you've got to disengage from the shopping process to read it. Or, you've got to know LLBean.

Eddie Bauer - Just like the other big retailers, there is no overall "shop with confidence" message when you hit the home page. When you get to the product page, there are no point of action reassurances. There's no word on the shopping cart page either (although you can check out shipping information here). Nevertheless, you may decide to check out, and begin filling in all sorts of information before you even know whether or not they'll take the item you've selected back if you don't like it!

Let's review what we've seen, or more pointedly what we've not seen. If you aren't providing those critical little reassurances exactly where folks need to see them, you are leaving money on the table. You can't bank on all your prospects knowing your reputation. And it's not enough just to have your policies somewhere on your website. Folks want confidence, but they don't want to have to work for it. Your prospects are urging, "Don't make me think and don't make me have to work too hard."

Finally, after the sale, include return, shipping, and customer-service information along with your order confirmation. (You do confirm every order, right? And say "thank you"?) When you deliver, include an incentive to return to your site. This is when customers are most delighted with their transactions with you (hopefully), so it's when they're most inclined to return. They might need just a little push, and your incentive will do the trick. Oh, and why would they "tell a friend" before their experience with you is complete and delightful? Then don't ask them too soon. By all means, ask for referrals — but only at the right POA. When you do your part for visitors, they'll do their part for you.

Conversion Tip

3 Tips on Momentum

Tip #1: Tell your prospects what they'll get, not what you get if they click on a link

Rather than tell a prospect to "Register Here" (via link), tell them what they'll get if they register. Change the link to read "Download Kit" or "Read Whitepaper".

Tip #2: Stop pre-checking checkboxes

If you check the box for your visitors, then you are really forcing the prospect to opt-out. You've now put them in a "no" mindset. Just leave the checkbox unchecked and make the prospect do the "work". Why? 'Cause it's a major buying signal – it signifies commitment. Get them in a "yes" mindset and they are much more likely to act or transact.

Tip #3: Don't forget to reiterate your value proposition on the order or registration form.

When prospects arrive at an order or lead generation form few are 100% committed to filling it out. Don't make them click away to "remind" themselves why they got there. Instead:
- Reiterate your value proposition and what the prospect will receive at the top of the order form.
- Make sure your very first sentence starts with a checkbox with the word "Yes" next to it.
- Put a check box next to every ìI want to receive...î Put a border around this statement too.

Each time they reread a benefit or check a box, they've committed themselves even more to the task of filling out the form...and pressing submit.

- **Dave Cadoff**, Future Now, Inc.

"If you would win a man to your cause, first convince him that you are his sincere friend. Therein is a drop of honey that catches his heart, which, say what you will, is the greatest high-road to his reason, and which, when once gained, you will find but little trouble in convincing his judgment of the justice of your cause." - Abraham Lincoln

The New Frontier: Complex Sales

Research indicates most complex sales begin with online information searches. A complex sale may involve automotive, financial services, or real estate. It could also be a business shopping for new suppliers, real estate, or professional services. Many people prefer to break e-commerce into business-to-business (B2B) and business-to-consumer (B2C) websites. We prefer to categorize it into complex, straightforward, and impulse sales. After all, a business spends as much time considering the purchase of a $0.39 pen as an individual does.

Complex sales require a much greater degree of self-disclosure on the seller's part. That's why buying research isn't entirely performed on the manufacturer's website. Think automobiles. The Internet is the perfect place to dig for all the information necessary to make a more considered purchase. Yet based on a research study we're conducting, complex sales sites have plenty of work to do before they satisfy visitors.

Less-Complex Sales Benefit From Metrics

Consumer sites, even B2B e-commerce websites, receive a lot of attention. We attribute this to direct marketing metrics playing an ever-greater role in e-commerce websites. Yet what's now measured is largely confined to how many sales are completed. This in itself limits marketers' horizons.

E-commerce is very different from traditional direct marketing. Yet pure conversion metrics tend to ignore visitors who fail to purchase. Micro-action and branding metrics must be incorporated into the mix.

Assist Visitors with Complex-Sale Investigations

The Internet is a vast repository of information that aids visitors involved in a considered purchase. Before the Internet, considered purchases relied much more on established relationships and were difficult to research. When shoppers seek to fulfill their needs, logic would dictate once they find exactly what they're looking for, they'll buy. Persuasion helps them realize what you offer is what they need or want.

A salesperson can meet a prospect, build rapport, and qualify her needs or wants, and then present based on the qualification. If the salesperson did a good job, the closing feels natural and comfortable to both parties. Can a website do that? Of course! That's what persuasion architecture is about.

The Internet, as a marketplace, is unique in three fundamental ways:

Almost every visitor to a commercial website is there voluntarily.

A website is non-intrusive, unlike radio or TV.

Visitors must participate. If they don't click, there's no way to reengage with them. When visitors refuse to participate by clicking, communication ceases.

That's a loss of persuasive momentum.

Consider Persuasive Momentum for the Complex Sale

The essence of the Internet experience is how visitors click from one hyperlink to the next. How they feel about that experience is determined by whether each click fulfills the visitor's expectations and needs. Satisfaction with each click (a micro-action) increases their confidence they'll get what they came for (the goal, or macro-action).

Websites offer many products and services, and serve multiple audiences with diverse needs. The dilemma is how to build a persuasive experience so each and every visitor can fulfill his individual needs on the same website.

Most complex sales websites develop as a result of a group of people from different departments compromising on what elements their website "needs" to have. Then, they compromise on a look and feel. Their visitors see the elements as they're presented, not necessarily as they want them to be presented.

Under these conditions, visitors do as they please. They look where they feel like looking and click wherever they want. What's left to measure but randomness and inferred intent?

Boost ROI by Developing and Testing Buying Scenarios

Place every word and pixel deliberately to control where visitors click. Clicks focus shoppers in the direction they want, and you want them, to take. Controlling variables later permits A/B testing, as you can change one variable at a time. The metrics you really need to track to optimize the scenario become obvious.

If you can't control a process, you can't improve it. If visitors don't click in the specific direction or pattern you predicted, assumptions are wrong. Because you controlled the variables, you can create a variation on the scenario and tweak it until you meet business objectives.

Deconstruct how and why visitors took a particular action. You'll get a clear picture of the road and the obstacles on it.

Continually research and analyze click-through errors (clicks not part of your scenarios) to help incrementally reduce cost, boost success, enhance customer relevance, accelerate the rate of improvement, execute strategic change, and provide insight into the "right" metrics.

In the long term, this propels you toward perfection. You can use failure to your advantage. A winning racehorse yields 10 times more than the runner-up. Not because he's 10 times faster, but because he's incrementally better. Scenario design helps improve every aspect of your website, incrementally, until you outrun the competition and garner far greater results.

Hopefully you'll keep all these points in mind as you focus on complex sales. These are different in some ways from other sales categories, but still involve the basic components of the sales situation – a seller, a potential buyer, and a product or service. Recognize the complex sale for what it is, but realize that at its essence, it's still about people, their wants, their logic, their emotions and their needs for reassurance and safety.

"Communication is a continual balancing act . . ." - Deborah Tannen, You Just Don't Understand: Women and Men in Conversation

Communication

Communication isn't what you say or write, it's the message received. And although the Internet is a powerful, fast, and flexible communication tool, many of the same principles that make other forms of communication effective apply equally well to the Web. Communicating effectively involves improving your writing and writing style, evaluating your balance of images and copy, expressing value, setting the appropriate mood, developing policies and procedures that instill trust, selling style versus substance, timing your messages for best effect, incorporating scannable and skimmable text, effectively managing your follow-up communication, knowing when you should use long or short copy, and much, much more.

To enable you to tackle the task of communicating online, we'll provide a perspective on what constitutes effective copywriting, look at the selling process, the buying process, and how to combine the two so both the customer and the website achieve their goals.

The secret to communicating is understanding your visitors, their needs and motivations. Convey that in everything from your copy to your design, and you'll enjoy higher conversion rates and more satisfied customers.

We've highlighted the important principles here, but for a more in-depth look at online copywriting, we refer you to our book, *Persuasive Online Copywriting: How to Take Your Words to the Bank.*

"The secret of all effective originality in advertising is not the creation of new and tricky words and pictures, but one of putting familiar words and pictures into new relationships." - Leo Burnett

Does Your Online Writing Have What It Takes?

To get the most from your online writing, make sure it's relevant, persuasive and effectively presented.

Reading is the primary activity folks engage in on the Internet. Some may click, some may register, some may purchase, some may send an inquiry, far too many will take a hike. But everyone who lands on your website has to read it (or have it read to them).

Speaking in the post-modern idiom, I have to admit that folks "read" in lots of ways. They "read" images, colors, style, look/feel … you get the breadth of potential meaning. But in a very practical way – in one of the easiest ways you can manage – people read words. Those words must be relevant, persuasive and placed about the site in a way that folks can find them. And they must be suited to the medium.

You have spent a great deal of time and hard-earned money to get people to come to your site. What will they do when they get there? That depends on what they read.

Relevance

You can string words together until you're blue in the … ah … tips of your fingers, but if they aren't the words that matter, you're wasting time and money. On top of that, those no-matter words fail to persuade, so you won't be rolling in nearly as much dough as you could.

The key to everything you do in cyberspace is relevance. Understand what your audience wants and what they really need to "hear." These aren't necessarily the things you think they want. Which is why we are fond of saying, "Speak to the dog in the language of the dog about what matters to the heart of the dog."

Want to know the real kicker in all this? Relevant mediocre writing always out-performs irrelevant but technically competent writing. So much for me being a sanctimonious stick-in-the-mud about grammar, you say? Well, just imagine the effect of competent writing that is also relevant!

Persuasiveness

Only when you have tapped the gold mine of relevance are you in a position to "speak" to your audience persuasively.

You speak persuasively when you acknowledge that not everyone approaches the decision to buy in exactly the same way. This involves understanding how words and phrases appeal to the different personality types that make up your audience. For example, "logical" means a lot to the Dr Spocks of the world, who could really care less about "what others have to say." Then there's Uncle Fred who deep down cares about getting "only the best." The words you choose have to "feel" right — on the same site, you need to speak effectively to the Dr Spocks and the Uncle Freds out there.

You speak persuasively when you employ language that captures the interest of your audience and motivates them to continue deeper into your site. The keywords and trigger words your visitor absolutely needs to see must be woven effectively into the copy and paired with calls to action that persuade her to take the next step. The style of your writing must communicate enthusiasm as well as generate an experience of empathy.

You speak persuasively when you answer the questions your visitors are asking, right when and where they are asking them. This includes Point of Action assurances and textual hyperlinks. And never forget that you speak persuasively when you promote benefits over features (from a rewrite for Volvo):

Double-filtered cab air system [feature] lets you breathe fresh and easy, even in dusty conditions [benefit].

Improved noise insulation [feature] effectively blocks out external noise, keeping you alert and focused [benefit].

Effective Layout

It don't mean a thing if it ain't got that swing. So, you take your relevant, persuasive writing and present it so folks can read it. Being able to read it relies on being able to find it – and on wanting to read it once it's been found. This is where you need to pay attention to layout techniques that promote scannability and skimmability in this screen-based medium. The techniques you choose could include:

- White space
- Headlines
- Embedded links
- Pull quotes
- Highlighted text
- Bulleted items
- Short text blocks

Around here, we talk about copy being "visually available." You may well have put the important copy your visitor needs to see on your site, but that doesn't mean he'll actually see it. And if he doesn't see it, it's effectively not there. Don't let that happen!

Before and After: Examples of Persuasive Relevance

X-Arcade makes a video-game controller. Here's a snippet of copy from their old home page:

Play Thousands Of Arcade Classics On Your PC
Relive your favorite classic arcade games, like Ms. Pac-Man, Space Invaders, Robotron, Galaga, Donkey Kong and Street Fighter! The X-Arcade Kit includes all the hardware and software you need to play thousands of arcade classics on your PC for free!
Never Purchase Another Arcade Controller Again
The X-Arcade separates itself from the crowd with the video game industry's first lifetime warranty, indestructible parts and support for any video game system or PC. These great benefits will ensure the X-Arcade is the last joystick you will ever need to buy!

Here's their new copy:

> Relive Thousands of Arcade Classics
>
> X-Arcade is a line of bulletproof industrial quality game controllers and gaming products that inject the ultimate arcade experience into your PC, MAC or game console...
>
> Install your X-Arcade and instantly relive those adrenaline-pumped moments in the arcade, battering the joystick, pounding the buttons, grinding your teeth, and tasting the thrill as you make your mark as the game's top scorer. Your X-Arcade Kit arrives stuffed with all the hardware and software you need to play thousands of arcade classics on your PC.
>
> The only thing missing is a place to drop in your quarters....
>
> Built like a friggin' tank!
>
> Flimsy plastic is swell for Tupperware and skirt hangers, but shouldn't you be demanding MORE from your game controller?
>
> Every molecule of your X-Arcade product is constructed with industrial grade materials, no dollar store plastic. It literally feels like an arcade game machine.

Volvo manufactures and sells some cool cars ... also some honkin' big construction equipment. Here's the original copy for Volvo Wheel Loaders:

> Powered by the Volvo D4D high performance, low emission engine, this all-rounder provides high rimpull, excellent penetration and fast acceleration in whatever you do. With its superb low RPM performance, the Volvo engine responds immediately to the operator's commands, making your operation more productive.

Rimpull? Here's the rewrite.

> MOVE IT — WITH EASE, SPEED & COMFORT
>
> It's our job to help you do yours — no matter how big. And the full line of Volvo Wheel Loaders is always up to the task. Whether you move rock, earth, timber, sand or snow, a wide range of Volvo Wheel Loaders and attachment options are available to help you conquer the elements.
>
> Dig deeper in this section to find the perfect Volvo Wheel Loader for your operation ...
>
> Climb into the cab of a Volvo Wheel Loader and get to work. Along with unmatched production and power, Volvo Wheel Loaders help you move it — with ease, speed, cost-efficiency and comfort.

Our Take on the Copy Examples

See why these "afters" work better? If you do, then great, we've made our point. Business doesn't have to be dull and ordinary. In fact, it really shouldn't be. When have lack-luster presentations and restatements of the obvious ever gotten you juiced? Your online copy makes a huge difference in the blackness of that bottom line. So start slamming some joy sticks and conquering some serious earth-moving. Both you and your visitors will feel the better for it.

Conversion Tip

Understand What Your Prospects are Hoping to Achieve RIGHT NOW

We've all been told to 'Know your customer'. However, a general "knowing" gives few clues to what any individual wants to buy or find right now. So, here's how you learn enough about your customers to take action:

- Study the keywords and phrases used by millions of users on the major search engines, to get insight into what people are looking for today, right now.
- Make sure that when someone lands on a page in your site via a particular keyword or keyphrase, he or she feels, "Yes, I'm in the right place."
- Write copy to match the keyword search. Yes, it probably means creating multiple landing pages, depending on the search term being used.

Result: Your page is immediately recognizable as relevant to that visitor.

- **Nick Usborne**, online copywriter, author, speaker and consultant

"Language can only deal meaningfully with a special, restricted segment of reality. The rest, and it is presumably the much larger part, is silence." - George Steiner, Language and Silence

Some Final Thoughts on Language

Message Must be Relevant

Identify what really matters to your visitors. What motivates them to seek you out? What problems do you solve for them? What friction points do you reduce for them? Identify the benefits and value of your products or services. Find your visitors' buttons, then push them by serving up a relevant message!

No Jargon

Unless you're marketing to a select audience that absolutely requires you to communicate credibility via insiderspeak (jargon), stay away from the stuff. Jargon convinces folks you aren't really interested in talking to them, so they're far less likely to listen in the future. If you must include specific terminology, give it a low profile. Those wanting to know if you can really talk the talk will look to find it. If you're not sure how folks talk or think about your products or services, conduct online consumer research. Using your customers' language on your website may help your chances with the search engines.

Don't "We" All Over Yourself

The first rule of online success is it's never about you. Brilliant as you and your business are, focus on visitors. Let them know you understand what matters to them. Put them center stage. Want a thumbnail view of how customer-focused the language on your site is? Try the customer focus calculator on our website. It sees how often your copy brags about things like, "We are the best, we are the original."

Keep It Need-to-Know

Ask for as little information as possible. You probably want to request customer information that includes everything from name to shoe size. You can certainly ask for it. But the more information you ask for, the less likely folks are to fork it over. Conversion rates are generally proportional to the amount of information requested. This holds especially true for lead-generating conversions. Lead generation is a value exchange. Your visitors expect to get something of value from you in exchange for their information. What they have to provide should not be one iota more than they perceive necessary! If you want more information, provide more value in proportion to the request. You want my shoe size for your newsletter? Offer me a free pair of socks after I've received the newsletter (let me know if you do this... I could use a free pair).

Help Them See It

No two ways about it, if visitors can't quickly make visual heads or tails of your content, they won't stick around and you won't generate a lead. Layout matters. Evaluate text scannability, and use eye-tracking principles to encourage visitors to engage with your site.

Think of a prospect as a hungry dog on the scent of his favorite food (meat). When you speak to the dog, speak in the language of the dog, about what matters to the heart of the dog. The dog cares about meat. Don't tell him about grooming. He'll get irritated and go elsewhere.

Make this the centerpiece of your site's language guide. If you don't have the time or resources to take advantage of all five tips, try at least one.

Conversion Tip

Why Are Customers So Indecisive?

It's a factor called the Full Story. While every single one of those arborists provided us with quotes, not one of them gave us a single reason to choose them. Any reason would have been better than none. Ten reasons would have clinched the deal, even with a higher price.

This is one of the main reasons why most deals seem to disintegrate before the eyes of most business owners and sales people. We fail (and fail miserably) to educate our customers about the unique advantages of working with us.

It's An Impossible Puzzle If It Doesn't Have The Pieces

People need to be gratified psychologically. Our brains are dying to know more about the companies that bid and all we get are terms and prices. The arborists should have educated me about the quality of their cutting, their comprehensive insurance policies, their warranties, their skills, and their service guarantees in detail. I needed to know anything and everything that would help me decide in someone's favor. Not one of those bids included that kind of information.

Look at yourself. Let's say you hire someone for your firm. How little would you like to know about him? Or say you go out on a date. How little do you want to know about your partner? Every piece of the puzzle is absolutely necessary. Don't forget to give your customers a reason to buy from YOU. Tell them about yourself. Provide all the juicy details, and you will leave your competitors crying in their beer.

What Is The Psychological Reasoning Behind The Whole Story?

The strong, silent type is the one our mamas told us to watch out for. We instinctively trust people less who tell us less. Even if we do like the person, we want them to open up. If you want people to trust you, you have to tell them about yourself.

This instinct of distrust is hardwired in our brains, and you'd do well to pay attention to it. A lack of adequate detail doesn't help to build trust, which is why customers go from hello to sayonara very quickly. Once you have their attention, stop saying stupid things like, "Buy from me," and start giving them all the reasons WHY they should buy from you (read the article on The Power of Why). Add spices to your marketing strategy curry, and your customer will be captivated by the aroma. Churn the gastric juices in their brains. Make them salivate. Get them to drool. And when they're ready to eat, feed them well.

- **Sean D'Souza**, excerpted from his PsychoTactics article of the same name

"Good advertising for a bad product is hucksterism. Good advertising for a good product is honesty. Bad advertising for a good product is incompetence. Bad advertising for a bad product is sweet justice." - Brett Feinstein

Buying: The Flip Side of Selling

We've explained the five-step selling process. The flip side of this process, seen from the customer side, is the buying process. Each of us engages in this process numerous times a day, whether we are buying a can of soda or making a more complex decision, such as buying a new car. Whenever a customer makes a buying decision, that decision represents the culmination of a process. It may take place almost instantaneously or stretch out over a long period of time, but it's a process, not an event. Recognizing this, savvy marketers understand how to address and package the buying process within the selling process.

No matter how long the process takes, the buying decision always begins when folks become aware of a need. Once they have identified that need, they begin to search for and explore possible avenues for meeting it. While gathering information, they refine and evaluate all the buying criteria that will affect the decision to purchase and narrow the field of choice to the "best few" alternatives.

Once they reach a decision and choose, they take action by making a purchase. (Keep in mind those horrid shopping cart abandonment rates – making a decision to purchase is not the same thing as completing the purchase!) The final step in the process involves a reevaluation of the decision and its results.

To summarize, the steps of the buying decision process are:

- Identify
- Search
- Evaluate
- Decide
- Purchase
- Reevaluate

To successfully get your prospect to take action, you must be able to see the world from your customers' buying point of view. Know what questions they are asking and answer those questions. You must answer their questions and provide them with the information they are seeking first, before you provide them with the information you want them to have (the selling process).

Buying and Complexity

The way customers make buying decisions depends on the complexity of the problem they are trying to solve and the complexity of their decision process. This complexity affects how you manage the sale.

If the customers' needs and the decision-making process are simple, all you need to do is make them aware of you, build confidence, differentiate yourself, demonstrate value, and make buying quick and easy. This is why branded products sell so well. Think of buying a book from Amazon.com.

If the needs and decision-making process are highly complex, then you need to approach the sale only slightly differently. This type of sales requires you to make customers aware of you; build relationships; educate your customers (perhaps many different individuals within the same organization); show sensitivity to the different decision makers, influencers, and groups; and resolve conflicting needs so that you can custom-tailor your solutions and make the buying process as painless as possible. Think of purchasing a multimillion-dollar piece of equipment that needs five departments to sign off to close a deal.

Merge the Buying and Selling Process? How?

When a consumer becomes aware of a need, he or she must also be made aware that you offer a solution to his or her problem. In a consumer sale, it may be enough to make consumers aware that a Coke is refreshing or a printer is fast. In a more complex sale, your branding will have to be more specific and must speak to a deeper need. What comes to mind is something like, "Nobody ever got fired for buying IBM." Does your Web site convey effectively that you satisfy your customer's deeply felt need?

Only when the customer knows that you provide a value that matters to him or her can you undertake building the foundations of a satisfying relationship by establishing rapport and trust.

When a consumer comes to you to explore avenues to meet the needs he or she has identified, you have to ask questions that help qualify what the customer really wants and how the customer's needs can best be fulfilled. When the customer narrows the field to the best few alternatives and possible solutions, you use information that you have developed in the qualifying stage to present recommended solutions in your customer's language so he or she understands your value immediately.

As the buyer moves through each step of a buying decision, you seek the buyer's commitment to a logical next step and provide reassurances that he or she has made the right choice.

The persuasive architecture of your entire website must recognize every step of the consumer buying process. Each step feeds and leads to the others. Although the process ultimately is linear, there can be feedback loops within the process as the customer re-evaluates information. So, it's not unusual to address two, three, or even all five steps on a single page.

It is helpful to think of the process as operating simultaneously on both a micro level (the individual page) and a macro level (the overall buying and selling experience). You should always acknowledge and address the needs of the buying process at both levels.

Above all, remember you haven't completed your selling job until the customer has completed their buying process. Although you may be doing a great job on your part, you cannot just quit and pack up until the buyer is finished. It would be like an expert first violin finishing the symphony ahead of everyone else, and leaving in the middle of the performance. Stick with it until the job is done.

"Value is the most invincible and impalpable of ghosts, and comes and goes unthought of while the visible and dense matter remains as it was." Investigations in Currency and Finance, W. Stanley Jevons, British economist, logician

Value

Value is not the same as price, and price alone is actually a lower priority for most buyers. Whether you will get the sale and your "buyer" will turn into a "customer" is determined by the value the customer finds. Are you effective at selling your product's benefits instead of just its features? Does the style of your website equate with your value proposition? Do you delight customers with the way you fulfill their orders, or do you merely satisfy or, even worse, disappoint them? Do your website's products and/or services address your customers' deeply felt needs, or are you trying to push something they may not even want? The customer must be able to readily determine your value, not have to guess at it.

It's also helpful at times to realize that the determination of value is not just a buyer-side issue. In selecting the best ways to connect with potential buyers, you have to distinguish between actions that actually deliver value, and those which only appear to do so. For that reason, we'll start this section with a story of two metrics, only one of which really delivers on the promise of value.

"A wise man sees both sides of a matter. The fool sees only one." - Anonymous

'Good Enough' Conversion Rates?

A client trying to sell his company's services through its website contacted us and asked two seemingly simple questions: "What is your other clients' experience?" and "What is the average number of visitors it takes to make one sale?"

We advised him to ignore other people's experiences; they'll prove worthless. Every website is different, and nobody is selling exactly the same thing in the same way to the same audience. We've found over 1,100 variables that affect conversion rates (number of visitors taking a desired action) on a website, and those variables can be broken down into even more detail.

Thousands of such variables exist on every website. Some have major impact; some only incremental. Ones that work for your widget business may not work for your friend's whatzit business. Sometimes a change will move your conversion rate only a bit. That doesn't mean your choice of variable had no impact. It could mean your choice of solution had no impact. Always identify the variables. Systematically measure, test, and optimize.

The reader who called told us his conversion rate is now 2.31 percent, and he was proud of himself. Working on it himself, he improved conversions by nearly 20 percent. We told him to use that as his baseline and focus on improving it.

His website's conversion rate was fairly typical, and by industry standards many might consider it to be good enough. We were sincerely paying him a compliment for his initiative and focus. Nevertheless, he called back later to say we wouldn't be working together. His boss felt the conversion rate was good enough already and they would be using their budget for more pay-per-click listings.

A red alert goes off whenever we hear "good enough." Good enough shields the status quo. Good enough masks mediocrity and rewards the unmotivated and lazy. But don't be fooled by those who say, "It's not good enough yet." That's often the procrastinator's mantra. Sometimes good enough is good enough, such as when refinement will only delay — but not significantly improve — or when deadlines don't allow for better.

To clarify, let's contrast two news stories:

News Item 1: TeaLeaf Technology, provider of systems to measure the availability of Web content, commissioned a new study from Business Internet Group of San Francisco. The study found nearly two-thirds of e-tailers (representatives of the Keynote E-Commerce Transaction Index) still present users with some kind of error that interferes with or prevents the completion of a purchase. Each failure is estimated to cost an e-tailer as much as $278.

The study is no fluke. A similar study found a failure rate of 72.5 percent. Some of the errors found were: inability to purchase after comparing products, blank pages, wrong pages, incorrect items, and an assortment of technical errors.

News Item 2: ComScore Networks reported online retail spending for the week ending August 10, 2003, grew to $969 million from $762 million the same week a year before, a 27 percent increase. In the first half of the year, online spending grew at a 15 percent clip; it expanded to 25 percent or better each week in the second half.

A rising tide lifts all ships. Many companies have finally broken through and are making money online. They are congratulating themselves for having "figured it out" and singing the praises of following best practices. Yet have they truly figured it out? We've seen survey results indicating 66 percent of respondents don't even know their own conversion rates, much less how to improve them.

Sam Decker, senior manager of Dell's Consumer eBusiness told us:

One of Dell's foundational principles is constant improvement of our customer experience and our business. We have many measures — especially from our Web site — and anything that can be measured can be improved. So we are constantly testing, analyzing, and improving; managing a portfolio of small and large site improvements. The cycle never ends, and it never should. Besides, it's fun that way.

Decker is among those responsible for increasing not only traffic and sales but also conversion rate year after year. Dell's online consumer business does over $3 billion a year in sales and doesn't think that's good enough.

Based on experience, we are only impressed by conversion rates greater than 10 percent. They're not unheard of, and some major sites report conversion rates from the low teens to over 30 percent. Failing to convert most of your traffic is largely accepted as good enough. What would happen to your conversion rate if you looked at every visitor who didn't convert as an error that needs correcting?

Conversion Tip

Use the Initial Buying Experience to Convert One-Time Buyers into Multi-Buyers – 4 Tips/Best Practices

Tip #1: Use a welcome kit to bring them back

One-Time buyers are a costly investment for retailers. And online retailers appear to have a much higher percentage of One-Time buyers than the 40% average experienced offline. But you can do something about this situation — create a first-time buyer "welcome kit" for every new customer shipment.

What a welcome kit does is force the customer to create a specific persona for your business. You can either let the customer completely control the image they create in their mind of your company — good or bad — or you can try to control what the customer imagines by giving them a welcome kit. The kit typically includes:

- Welcome message, "thanks for becoming a customer, we appreciate your business very much..."
- Who the people are behind the company, "In the beginning, I built every product by hand, and wife Marge shipped them out..."
- What the business beliefs of these people are, and how these beliefs impact the customer and products or services, "We take great pride in the quality of our products. They may be a bit more expensive than others you see on the web, but we believe you will appreciate not having to replace them..."
- Company history, if appropriate, "with 40 years of experience..."
- Member card or ID, phone stickers, info magnets, etc. if appropriate

A properly put together new customer presentation can increase 2nd purchase rate by 50%. It is the most important "customer marketing" you can do.

Tip #2: Surprise gifts

Good surprise gifts are related to your company or products, useful to the customer, but do not have your logo or phone number on them. If you send magnets or whatever with your info on them, you need a surprise gift as well. You might consider a different, more valuable gift for high-ticket 1st time orders — these people are typically your future best customers. By the way, just in case it's not clear, new customer offers are not surprise gifts. "Every new customer gets a blah blah" is not a surprise, it's an entitlement.

Tip #3: The appropriate use of samples

Sample anything you have that is related to the purchase and consumable.

Don't give a customer a sample of something they purchased; have a number of different samples so each new customer gets a sample of something they did not buy.

The catalog industry has tested this stuff for decades — it works.

Tip #4: Don't forget the importance of packaging

When you send something, pay attention to the first thing your new customer will see . . . the package. If at all possible, use fresh clean "blank" boxes (unless you can afford to customize boxes with your logo), kraft tape, and blank newsprint/peanuts to pack.

Sure, it will cost you another 60 cents an order, but what are all those 1x buyers costing you? Opportunity, that's what.

- **Jim Novo**, author of *Drilling Down* and co-author of *The Marketer's Common Sense Guide to E-Metrics*

"The customer is the immediate jewel of our souls. Him we flatter, him we feast, compliment, vote for, and will not contradict." - Ralph Waldo Emerson, Address Delivered in Concord on the Anniversary of the Emancipation of the Negroes in the British West Indies

The Golden Rule of Online Persuasion

In the film "City Slickers" the old-time cowboy shares his secret to the meaning of life. He holds up his index finger and explains how to ensure success in life, "One thing. Just one thing. You stick to that and everything else don't mean s*%t." We'll, like the cowboy, we know that one secret.

We call it our golden rule. He who has the gold, rules. In the online world, the one with the gold is your potential or existing customer. She is all that matters to herself. It's about her: her ease of use, her experience, her expectations, her idiosyncrasies, her preferences, her personality, her energy level, and her needs or wants. It always has to be about your customer. Always! This is more critical online than ever before.

You can trace the development of the art and science of sales and markets, from early barter economies to the invention of currency, from nomadic markets to retail stores and huge malls, from road shows and door-to-door sales to telemarketing and TV shopping. In each case, the medium was new and sometimes even amazing. But the message, the systematic process of getting a customer to buy, was the same. QVC and HSN didn't succeed by forcing a new technology on customers and demanding they adapt. They adapted the technology so it would serve customers the way they've always preferred to be served, only better.

The Internet doesn't change the fact people want to be sold (in the sense of helping them identify what they want, then presenting exactly that). Buying is fundamentally an emotional decision. To be successful sales must stay in touch with its human-centered roots — regardless of the medium. Time-tested sales and persuasion principles work offline, and they work online, too.

People have employed every communications medium as a sales tool. Each evolution reduces friction for the consumer and puts a greater onus on the merchant. By "friction" I mean the physical, cognitive, or emotional efforts required to satisfy wants and needs. Today, consumers have more choices. They can shop anytime and virtually anywhere with minimal effort. They can buy with just a single click.

Merchants deal with people's perceptions and motivations. We meet business goals by meeting our customers' goals. It's not easy to do. It takes a lot of hard work and planning. To get high conversion rates, set the hurdle high.

Recently, websites have replaced the human-centered sales process with lots of non-human-friendly technology. Some websites are hard to buy from. Successful selling is human-centered — people meeting the needs of people based on a series of steps understood, explicitly or implicitly, by all participants.

Websites with high conversion rates have a dominant characteristic: a high degree of empathy for the visitor. Here's how they do it:

- These websites sell a product or service for which there's a truly felt need or want.
- They are built with the understanding that the visitor is there voluntarily; website activity is based on participation, not coercion.
- Their presentation doesn't assume the visitor knows anything, but it doesn't insult her intelligence either.
- Their owners understand you can lead a horse to water, but you can't make it drink. You can, however, entice it to take one sip at a time.
- They present visitors with necessary information when it's needed.
- They anticipate questions the visitor may ask and address his fears and concerns.
- They use copy that emphasizes consumer benefits and helps involve the visitor's senses in an "intangible" type of sale.
- They use copy that helps them rank well in the search engines, because it's relevant to a visitor seeking a way to solve her problems.
- They employ hyperlinks filled with keywords that speak to her questions. They're laced with benefits that jump out at her. They let her know she's on the right track to achieving her goal.

You can't sell ice to Eskimos on the Internet, or elsewhere. No matter how well designed the website, how persuasive the copy or how usable, if you can't find a way to meet customers' needs, they won't buy. They are looking for value. Customers who vote with their mice have already proven they're not interested in "solutions" that are long on sizzle but take forever to load and only delay what they came to do: buy.

Why have we all seen horrific websites that sell successfully? Despite their obstacles, they meet customers' desires and motivations with merchandising or brand identity. If your brand is so cult-like, your price so ludicrously low, or the need for your product or service so insatiable, you may get away with a website that persuades poorly. If your product or service doesn't fit one of those categories, remember just one thing: Follow the golden rule.

"Goodness is the only investment that never fails." - *Henry David Thoreau*

Increase Your Pay-per-Click ROI

In the "virtually" frictionless environment of the Web, a customer is a self-service volunteer with lots of choices and access to any of your competitors with a single click. Nowhere is this more true than in search engine marketing (SEM).

To meet your business objectives online you must first meet your customers' objectives. Every click must provide relevance. They look for relevance when they come to your website. They have a need or problem or are in search of a solution. They are looking for someone who will provide enough information and comfort so they can make a buying decision the in the way they're most comfortable making one.

A website's persuasion architecture leads each person, along with her individual approach to making buying decisions, comfortably along the sales process. It's mapped to a decision tree users find relevant and persuasive at every click.

Here are seven tips we share with clients to optimize their pay-per-click (PPC) campaigns:

1. Track on a macro-action basis. Track every keyword/key phrase to conversion on a macro-action basis. A poor result for a particular keyword or key phrase doesn't mean you should drop it. It means your website should better accommodate it.

2. Track on a micro-action basis. Track every keyword/key phrase to conversion on a micro-action basis. This clarifies how your visitors interact with your website's persuasive dialogue. Micro-actions are key decisions that must be made before a visitor can decide to buy — the action that's your ultimate goal. It lets you optimize your website's dialogue to terms you use with persuasion architecture.

3. Select keywords based on buying process. Choose your keywords/key phrases based on an understanding of the buying process for your product or service.

4. Use visitor latency. Some terms won't immediately convert well in a campaign, so track macro-actions and micro-action factoring in latency. In a recent study with a shared client, Jim Novo documented how visitors came in cycles of 14 days from PPC engine to actual purchase. PPC ad campaigns are just that — campaigns — not one-off tactics.

5. Define metrics clearly. Calculate return on investment (ROI) correctly. Divide the amount you spend per keyword/key phrase by your gross margin (gross profit minus cost of goods sold) on products or services bought from that keyword/key phrase. If you want to generate leads, establish a base amount every lead is worth. Divide the amount you spend per keyword/key phrase by your value per lead.

6. Go broad. Focus on those keywords/key phrases with the greatest ROI before those with the most traffic or gross sales. You don't need to be ranked number one.

7. Engage visitors in persuasive dialogue. Use persuasive architecture to anticipate visitors' frame of mind, plan the action you want them to take, and tell them what they need to know before they can take that action. Match ad copy closely with keywords so the visitor perceives the relevance. Then, make sure the persuasive dialogue on your website is the dialogue your visitor wants to engage in.

Whether you're a brand marketer, an online retailer or responsible for generating more business leads, PPC is a medium you can't ignore.

Not every merchant ships custom printed boxes. This is unfortunate since the experience doesn't end with checkout. Your packaging is part of the customer experience. There is no doubt of what is being delivered when you see the famous cow-pattern on the Gateway boxes or the Amazon.com logo. We have often heard from merchants that this is because of a shortage of resources. Order custom printed packing tape; it will deliver a substantially better experience for only a few cents more. - Future Now, Inc.

Are You Providing Value?

Humans have some interesting notions about what constitutes value. If they pay a lot for something, they either think they've purchased a high-quality product or they've just gotten ripped-off. Stuff with bargain-basement price tags is considered . . . well . . . bargain-basement. Find a high-quality product at a substantially-reduced price, and, hey, you've just found value!

This is just one view, not remotely the complete picture. And online, it's still believed that value is all about price, although this has been shown as untrue offline years ago. Sure, you might get lucky and make a few sales based on a super-discounted price alone. But if that's all you're offering, you're building zero loyalty and you're begging for competition. If you want lots of delighted, loyal, repeat customers, you have to realize superior value goes way beyond price, and it's superior value that keeps them coming back. Just look to the recent success of cross-channel promotions where the customer can order online and pick the product up offline. All those sales weren't to least-cost buyers.

Try on the idea that you are not just offering your customers a price proposition; but rather that you are actually offering them a value proposition. It's a complete package, filled with lots of human-friendly usability elements, attractive but fast-loading and functional design, great information, great products, appropriate prices, top-notch customer service, plus lots of nice little guaranteed-to-make-them-smile extras you devise to set yourself apart from the guys and gals that just offer, well, price.

If you still think online isn't about sustainable value, consider the results of an MIT study of online buying that discovered "only 47% of the consumers ... bought from the lowest-priced seller ... in fact ... price was the least important factor."[1] And what beat price? The biggest factor was whether the customer had visited the site before (see why I go on about making the right impression with your website?), followed by the company's familiarity, then shipping time (think "service").

Truth is value is so subjective you can often be more successful charging higher prices, provided you pay close attention to all the other factors that influence the buyer's perception of the value of your product. A lot of that perception hinges on your market position: if you're selling coffee, are you a corner lunch counter or a Starbucks?

Remember image alone won't do the trick, particularly online, where it's that much harder for your prospects to bask in your fancy ambiance. Folks flat out demand real substance, and they consistently vote with their mice.

". . . tell him there is measure in everything. . ." - William Shakespeare, Much Ado About Nothing

Accountability

"What gets measured, gets done." If this is true, then we really need to pay attention to what we choose to measure. Because measurements not only show us the dimensions of outcomes attained but also appear to focus and motivate those who are responsible for the outcomes. Stated differently, "Who gets measured, does." This is the essence of accountability.

This section of the book will make an attempt to sort out the confusing array of metrics that appear in the context of e-commerce discussions. We'll begin with those metrics that are used to measure business success in general, and how they apply to e-commerce. Then we'll take a deeper look, further down the causal chain, at those metrics which may be unique to e-commerce. The former are more strategic in nature, in that they focus on the success of the business. The latter are more tactical, and focus on what must be done at the operational level to set in motion the behaviors of buyers and sellers which lead to business success.

And, along the way, we'll throw up some caution flags when we identify metrics that have the potential to mislead, or which may simply be misunderstood. Let's take it from the top.

"If you torture the data long enough, it will confess to anything you want." John Thompson, *President of BestBuy.com*

E-Commerce Metrics: Drowning in Your Own Data?

While interviewing a prospective client, the authors had an interesting insight regarding metrics. The prospect, a senior vice president of marketing and sales, confessed to being overwhelmed with all the data her staff produces. So, we decided to go back to basics. And to keep it simple, we organized our response to her into three categories: objectives, strategy, and tactics. We told her:

- The objective is to make a profit.
- The strategy is to buy low and sell high.
- The tactics are how you run your business.

Getting a handle on your data and distilling lots of it into meaningful and manageable information — it's really that simple!

First, recognize that the order in which we've presented these categories is not random. There is an implied hierarchy. Second, accept that each category has its own set of key metrics and a set of "players" that use them to guide their work. Finally, understand that performance metrics at each level of the hierarchy are supported by performance at the level below, if one exists.

Now, let's look at each category again, and see which metrics and "players" are specific to each level:

- **Objective.** The board and executives get the cash flow, profit and loss, and balance sheet reports.
- **Strategy.** Management gets the gross and net sales, cost of goods sold (CGS or COGS), sales per visitor (SPV), cost per visitor (CPV), and customer conversion rate (CCR) reports. The first three, gross and net sales and cost of goods sold drive the metrics shown at the Objective level above.
- **Tactics.** The staff gets all the raw data that feeds the management reports, built up from the overall site performance, individual promotions, fulfillment, customer service, and so on.

"But," you say, "what about this report or that metric?" We'll happily take the credit, but it wasn't Future Now, Inc. that developed the science of management reporting. For a management reporting system to be meaningful, everything must flow into the financial statements. If you can think of a metric that doesn't seem to be a subset of one of these management reports, let us know. If we can't show you how it is a subset, we probably can show you why it's not worth measuring.

Now that we've determined which metrics fall into which categories, let's take the next step and define each of one at the Strategic and Tactical levels:

- Gross sales: This is your total sales at the prices you originally invoiced (you know darn well you'll probably never see all of it).
- Net sales: Net sales equal gross sales minus discounts, returns, allowances, and any other adjustments your customers were able to squeeze out of you.
- Cost of Goods Sold (CGS or COGS): Also called cost of sales, this is traditionally a measure of the cost of buying raw materials, if any, and of producing your finished products. Included are direct costs, such as labor and overhead. You deduct your CGS from your net sales to arrive at your gross profit. If you have no employees and no overhead and your product costs nothing to create, your net sales and your gross profit are the same. Call us, we'd like to invest.
- Sales per Visitor (SPV): The SPV shows the actual average dollar amount purchased per visitor (not per order). This measures both marketing efficiency and the ability of your website to close orders. You don't need us to tell you that you want this number to be as high as possible.
- Cost per Visitor (CPV): Divide all those maddening marketing expenses (or marketing expenses plus Web expenses) by the number of unique visitors.
- Conversion Rate (CR): This is the ratio of orders to website visits, sometimes called the sales closing rate. It measures how well your website can turn a visitor into a buyer. The buck starts here.

Why are these the key metrics you need to manage your business? Well, let's look at gross sales, net sales and CGS. If you buy low, say $10 per unit, and sell high, say $15 per unit, $5 is the difference. If there are no discounts, returns or allowances, meaning gross sales equal net sales, then Voila! You've found your gross profit. No gross profit, no business. It doesn't get any simpler than that.

Next, let's look at Sales per Visitor (SPV). The idea is to increase your SPV (sell high). Factors affecting this include the quality of your traffic and merchandizing. You can improve your SPV by increasing your Conversion Rate (CR), your average order size, or both.

Now let's look at something that takes cash out of your pocket, Cost per Visitor (CPV). Naturally you want to lower your CPV (buy low). Factors affecting this are the effectiveness of your online presence and merchandizing. You can also improve (lower) your CPV by increasing your CR, decreasing your marketing expenses, or both.

Finally, there's Conversion Rate (CR). This is the heart of the matter, and where we'll be focusing a lot of attention going forward. Put a system for increasing your CR in place as an ongoing exercise. This exercise, more than anything else, will help you buy low and sell high. Nothing you can do will affect your profit and loss statement as dramatically or increase your return on investment (ROI) as much as improving your CR.

E-commerce is a numbers game. The trick is to focus on the right numbers so that you can make accurate decisions about how to improve your website and, ultimately, your CR – which we see as the foundation metric for performance improvement. Our experience has been that few companies are collecting the right data or, like the executive mentioned above, are so overwhelmed with data that they don't know what to do with it. It's up to you: Will you drown in data that's voluminous but useless, or will you reap the benefits of meaningful information?

For those who like pictures more than words, take a look at the roll-up of business metrics at ABC Co.

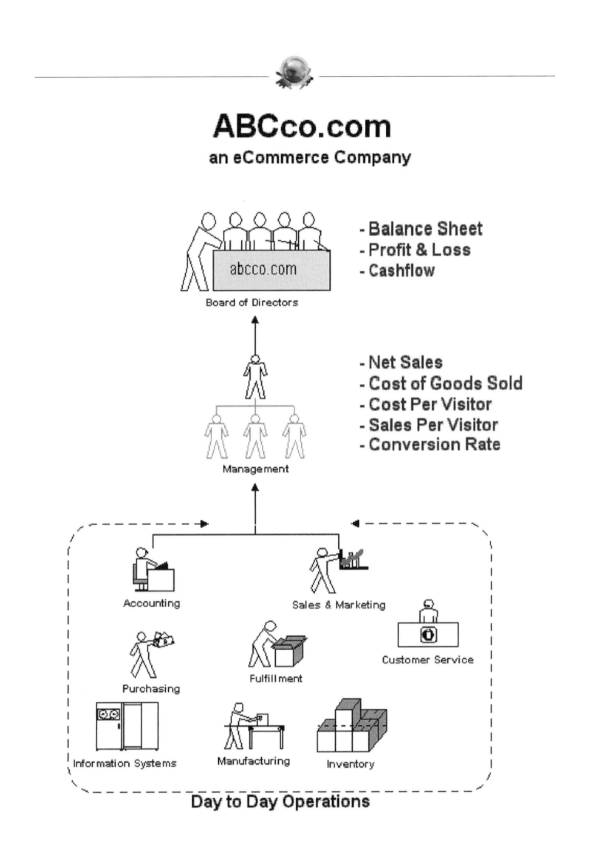

ABCco.com
an eCommerce Company

- Balance Sheet
- Profit & Loss
- Cashflow

Board of Directors

- Net Sales
- Cost of Goods Sold
- Cost Per Visitor
- Sales Per Visitor
- Conversion Rate

Management

Accounting

Sales & Marketing

Customer Service

Purchasing

Fulfillment

Information Systems

Manufacturing

Inventory

Day to Day Operations

Conversion Tip

3 Tips on Metrics and Accountability

Tip #1: ROI is a blunt instrument

Is ROI is the only measurement (for keyword effectiveness) that really matters? While ROI is indeed important, it suffers from being too crude in many instances, especially for search engine marketing. This is a pretty contentious thing to say, so let's look at an example:

A store selling a range of gourmet foods is buying keywords for Olive Oil. When doing ROI analysis this keyword shows poor results; that is, lots of clicks but very few sales. A closer investigation however might reveal that the olive oil comes in ornate glass bottles — attractive, but heavy and expensive to ship. The lack of sales results from the high shipping costs, not the keyword itself.

Tip #2: Don't blame the messenger

Search keywords often correlate directly to a product. Lack of conversion may well be related to the product itself or an attribute of it, and not the keyword itself. Proof of this for the example above would exist by examining the abandonment rate from the shipping confirmation page of the cart. Unfortunately extracting this data for each keyword, for each product will most likely be very time consuming, even if the analytics app can support it.

Tip #3: A different metric — ATOS

What's needed is a metric that can quickly be applied to all keywords and that indicates propensity to buy instead of actual purchase being made. In our experience this best single value that indicates this is 'average time on site' or ATOS. As an absolute value it doesn't mean much, and even expressed as a trend it's not a lot better. It could be argued that a long time on site is a bad thing because it indicates the site has poor usability. However, when viewed across search engine keywords, or segments of visitors, or different campaigns, a longer time indicates greater interest in the product/website. Since we assume usability problems are the same across all keywords the metric is valid when used for comparisons like this. People do not waste time browsing for products they have no intention of buying. They may decide against purchasing because of cost, shipping, return policy or phase of the moon, but that's not the fault of the keyword. ATOS is the single most efficient way of proving this.

- **John Marshall**, CEO of ClickTracks

"The "art" in website analytics comes when "interpreting" the reports — reports which are hopefully set up to answer the real questions at hand accurately. It's all about the experience you have in looking at these reports. This art is developed through the success you have with decisions made based on these reports over time. The only time you have to "read tea leaves" in web analytics is when you have reports that have not been set up correctly and there is no way to go back and re-run the data."
- Jim Novo

Web Analytics for Retailers

The Basics

One of the first questions clients usually ask is, "Do we have the right Web analytics solution?" For retailers, we recommend they first have the right person in place before investing in a new analytics solution. A 2004 Jupiter Research study revealed only 27 percent of online businesses surveyed don't have a dedicated tech person on staff. Yet 63 percent don't have a dedicated analytics staffer.

Jupiter Research asked executives to identify the top challenges facing their sites. Three of the top six are the need to collect, understand, and act on data.

The Art of Web Analytics Interpretation

There's an art to Web analytics. First, you must ensure reporting is set up to answer those questions you want answered. Do you want to exclude search spider activity? Is a page refresh counted as a page view?

What do you want to know? If you're not sure, don't just ask some IT guy to set up your reports or run them in "default" mode (as so many do).

Retailers Lag Behind

Unfortunately, many retailers either don't have the tools or people to benefit from their Web analytics. Successful online retailing depends on consistent and regular test, measure, and optimize cycles. The e-tailing group inc. found 14 percent of respondents in a 2003 survey didn't know their conversion rates, and 43 percent didn't know their shopping cart abandonment rate.

Online businesses must emphasize running things by the numbers. As the e-tailing group points out, "The most frequently used measurement methods were based on sales results and site activity/traffic reports, many of which are overly simplistic in nature."

Implement Key Performance Indicators

Retailers must first establish key performance indicators (KPIs). These are the backbone of ongoing optimization efforts. KPI reporting is really the only meaningful link between the numbers you generate and your business goals. Jupiter Research's Eric Peterson elaborates on the qualities that compose a useful key performance indicator:

- Offers a succinct definition that summarizes the nature of the relationship between the data that are compared (meaningfully compared, naturally!)
- Establishes an expectation for performance by using business-relevant comparisons over time
- Is capable of revealing a meaningful change in activity for a selected period
- Is capable of influencing remedial action

Some useful KPIs for online retailers include: sitewide conversion rate; percentage of new and returning visitors; sales per visitor; average order value; average number of items purchased; shopping cart abandonment rate; and repeat order rate, which can help on the way to calculating lifetime value.

Most of these metrics have some correlation to your P and L statements. Most also provide an incomplete picture of customer behavior. Allen Crane, Dell Computer's senior manager of business process improvement, says, "The Holy Grail is a suite of quantifiable, actionable e-metrics that captures behavior patterns and accurately relates them to the key transactional business levers of units, revenue, and margin."

Start With Reporting Basics

Not all reports are created equal. Many products allow users to generate custom reports, making millions of potential reports available. Even at their default setting, hundreds of reports are offered — too many to start taking action. So let's get a sense of the first five reports retailers should be looking at:

- Single page visits. This report is one of the most critical. Monitor key entry pages, such as home page, category pages, and important landing pages, to ensure visitors aren't just landing and exiting without any additional action on your website. This would indicate either the page wasn't relevant to visitors or they couldn't find what do to next.
- Entry pages and exit rates. Monitor traffic sources, what website pages visitors enter on, and if any entry pages have high exit rates. A top-50 retailer we worked with recently had a category page that was a top entry page (for a common, under-$30 product). Yet the page had a 91.3 percent exit rate. We found the cause was the product image; once it was replaced, the exit rate dropped to 61.5 percent. Originally a cause of visitor frustration, this page now accounts for a healthy income stream.
- Traffic by product category and individual products. Determine if key product families get the visits they deserve. If a key product category that's critical to the bottom line is underperforming, consider restructuring navigation.
- Products by search engine. This report helps evaluate activity based on the most recent search engine activity. It tells you which search engines people use to find your products and what kind of income they generate. Use this report for search engine optimization (SEO) and ranking.
- Scenario/shopping cart analysis. How do visitors move through the various stages of the shopping cart and checkout process? Obviously, you want to reduce the number of visitors who abandon the process. We know from the Fireclick Index that the average shopping cart abandonment from December 2003 to March 2004 was upwards of 70 percent across Fireclick's client base. If you have a cart abandonment issue, review the 20 tips to reduce abandonment.

This list isn't exhaustive, yet it provides a glimpse of the power and flexibility Web analytics can offer retailers when it comes to monitoring and optimizing websites.

Intermediate

You'll find Web analytics solutions fall into three distinct categories: basic, intermediate, and advanced. The levels are applied based on client sophistication, the effect reports and solutions have on increasing the number of visits and the revenue per visit, and the frequency with which analysis is performed. This week, we'll explore these reports through the words of several Web analytics users, with different vendor platforms and different needs.

Royal Appliance Manufacturing develops and markets the Dirt Devil brand of floor-care appliances. As a company, it believes a household is generally in the market for a new upright vacuum cleaner every four years, and selecting and purchasing a new cleaner takes about two weeks. The challenge for an interactive marketer, then, is to understand at what point in the consumer's buying cycle the website begins to play a role.

Basic analytics takes Dirt Devil to a partial answer. Following careful segmentation, the company examines the length of time website visitors spend on product information pages versus store locator page. This can shed light on whether visitors are in research or purchase mode.

Though invaluable for uncovering flaws and dead ends in a website's structure and content, basic analytics, such as click stream and scenario analysis, can't always take the next step away from a website's tangible aspects toward more abstract knowledge, such as where in the buying cycle a visitor is or how soon after a visit to the website follow-up communications should be sent. To uncover this type of understanding, Dirt Devil turns to a set of reports that shows actions, such as a single visit or purchase, in a temporal context.

Sales-Cycle Reports

A number of sales-cycle reports are available in WebTrends. They automate the onerous task of calculating how much time, in days, elapsed between a consumer's first site web visit and the purchase visit (otherwise known as latency). Combined with click-stream information from the first website visit, these reports provide a clear picture of how long Dirt Devil has to convince visitors to complete the sale. Results are revealing, and sometimes a little scary.

Michael Crowdes, manager of interactive marketing and e-commerce at Dirt Devil, said:

"We look at the Sales Cycle by Product report as being the most accurate for this information, since it can uncover important differences between product categories. For instance, for a $200 upright vacuum, there may be as much as 15 or 20 days between the first visit to the site and the visit in which the sale is made. On the other hand, some specialty items, which are at price points that make [consumers] more prone to impulse buying, are overwhelmingly sold on the first visit. Not much time to close the sale there. With only one shot, we need to make sure not only that the information on those pages is making up the consumer's mind to purchase, but that taking the next step is as clear and easy as possible."

Internal Search Keywords and Failed Search Keywords

Pat McCarthy of Palo Alto Software said:

I use WebSideStory's HBX Internal Search reports to see what users are wanting to find. I often check to see what the results for these queries are, if the actual results make sense, and are the best possible. [I] tweak the results and also track conversion rate from the search results. If we don't have good content in that particular area, [we] try and improve that weakness. If a search fails, we need to add content/products if it's a worthwhile query.

Next-Page and Previous-Page Flow Reports

Omniture's page-flow reports graphically illustrate two levels of the most popular pages visitors view after leaving the analyzed page. The report also highlights when visitors exit the website. This is all the information necessary to perform a next-step analysis that identifies the steps visitors take most often after viewing a selected page. I use this report by looking at the top entry pages to see what holes visitors leak through.

Use this report to understand what steps are taken most frequently after viewing a selected page; to optimize website path design to funnel traffic to a desired goal page; and to identify where visitors go instead of those desired goal pages.

Marketing Effectiveness Dashboards

Retailers who constantly evaluate marketing spend in areas such as affiliate marketing, paid search, paid inclusion, e-mail marketing, and banner advertising. By tying the effectiveness of these campaigns to purchase behavior, marketers can quickly optimize their spending to increase website traffic. These dashboards provide easy access to accurate, unbiased performance metrics for thousands of simultaneous marketing programs. Retailers can compare, optimize, and negotiate pricing based on revenue for all online marketing initiatives.

"The Coremetrics Marketing Management Center guided us through a rapid process of cutting out poor-performing keyword buys and reinvesting in top keywords," said Heather Blank, director of e-commerce and business development at PETCO. "Applying this process to just one of our cost-per-click search engines, we boosted order volume and increased gross margin contribution."

Look-to-Book Ratios

Retailers also measure merchandising effectiveness by tracking abandonment rates and look-to-book ratios for products and merchandising categories. Merchandising analysis allows direct marketers to monitor the effectiveness of product pages in driving purchases:

- High visits/high conversion. Don't waste your energy here. Obviously, you have a winning product.
- High visits/low conversion. This is the Holy Grail of this report. Consider better merchandising, improved copy, and testing price points.
- Low visits/low conversion. This indicates either there's little interest in the product or visitors aren't finding these products on the website. Consider removing or replacing the item.
- Low visits/high conversion. Consider bundling these items with other top-selling products to increase their visibility and drive more traffic to them.

There's an art to Web analytics. What do you want to know? If you're not sure, don't just ask some IT guy to set up your reports or run them in "default" mode (as so many do). Hopefully you've had time to read about the most basic and intermediate reports retailers use Web analytics to review. Now, a look at some of the more advanced reports needed to optimize conversion rates and maximize online sales.

Merchandising Reports

Review your Web analytics reports regarding which brands, categories, and products sold best, and study up- and cross-sell reports. You'll identify which products are most popular and which are likely to be sold together. By identifying top items sold together, you can more effectively price and place products to increase average order values.

Multichannel Reports

Retailers must understand how their customers behave in all channels. Those who don't adopt a multi-channel customer view risk making uninformed decisions. They aren't taking the whole picture into consideration. The ability to import and export online customer profiles to create a single view of the customer is critical to advanced Web analytics.

First-Time vs. Repeat Buyers by Products Purchased

Michael Crowdes uses this WebTrends report for additional insight into what point consumers engage with the company's website.

"More purchases of new models from our website come from people who have already purchased something from us in the past. We sell relatively few models online, so it makes sense that most new buyers come to us for replacement items for a purchase they made at a retail store," said Crowdes. "This shopping behavior seems to indicate that once a consumer has made an initial purchase from our site to support a product they already own, they're more open to the idea of expanding that behavior to include purchasing completely new products."

Segmentation Analysis

Every online business has many segments of daily visitors. Some know exactly what they want, some know approximately what they want, others are just browsing or repeat customers. As Eric Peterson says in his excellent book, Web Analytics Demystified, "It is a mistake to lump all visitor value groups together and use that information to try and understand how to best serve the groups providing higher value — thus the need for visitor segmentation tools."

The most advanced Web analytics are performed via profile-based segmentation that uses historical records of online customer activity. Customer profiles allow clients to target marketing efforts based on displayed behaviors. Targeted marketing increases customer retention and lifetime customer value on a daily basis. To do so, employ targeted e-mail campaigns, invest in website tools that high-value customer segments use, or correlate online behavior with offline systems to deliver recommendation engines in the call center.

CompUSA segments with Coremetrics' Web analytics platform. "Our relationship with Coremetrics has improved CompUSA's online business performance immensely because we have access to a powerful customer analysis platform which helps us identify and optimize for high-value customers," said Al Hurlebaus, director of e-commerce. "Using Online Analytics 2004, we learned that Product Compare users represented a key customer group for us, sparking an initiative to improve access to that function as well as its capabilities. Coremetrics helped us increase annualized revenues by $2.2 million."

Learn how different segments behave on your site. Do they view different pages or products? Do they convert at different rates? Do they use different site functionalities? Are the order values different? These are just some of the questions you should be asking.

A/B Testing

Most people end up conducting A/B testing for a simple comparison between two related groups or segments. Instead, they should focus on a true experiment with a hypothesis and evaluation criteria defined before tests are run.

Mayer Gniwisch, vice president of Ice.com said, "Visual Sciences allows us not only to segment a portion of our traffic that will be tested but it also give us the insights to set up proper experimental design and the analysis tools to tell how long the test must run to show statistical validity."

The tool should allow you to measure actions (conversions) to visitors and calculate based on profits that require the integration of costs, returns, cancellations, discounts, and actual shipping costs.

Keep in mind a few important considerations when considering any of these reports. Accurate tracking of individual users is critical. If IP addresses were used to track individual users instead of unique cookie values, orders might be over-allocated to just a handful of users coming in from large ISP proxy servers. Also, as in our case, the longer the overall lifetime of the product, the more important it is to have a significant amount of historical data to include in reports.

The right reports are critical to achieving a high return on investment from your store. Are you getting them?

Conversion Tip

The Explosive Power of Look-to-Book Metric

If you are selling products online, then get to know the "look-to-book metric". This metric is incredibly powerful and tremendously under-used (or not measured at all).

"Look-to-book" or "browse-to-buy" is the measurement of how many visitors are browsing a product versus buying it. This is also sometimes referred to as a product's "conversion ratio". For example, if 100 people browse a product and only 1 of them buys it, then the conversion ratio is 1% and the look-to-book ratio is 100:1.

Why is this important? Well, can you think of another channel besides the online channel where you can exactly measure how many people look at an item versus buy it? You can't do this with catalogs. You can't do this in stores (well, you can, but not for every product you sell and not without looking like a detective to your customers). But online you can have near-perfect information about this valuable behavior on a 24x7 basis.

How do you use this metric? One Coremetrics' client, a multi-billion dollar specialty retailer, looked at their Coremetrics merchandising report and sorted their top 100 products in descending order by the "product views / items sold" metric (i.e. "look-to-book"). They then did extensive research to find out why so many customers were viewing these products and so few were buying them. What they eventually found out was that they were being dramatically under-priced by their competitors online. They then executed a series of tests, reducing the price until they maximized their gross margin contribution (i.e. the typical business school analysis executed in "real-time" with a real, unbiased "focus group" of customers). Their results? They increased the gross margin contribution of those top 100 products by 90%. A 90% gross margin dollar increase driven directly to their bottom line results! This could easily be a Wharton or Harvard Business School case study.

In short, their results were phenomenal and they used this same methodology on their next 100 products, and the next, until they had significantly increased online profits and customer satisfaction. It also resulted in a promotion for the employee that drove these results at this retailer.

- **Brett Hurt**, founder of Coremetrics

"I once used the word OBSOLETE in a headline, only to discover that 43 percent of the people had no idea what it meant. In another headline, I used the word INEFFABLE, only to discover that I didn't know what it meant myself." - David Ogilvy

An In-Depth Look at Conversion Rates

In the previous section, we went back to basics to understand how the key business metrics fit together. Central to that discussion was the idea that we start by understanding business objectives. It follows, then that website objectives should, in some way, support the business objectives.

So, what are the website objectives? The responses we hear are many and varied. Some say "to sell stuff." Others might say "to drive leads, offer self-service, or offer information." Responses used to favor selling stuff, but lately driving leads has reached parity. There are also a few self-service and media companies around. Each has unique key performance indicators (KPIs), but they all have one thing in common ? Conversion Rates (CR) ? which we previously indicated to be our foundation metric.

Conversion Rate: The Most Important Metric?

Some would argue conversion rate should not be the main measure. To a point, we agree. It's only one of many metrics we focus on with clients. Nevertheless, we believe it deserves special consideration.

As we make our case, please understand that we recognize the limitations of CR as well as its strengths. Conversion rate is like taking your temperature when you're sick. It won't tell you what's wrong. It only indicates whether you're too hot or cold, based on a standard. And yet, like temperature, it lets you know whether action is required or not.

Conversion rates are calculated by dividing the number of website visitors who took the action you wanted, by the total number of visitors. Therefore, conversion rate is a measure of your ability to persuade visitors to take the action you want them to take. It's both a reflection of your effectiveness and customer satisfaction with what you've presented. For you to achieve your goals, visitors must first achieve theirs. When you take actions (reflected in the website) that your visitors appreciate, they express their appreciation by taking the actions you desire them to take.

The "Macro" and "Micro" Elements of Conversion

Prospects that come to your website may not be ready to buy now. They may be only searching for the right place to buy, and return later to complete the purchase. When they're ready, they'll buy.

Sometimes we get so focused on the end point (the sale), though, we forget there was a journey to achieve that end point. You see, not all your visitors know exactly what they want when they land on your website. On top of that, they are each in different stages of the buying process. They might not be ready to take that macro action right off the bat.

In fact, to complete a macro action (the Big Picture Conversion), your visitors take any number of steps. "Micro" actions. And every one of those is a conversion tool.

When you don't appropriately track those visitors (more on this later), it may mean you've converted customers your metrics consider lost.

Let's focus on an example which clearly illustrates the whole "micro/macro" construct. To do so, we're going to take you to our own FutureNow website:

- Step 1: You land on our home page, read all that text and are persuaded to click through on the "Conversion Assessment System" hyperlink (a measurable conversion point in the process, but not the goal).
- Step 2: You land on a page that gives an overview of the value and nature of an assessment. If you can't be bothered with the text, you are offered the option of going directly to the assessment information via the top navigation; you can select from itemized options in a bulleted list. After reviewing the options, you decide you want to convert more eCommerce traffic, so you click that hyperlink.
- Step 3: You land on a page that gives you a detailed description of what goes into an assessment. If you scroll down, you'll find a request form and the telephone number. However, and this is the most important point, the goal is not achieved until you have clicked "Contact Us" to submit the form.

One macro-action conversion is preceded by three micro-action conversions. And at each point of conversion, our visitors must be persuaded to take the next action. They're like the point of the spiral that starts the Yellow Brick Road.

Are you tracking and measuring these different points of conversion? They all matter. When you think of each step on your navigation paths as a conversion point you can test, measure and optimize, you will truly know if you are converting your visitors successfully through each stage of their journey.

Understanding and Anticipating Customer Behavior Can Dramatically Influence CR

Now that you know that you have to encourage the visitor at each step on the way to conversion, you may be asking "How do I do that?" You can influence prospects' need to buy from you by understanding their behavior. These behaviors can be traced to patterns or groups of patterns all customers perceive as their "experience." Understanding the experience is used to predict customer behavior and is key to developing actionable Web metrics. If you predict customer behavior using metrics, you can anticipate their next move — and beat them to it.

To better understand the importance of understanding and anticipation, let's journey to the bricks-and-mortar world for a short case study. First, let's focus on the nearly defunct Kmart. It doesn't correctly anticipate customer needs. It buys a new style of shirt and stocks it in pink, yellow, green, and blue. Blue sells out immediately. The merchant is left with inventory of three other colors. Kmart doesn't reorder the blue ones as 75 percent of its inventory remains unsold. It's still got plenty of that style of shirt to sell!

Wal-Mart, on the other hand, would order a new shipment of blue shirts. Its model takes the customer into account, not the inventory. The merchant understands it's the color customers want, not the style (in this case, anyway). Wal-Mart currently implements RFID (radio frequency identification) to better understand what customers want from it. It's successful because it tracks, analyzes, and reacts to what customers want.

Listen, They're Telling You How to Increase Conversion

Customers tell you something each time they take an action on your website. If you don't develop expectations of what actions visitors should take, you can't optimize your website properly. Develop persuasion scenarios that allow you to pinpoint and optimize based on your assumptions. If visitors aren't doing what you thought they would, find out why. Analyze where the pitfalls are, then develop new scenarios.

Unlike manufacturing or retail, the Web doesn't have tangible deficiencies or expectations. You must develop hypothetical borders or limits to test within. Creating scenarios helps our clients see where they misunderstood the needs and motivations of website visitors.

As far as we know, it's the only way you can judge what actions visitors really want to take and enable these in a Persuasion Architecture process. Most websites ignore their analytics and simply hope visitors will buy. The leaders in the field extract actionable analytics from inferred intent, not from comparing visitor behavior to persuasion scenarios.

Use analytics to tell you what your customers are looking for. Did they get what they were after? Most understand the macro level (buy the product/service) but don't see the minutiae.

Web Analytics Measure Behavior

Conversion starts with a single click, even before a visitor lands on your website. If she gets what she wants, she'll click again. With each click, she's more convinced you have what she wants. Implement the conversation she expects, and she'll be delighted. She wants to buy from you. All she needs is confidence. Jim Novo explains:

The customer raises [their] hand, the marketer Reacts. The customer provides Feedback through Action — perhaps they cancel service, or perhaps they add service. The marketer reacts to this Action, perhaps with a win-back campaign, or with a thank you note. It's a constant (and mostly non-verbal) conversation, an ongoing relationship with the customer which requires interaction to sustain. It is not a relationship in the "buddy-buddy" sense. Customers don't want to be friends with a company, they want the company to be responsive to their needs ? even if they never come out and state them openly to the company.

Your responsibility to visitors is to figure out what they will ask and where they'll ask it. Then, track the correct data. Use it to optimize your website based on what visitors want.

Be Proactive to Boost Conversion (and ROI)

When you encourage a customer to buy something, you want specific behaviors to occur. You can never change customer behavior, but you can predict and accelerate it. That's where you can increase your return on investment (ROI).

When you can predict a visitor's likelihood to take specific actions and accurately encourage specific behaviors, you can reverse drop-off before it happens. All you need to do is develop persuasion scenarios, develop models for predicting consumer behavior, and focus on increasing conversion.

Do You Know Your Conversion Rate?

If, by now, you've accepted our premise that conversion is important, you may be ready for the numbers, in this case the conversion rate (CCR). How many people know what their conversion rate is? According to a study from the eTailing Group, 58 percent of retailers rank conversion rate as being of prime importance for understanding how well a website performs. But 19 percent of respondents don't know their own conversion rate. What we find most troubling is that people running lead-generation or self-service websites are even less aware of their conversion rate than average. At least retailers are accustomed to tracking these numbers.

When we ask our clients and colleagues "What's your conversion rate?" we not only get a few dull stares, but some challenging questions in return. "What's an average conversion rate?" "How do I know if I'm doing well enough?" The way we address their questions is typically by asking another question in return (Don't you hate that?), specifically "What's your industry vertical?"

Average Conversion Rates by Industry Vertical

The only way to get accurate data about average conversion rates is to have access to Web analytics. Many self-reported industry surveys seem suspect. It's not that they're too high. We're suspicious because in our experience, most companies aren't measuring correctly, many don't have their analytics set up properly, and reporting isn't standardized.

Below, the latest conversion rates from the Fireclick Index (made available to its clients). They're aggregated from Fireclick's actual Web analytics retail customers, spanning December 1, 2003 to March 1, 2004:

Vertical	Conversion Rate (%)
Catalog	6.1
Specialty Stores	3.9
Fashion/Apparel	2.2
Travel	2.1
Home and Furnishing	2.0
Sport/Outdoors	1.4
Electronics	1.1
All Verticals	2.3

The data confirms what we've long believed — catalogers do it best. Knowing how to sell something in an intangible environment is half the battle. Sadly, many sit smugly at the top of this chart and fail to exploit all the advantages the new medium offers. They just apply the same direct marketing principles they learned offline. Traditionally, catalogers are constrained by space and mailing costs. Neither issue is the same in the online environment. Yet we can learn from what catalogers do right.

As an example, many retailers measure shopping cart abandonment. Learning from analogy, lead-generation sites should measure form abandonment. But the news from the retail front is not all good. The E-tailing group's survey reports 47 percent of retailers don't know their shopping cart abandonment rate. Fireclick's data shows an average 70 percent shopping cart abandonment rate. There are so many ways to improve shopping cart abandonment that we will discuss later.

Segmenting Your Conversion Rate

The most interesting data usually shows up when you start segmenting conversion rates. If you work with us, we'll want to know things like conversion rate of new visitors versus that of repeat visitors and conversion rates of visitors who use your internal search engine versus that of visitors who browse.

We've found significant differences in conversion rates by search engine. Last year, in a report titled "What Converts Search Engine Traffic" (for WebSideStory's StatMarket), we found AOL (3.49 percent) and MSN (2.35 percent) to be the top major search engines for overall conversion rates. When we looked at this report segmented by electronics retailers, we found CNET (1.64 percent) and AOL (1.28 percent) to be the top engines. In fashion, AOL (1.87 percent) and Google (1.68 percent) were the leaders.

Unfortunately, the same type of data isn't readily available for lead-generation and self-service websites. We suspect these numbers would be all over the place, based on type of lead, cost of product or service sold, and marketing efforts. When you sell "stuff" online, it's much easier to compare apples to apples. It's not the same when dealing with lead-generation or self-service. But, you have to start somewhere.

Conversion Tip

Track the Conversions that Happen Offline

Just because they aren't converting online doesn't mean the site is ineffective. It is important to look just as closely at offline conversions as we do those that happen online. To do this, employ multiple 800 numbers. Specifically:

- Have a single 800# that is only on the web site, then track inbound calls for quantity, closing rate and closing value.
- Assign different 800# to different parts of the site based on product groups or level of exploration (unique number only on the shopping cart page).
- Assign a different 800# for each different campaign to measure effectiveness.

- **Jason Burby**, Director of Analytics at Zaaz

". . . when the band spread out the tracking was much harder. . ." – Theodore Roosevelt, Hunting Trips of a Ranchman IX

The Ideal Tracking System

So far, we've spoken about conversion rates, how to determine good performance from bad, and how conversion supports a hierarchy of metrics that goes all the way to the top of the chain – financial performance of the enterprise. Now we'll turn to the actions that allow you to influence conversion, first of which is active tracking and evaluation.

Think of conversion as a system with many components, directed by those responsible for its performance like a musical score. An effective conversion system successfully addresses all the complex requirements of a user when he or she is interacting with your website and undertakes a decision to act. What you must decide is how to orchestrate the three critical components that make up the conversion system: WIIFM (what's in it for me?), AIDAS (attention, interest, desire, action, and satisfaction), and the five-step professional sales process. If these core components do not work in concert, your website won't achieve anywhere near its full conversion potential. That is what we do in Persuasion Architecture.

If we think of conversion as a comprehensive system that carries a visitor from start to finish, from landing (the driving point) to close (the conversion point), we can start asking questions about how we evaluate that system. How do we know that we have each instrument tuned to perfection? How do we know that we've established the correct rhythm? How do we know that our melody and its thematic variations are presented to best advantage?

The answer is tracking what you planned in your persuasion Aachitecture. And not just end-result tracking, or bail-out tracking, but a more comprehensive system of tracking that allows you to know all the what's, all the where's, and all the why's — everything you want to know when it comes to fine-tuning the musical score of your website. Only this level of fine-tuning will ensure that your conversion rates are the best they can be.

Following the Visitor

Your visitor brings to your website a personality, character traits, temperament traits, and an entire psychographic profile, as well as the ephemeral "mood of the moment." Assume that marketing has done its job well and delivered a qualified visitor; your website still has to present the composition your visitors want to hear, a composition that may have little to do with what you've been practicing and intending to play. Only your visitors can let you know if you are in tune with them. Since they aren't going to call you up to let you know why they did what they did, the only way you can figure it out is to follow their every move and make inferences.

The principal difficulty in evaluating the conversion process is that most websites focus on measuring the end result — the customer conversion rate — without tracking the click-through path taken by individual users on the way to that result. The length of the path taken by visitors is a key variable. Generally the fewer steps required in the conversion process, the easier visitors are to track. Also, the fewer the steps, the greater the likelihood is of a sale. To be most effective, a website will employ the fewest number of pages necessary between the driving point where the user arrives and the conversion point where the sale is closed.

Once a user arrives on a website, the conversion process becomes a conversion funnel, but it's a funnel with holes. At each step of the conversion process, the website is going to lose some percentage of its visitors. It's the leaky-bucket metaphor, where traffic fills your bucket like water, then leaks out of the holes. You want to plug as many of the holes as possible. If you make the effort to track the actual paths of users through your website, you stand a much better chance of figuring out how to plug those holes.

You need a tracking system that allows you to determine the location and information being viewed by visitors at any point in the process, as well as the point where each leaves the process. A system of this nature maps the decision-making process, providing a decision-tree record of each visit that can open insights into why your visitors stay or leave. To have the greatest degree of control over the conversion process, your website must employ such a method for tracking each user's path through the website — to locate those internal factors that are impairing conversion, to assess them, and to suggest remedies that can boost your end result.

In short, a good tracking system helps you answer questions that make a difference. To illustrate the types of questions that you might be trying to answer with your tracking system, consider the following:

- What percentage of your visitors fit each different personality profile?
- Does your home page meet the needs of each personality profile and offer each an entry into your conversion process?
- Why do methodical visitors bail out by the third page, but assertive visitors generally remain long enough to take action?
- Do certain features of your website appeal to all visitors?
- Where and why does any given visitor bail out?

If you construct your website with Persuasion Architecture it will reflect an understanding of consumer psychology, and if you have a comprehensive tracking system in place, you'll be able to infer useful answers to these questions — and many more. You'll be able to make efficient use of your resources as you work at reducing the leaks in your bucket. And you'll find yourself with much higher conversion rates.

"The wish to acquire more is admittedly a very natural and common thing; and when men succeed in this they are always praised rather than condemned." - Niccolò Machiavelli, The Prince

Measuring Your Sales Success

Now that we've covered strategic metrics, the complex topic of conversion, and provided some guidance on tracking systems, let's turn our attention to metrics at the tactical level. A great place to start is your home page, where you want to effectively engage visitors and help them move along the path to a purchase. The obvious question now is, "How can I tell if my home page is effective?"

Watching Your Web Trends

We recently spoke with a client who was concerned with the low conversion rate of the company website ? well under one percent. However, this particular client spent no money to drive visitors to the website; visitors come to the website from the marketing overflow of the company's other distribution channels. And, in spite of the low conversion rate, the client was doing several million dollars' worth of sales in high-ticket, high-margin consumer goods. What we were confronting was a website with lots of potential for improvement.

To get a snapshot of what was going on with their online business, we asked them to run some website reports based on their server logs, even before we spent any time looking at their website. Those logs ? and yours, along with some of your other management reports ? contain a gold mine of information, if you know how to look for and analyze the right data relationships.

That's the focus of this particular section – learning what to look for. We'll do so using a baseball analogy, allowing you to round the bases, and make it home. To help you, we'll introduce two new tactical metrics along the way – Site Penetration Ratio (SPR) and Clicks to Buy (CTB). There are more, but these will serve our purposes for now.

Getting Hits, Making It to First Base

The simplest measure of the effectiveness of your home page is your website penetration ratio (SPR). It comes as a surprise to many e-commerce website owners that most visitors to most websites never get past the home page. You spend lots of marketing dollars driving traffic to your website, yet visitors leave immediately. In fact most may leave even before the page is done downloading.

Monitoring your SPR is essential to understanding the effectiveness of your home page. To calculate your SPR, all you need to do is divide the number of unique visitors who click to any interior page by the total number of unique "hits" to your home page.

Let's return to the client we introduced above, the one with the one percent conversion rate. What we found when we looked at the client's numbers was that almost 40 percent of visitors never got past the home page. Here's a little clue: The client's got a big home page problem!

Running Around the Bases, Chasing the CR

Paco Underhill, a leading expert in consumer shopping behavior, has a wonderful quote we like to use: "Conversion rate is to retail what batting average is to baseball." Shop.org reports that the average order conversion rate for its members (many of the very top e-tailers) is 1.8 percent. Imagine, fewer than 2 people out of every 100 who visit Shop.org's Web sites actually make a purchase. Should we stop at first base, and say, "This is far enough."?

Consider Ted Williams. He became a legend for hitting above .400. That's over 40 hits for every 100 times at bat. And that's the type of number you would see in an effective brick-and-mortar store (about 48 percent, according to Underhill). Hmmm, imagine that...

A conversion rate of less than 2 percent is akin to that of the direct response business – in which the seller pushes out solicitation letters, postcards, or catalogs, and then hopes you buy on your own initiative. What's scary is that if the average is under 2 percent; just imagine how bad some of the websites out there are doing.

So here's a question for you: Are you pushing your website on people, or are they seeking it out? Is your website nothing more than a direct response vehicle, or is it an interactive sales machine? If you could find a way to increase your conversion rate from 2 percent to just 4 percent (some of our clients reach CRs of 5-10 percent), you could double your sales without having to spend an extra penny on marketing.

But, does a relatively high CR mean there's no room for improvement? If you're getting very highly targeted traffic or your competition is negligible, your CR could be much higher than 2 percent, yet still be a tiny fraction of what you could be — no, should be — getting if your website were designed right.

Crossing Home Plate

Many e-tailers really take this baseball analogy to heart. However, when you take a close look at their websites, you realize they're confused. They have mixed up the teams in their heads.

What do I mean by that? The way their websites are designed suggests that they see themselves as the home team and their prospects as the "visitors." While "visitor" is the technically correct term for someone who comes to your website, they are not an adversary, as the baseball analogy would have us believe. As a merchant, you want to make sure that your visitors feel like a part of your team. And that it's you want to do what it takes to help them score.

Score what? Score whatever they came to your website to find. In other words, make it really simple for them to get to your website, find what they want, give you cash, and leave. Now, that's a home run for all involved.

Keep Score...

A simple measure that lets you know if you are helping your new teammates score is clicks to buy (CTB). CTB measures the average number of clicks it takes visitors to go from your home page to the completion of their purchase. Generally the fewer clicks the better.

Smart retailers have learned this lesson well. Why do you think Amazon.com fought so hard to protect its 1-Click Checkout patent? It realizes that one of the main causes of incomplete purchases and abandoned shopping carts is the long and tedious checkout process many e-tailers inflict on potential customers.

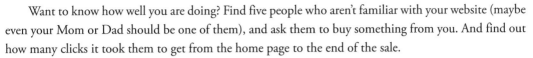

Want to know how well you are doing? Find five people who aren't familiar with your website (maybe even your Mom or Dad should be one of them), and ask them to buy something from you. And find out how many clicks it took them to get from the home page to the end of the sale.

Remember those commercials of yesteryear, "How many licks does it take to get to the Tootsie Roll center of a Tootsie Pop"? A lot of licks was a good thing. Now is the time to unlearn that lesson. Too many clicks may account for lots of lost sales. Know your CTB, and find ways to keep it at a minimum.

. . . And Keep on Scoring

Those are just a few of the ways you can keep an accurate score of what is really going on in your online business. Have fun proving to yourself how, as a coach with a new game plan, you can help customers score more runs, while you score big all the way to the bank.

"I hesitated long before I put this theory to the test of practice." – Robert Louis Stevenson, The Strange Case of Dr. Jekyll and Mr. Hyde

Making the Dial Move by Testing

A friend of ours has taken up hiking, and, being a shoe kind of gal, she has taken an intense interest in hiking boots. She's the first one who will tell you, "They may be a dream on the shelf, but you really have no idea how they're going to work for you until you start trail testing them."

You could say the same thing about e-business. When you start doing business online, you enter the realm of "trail testing." And here is where you discover that the practical work of managing any online enterprise has just begun. Because no matter how thoroughly you think you've covered your bases in the development phases of your website or your email campaigns, you are about to discover countless opportunities for improvement.

By demonstrating a willingness to subject your most cherished and long-held beliefs (not to mention your writing and sense of style) to the dispassionate and unforgiving glare of public scrutiny, you truly "get" accountability. It's time to test.

Almost everyone buys into the theoretical value of testing. Few would argue with Claude Hopkins, author of "Scientific Advertising" (1923), who wrote, "Almost any question can be answered cheaply, quickly and finally, by a test campaign. And that's the way to answer them — not by arguments around a table. Go to the court of last resort — buyers of your products."

Hopkins couldn't market on the Internet, but you certainly can — and should. We work in a medium where testing really is king. It's incredibly easy and can yield powerful results. Online, marketers may be in the driver's seat, but consumers are doing all the steering.

The Basics of Testing

How do you take that first step in monitoring your performance based on all the little tweaks and fidgets you think will help? Maximizing your conversion rate is not simply a matter of making changes, it's about making:

a) The right changes,
b) At the right time,
c) In the right sequence, and then
d) Evaluating the results before continuing the process.

If you are not methodical in your approach to change, much of your effort will be wasted. This is one of those points in the process where you "go slow to go fast." So take your time, and keep these guidelines in mind as you test:

- Always be clear about what you are testing and how you are going to measure and interpret the results before you begin. You cannot measure success unless you know exactly what you are measuring (and naturally I hope you have a clear idea of what constitutes success).
- Make sure your test groups are of similar size.
- After the first test, always test against a control. The first time out, you are testing two unknowns, and you won't be able to determine the better option until the results are in. Once they are in, then you have a benchmark, or control, against which you can measure subsequent changes.
- Remember you can accurately test only one element at a time. Even if they all seem necessary, changes need to be made individually so you can track effectively the result of the change. While you might institute several changes and see an improvement, it could be a "net" improvement — that is, a 5% improvement could be the result of change #1 helping 10% while change #2 actually hurt by 5%. If you make one change at a time and then discover it doesn't help, it's easier to back up and try something else.
- If you are testing emails, send your test emails simultaneously to eliminate the timing variable. Ideally, at the same time, you want to test your website as well. Software platforms like Optimost and Inceptor can help with this.

Introducing A/B Testing

A/B testing — sometimes it's called an A/B split — is the simplest and easiest method of testing elements in your emails or on your website. You divide your audience into two groups. You expose one group to the original version of whatever you are testing. You expose the other group to an alternative version, in which only one element has been changed. Then you track the results.

For example, suppose you want to figure out the best subject line for your promotional email. Prepare two separate emails, identical except for the subject line. The email with the first subject line goes to half your list, while the email with the second subject line goes to the other half.

To gauge the effectiveness of your subject line, compare the open rates between the two groups. Once you find your winner, it becomes your control or benchmark. Test it against another subject line, and so on, until you are convinced you've found the best possible subject line for your messages. And the results may surprise you. In one of our testing scenarios, one subject line generated an open rate 300% higher than its closest competitor. A difference like that can have a tremendous impact on your bottom line!

For those who learn best from analogy, think of A/B testing as being like an eye exam. The ophthalmologist puts you in a darkened room, asks you to stare into the eyeholes of an evil-looking machine and then asks, "Which picture is sharper and easier to read, A or B?" When you indicate your choice, he makes a small change and again asks, "A or B?" Each time, he makes another small adjustment, always taking the better result. This continues until you can see clearly through the machine.

The problem with the eye test analogy is a doctor has population studies that establish the test's controls. The eye chart scales and the machines he uses are carefully calibrated to ensure accurate, predictable, replicable results. We have to make do with much less certainty. However, the results we can get are impressive.

One of our favorite test examples is one Amazon.com conducted well over a year ago. Below is the "ready to buy" area on its pages.

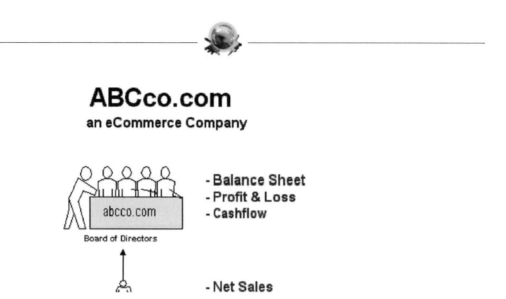

ABCco.com
an eCommerce Company

- Balance Sheet
- Profit & Loss
- Cashflow

Board of Directors

- Net Sales

The original website always used version A. The book section of the website removed the phrases in parentheses and removed some words from the buttons (version B). I'm not privy to the objectives behind the test, and I always recommend adding assurances at the point of action (POA), but for a long time you could still find versions of button A on other areas of Amazon's site.

Here's another example. ICE.com conducted a test using a Visual Sciences tool. It wanted to increase sales of featured products listed on its home page. It decided to test the copy beneath the featured product and measure the effect. It tested three variations against the control (no copy). The four variations:

A.	B.	C.	D.
14k Yellow Gold Multigemstone Bracelet	14k Yellow Gold Multigemstone Bracelet	14k Yellow Gold Multigemstone Bracelet	14k Yellow Gold Multigemstone Bracelet
$195.00	$195.00	$195.00	$195.00
5 payments of $39.00	5 payments of $39.00	5 payments of $39.00	5 payments of $39.00
	BUY NOW	VIEW PRODUCT	ORDER NOW

Which do you think outperformed the others? As is often the case in A/B testing, we fall in love with one idea and will it to be the winner. A/B testing provides real-world, data-driven, unbiased answers to a hypothesis. Early indications showed version D to be the hands-down winner. It resulted in thousands of dollars of increased spending.

Some Helpful Cautions and Guidelines for Successful Testing

You now see the value of testing, and have decided to put what you've learned into action. But you still have some concerns. How can you tell (and convince others) that your test results are valid? When you run any kind of test, beware the "fresh" factors: seasonality, even time of day. You must run tests concurrently, ideally for a couple of weeks. Be certain your sample size is adequate and results variation between tests is statistically meaningful.

Mike Sack, Executive VP of Inceptor, offers some tips on splitting traffic, stability and timing:

First step is to decide in what proportion you are going to split your traffic, 50/50, 90/10, or even 80/20. And you can split them randomly, by time of day or even by source (Google people to A and Yahoo! to B). Second, you must decide on test stability; in other words, if a visitor leaves your site and comes back, do they see the same test? You can choose for no stability, session stability, and cookie stability. At a minimum, you should have session stability, even though cookie stability is better for tracking latent conversions.

And here are our thoughts on sample size and criteria:

To decide your ultimate sample size, run a "null" test with your A/B test. The null test is really just an A/A test, where you are running the control against itself to determine where the convergence of results matches up (typically within 0.05 percent of each other, but that's up to you). When the tests converge, you'll have an idea of the volume of traffic you need to test.

You decide your criteria for success based on a certain number of conversions or sales, or you can measure results over course of time (e.g. two weeks). To know whether your test is showing a statistically meaningful impact on the variables, you have to know if you've demonstrated enough of a difference (delta) between the tests to declare a clear winner. As a rule of thumb, one result should be at least 3X the other (e.g., if A is 5, B should be 15).

A/B testing is powerful and there are all kinds of ways to do it:

- Use inexpensive scripts;
- Rout traffic to different servers;
- Use software and services that set up A/B testing services, such as Inceptor, Optimost, OfferMatica, and Visual Sciences.

You may wield the power to test thousands of variables, but remember only a few have significant effect on return on investment (ROI). Although tools make it simple to test, they don't provide the knowledge, hard work, and resources it takes to build successful tests. That part's up to you.

What should you be testing? It's easier to make a list of what you don't need to worry about, because that would be a blank sheet of paper. But here are some possibilities of elements that merit testing. This should get you started:

- Emails: bonus gifts, coupons, P.S. messages, guarantees, opening sentence image, closing sentence image, from-field, calls to action, opening greetings, type styles, layout elements, graphic images, etc.
- Websites: landing pages, language of copy (headings, body, calls to action, assurances), colors, location of elements, look/feel, hyperlinks, etc.

A/B testing is far from rocket science (and there are other more complicated and robust ways to test), but it has a sweet advantage: it isn't complicated. More importantly, it means you won't have to make potentially expensive decisions based on your gut reaction. You'll know, because you can say, "Here, look at the numbers!"

Conversion Tip

Do A/B Split-Testing on Your Ads and Landing Pages

Once you've set up a landing page – a specialized page designed to induce the shopper who responds to an ad to make the purchase — it's important to fine-tune it using A/B split-testing.

A/B split-testing is an approach that creates two (or more) pages that contain a single difference only. Then you randomly send one shopper to Landing Page A and the next to Landing Page B, and so on, comparing the sales conversion rate of page A to page B. (It isn't nearly as accurate to send the shoppers for two days to page A and the next two days to page B, since other factors can make a difference in the sales conversion rate.)

Over time, you'll notice differences between the sales conversion rates of page A over page B that can be scientifically attributable to the single difference between the pages. It's important to get enough data so that your results are statistically significant; if you stop testing too early, you are extremely likely to come to incorrect conclusions.

Two split-testing software programs stand out. For larger companies, Offermatica offers an excellent product that allows the merchant to insert small variable content sectors (called an mBox) into existing webpages. For smaller companies, Vertster allows merchants to redirect shoppers to two or more versions of the landing page undergoing testing.

Continual, unremitting testing is what is gradually separating the top online merchants' conversion rates from conversion rates of those who are trying to improve their sites and sales processes from seat-of-the-pants guessing. The lesson here is — test everything!

- **Dr. Ralph Wilson**, Wilson Internet Services

The Future Now, Inc. Conversion Rate Marketing Glossary

A/B Split

When the email list is divided into two segments (or two different versions of a web page are created), each of which is tested for different offers or the effect of changes in elements.

Above-the-Fold

The top portion of an email or web page that is visible without scrolling.

Acquisition versus Retention

The presentation and content of an email marketing message or campaign often depends on whether the objective is to acquire new customers or encourage loyalty and repeat purchases from existing customers. Acquisition efforts are more likely to focus on encouraging action, retention efforts on building relationships.

Active Voice

Active voice emphasizes the subject, the agent of the action; passive voice shifts the focus to what is happening. "Birds build nests" is written in the active voice and emphasizes the subject — birds. "Nests are built by birds" is written in the passive voice and emphasizes the action — building nests. Active voice uses strong verbs and involves the reader in the action, thus active voice is far more persuasive in driving action. "When you click the button, your order is immediately generated" is stronger than "Once the button has been clicked, the order is immediately generated."

Active Window

The central portion of computer screen real estate "above the fold" which constitutes the area your visitors are most inclined to focus on. It is the area in which you want to keep the visitor actively engaged in the conversion process at all times.

After Sales

No less a part of the professional selling process than closing the sale, everything that occurs after the "buyer" has taken action must not merely satisfy, but delight. This includes confirmation of the action taken, appropriate follow-up through exceptional fulfillment and opportunities for your customer to offer feedback and participate in viral marketing. The after sales experience of delight can be severely compromised if you fail to honor your promises, particularly those relating to guarantees and privacy.

AIDAS

"Attention, Interest, Desire, Action, Satisfaction" — elements of the conversion message that establish and sustain the prospect's persuasive momentum from initial contact up to and beyond the "close."

ALIGNMENT

Alignment is an organizational layout feature of the elements included on a Web page. Alignment allows a visitor to group and categorize different aspects of information. It also helps to define the coherence of each category of information. Alignment can be flush left, flush right, right/left justified, or centered. Indentations of topical information that echo the overall alignment scheme can help further subdivide information. Attention to alignment can dramatically improve the readability of a Web page.

AVERAGE ORDER SIZE (AOS)

Whether you're operating an e-commerce website or running an email campaign, it's important to persuade more of your audience to take action. But it also makes sense to persuade your customers to buy more of your product or service each time they do buy. As you refine your website or emails so they persuade and convert better, not only will your Customer Conversion Rate increase, but so will your Average Order Size, which will make each order more profitable.

AVERAGE VISIT LENGTH (AVL)

Why is Average Visit Length important? Simple: the longer people stay the more likely they are to buy. But be careful: despite what some developers would have you believe, extensive research proves that the people who are your best prospects are not looking for "entertainment." Nor are they looking for chat or any other gimmicks. In fact, they hate gimmicks. They came to buy. Isn't that what you want them to do? Then make it simple, comfortable, and fast. You build real stickiness by creating content that has value to your customers. If you try to build it artificially, by tacking on multimedia or other gadgets, the immediate impact is that you will slow the download (67% of shoppers aren't even at 56K and only 7% have broadband), and the next impact is that instead of drawing shoppers in, you will actually drive them away.

This is another extremely easy metric to determine. You should be able to get the data right from your logs or from any program that helps you analyze your logs.

BENEFITS VERSUS FEATURES

Benefits address a prospect's emotional needs and communicate how the product or service will improve his/her quality of life or make him/her feel better. Features address the attributes of the product or service. Benefits are more effective in driving action.

BLOCKING

E-mails that are blocked are not processed through the ISP and are essentially prevented from reaching their addressed destination.

BLOG

Originally, a blog – shortened from "weblog" – was an online journal charting the personal meanderings of an individual. As an opportunity to provide rich, hyperlinked, dynamic content, it is increasingly employed as an online marketing tool.

BROCHUREWARE

A website that is essentially nothing more than a form of advertising, providing information but failing to actively motivate its visitors through the decision to buy. Any conversion effort that does not capture, engage and motivate its visitors can, at best, only hope those visitors will choose to take action.

BROWSER COMPATIBILITY

The degree to which all displays and functions of the website work correctly in both past and present versions of principal browsers (Internet Explorer, Netscape, AOL, etc.)

BUYER

A lead currently in negotiation who has made a commitment in principle to buy, but has not yet purchased the product or service.

BUYING PROCESS

The buying process is the information gathering process the buyer goes through before they are ready to take an action.   Key factors for determining a persona's buying process include: motivation, fears/objections,   questions and information sought and stage of the buying process: Early – gathering information, Middle – comparing options, or Late- ready to buy.

CALLS TO ACTION

(see also Point of Action — POA)

Words that offer the opportunity for and encourage the prospect to take action. For example, "See CM3's new designer colors" or "Add this product to your wish list." Calls to action are motivations for the visitor to move further into the sales process.

CAMPAIGN

A coordinated set of individual messages delivered at intervals and with an overall objective in mind. A campaign allows each new message to build on previous success.

CELL TESTING

Most often used when a list is divided into a number of discrete cells to allow for a robust test across multiple variables. To determine optimum response, conversion rate is measured for each cell.

List Segment	A	B	C	D
Offer Received	Offer 1	Offer 1	Offer 2	Offer 2
Landing Page	LP 1	LP2	LP1	LP2

Clicks To Buy (CTB)

Similar to Clicks To Find (CTF, below), this lets you know how many clicks, on average, are necessary from the time a visitor hits your homepage to the completion of the checkout process. Fewer clicks are better.

You should get the data from your logs of actual customer visits, not from employee or contrived focus group experiments.

Clicks To Find (CTF)

This metric identifies how many clicks, on average, are necessary to get to a specific product or service on your site, with all options specified, ready to be ordered. Fewer clicks are better.

As with CTB, you should get the data from your logs of actual customer visits, not from employee or contrived focus group experiments.

Click-through

When a prospect takes an action and clicks on a link. Also known as CTR.

Closing Sentence

The last sentence of the communication, which must reinforce the desire to take action.

Color

That quality described by the viewer's perception of hue, lightness and saturation. Color can help visually organize elements and hierarchies of information on the website. It can be used symbolically and to reinforce communication of desired moods and meanings. The role of color in Web design is varied, but it should never be the sole feature of any page, nor any design. Successful persuasive Web designs will function when rendered in grey scale.

Color Theory

A body of knowledge concerning the ability of color to help create an appropriate psychological state and present information most effectively, in addition to engaging prospects and directing their progress through the process.

Content

All the copy, graphics and images that go into the presentation. Effective content is engaging, useful, informative, educational, professional and entertaining.

Content Site

One of four ebusiness categories. The basic objective of this category is to increase readership, the level of interest and the amount of time visitors spend on the site.

Contrast

The difference in lightness in the light and dark areas of the page design — the difference between black and white representing the strongest contrast. Contrast dramatically affects readability and the visitor's ability to spot elements critical to the persuasive process. Contrast is also an important consideration when designing so assistive technologies can render Web pages readable to those with impaired vision.

Conversion

1. A process whereby a visitor is converted into a "buyer" (used in the most general sense of someone who takes the desired action).
2. A system (i.e., website) for managing the process of conversion. This system includes not only tactics for persuading the visitor to take action, but also incorporates mechanisms for tracking the flow of traffic through the conversion process, so that areas needing improvement can be easily identified.

Conversion Rate

The key metric to evaluate the effectiveness of a conversion effort, reflecting the percentage of people converted into buyers out of the total population exposed to the conversion effort. For websites, the conversion rate is the number of visitors who took the desired action divided by the total number of visitors in a given time period (typically, per month). For email marketing, the conversion rate is the number of people who take an action divided by the total number of people who received the email. (Multiply these numbers by 100 to express the results as percentages.)

CPA (or Cost per acquisition)

A payment model in which payment is based solely on qualifying actions such as sales or registrations.

CPM (or Cost per thousand)

In e-mail marketing, CPM commonly refers to the cost per 1000 names on a given rental list. For example, a rental list priced at $250 CPM would mean that the list owner charges $.25 per e-mail address.

Cost Per Visitor (CPV)

Divide your marketing expenses (or your marketing expenses plus your web expenses) by the number of unique visitors to your site or recipients of your email. This is a very useful way to measure what your traffic is costing you. It is a simple calculation to get an important number that many companies overlook.

Customer

A person or organization who has paid for your product or service. In broader usage, a customer is one who has indicated an interest in what you offer, by taking an action you have motivated either on your website or via your email (opting-in, registering, subscribing, establishing an account, etc.).

Customer Acquisition Cost (CAC)

To determine your Customer Acquisition Cost, you divide your marketing expenses by the total number of actions taken by unique prospects over a specific time frame, usually monthly. For an e-commerce website, this would be the number of orders you receive from unique new buyers during the month. For an email, it would be the total number of orders, or subscribers, or other "actions" taken by the recipients in response to the email. For an email campaign, it would be the number of results over the life of the campaign.

With regard to the marketing expenses component of the calculation, some e-commerce companies include a monthly amortization of the cost of their website as well as the monthly cost of maintaining the site, while other companies only consider promotional expenses. Use the approach that works best for you. Notice that as you increase your Customer Conversion Rate by "teaching" your website or your emails how to persuade more of your traffic or your recipients to take the action you want, your Customer Acquisition Cost will go down automatically. Naturally, then, your profitability and cash flow improve automatically, too.

CUSTOMER ACQUISITION GAP (CAG)

This number is calculated by subtracting your Customer Acquisition Cost (another way of saying "Cost Per Customer") from your Cost Per Visitor (CPV - CAC). Again a reminder: a "customer" is not necessarily someone who buys a product or service, but rather anyone who takes the action you want them to take in response to your website or your email. The result will be a negative dollar amount, the size of which may surprise you. It is a way of measuring the cost of not getting customers from your traffic. As you work to improve the persuasive ability of your site or emails, your CAG will decrease (become less negative) and you will see the gap starting to shrink.

CUSTOMER ACQUISITION RATIO (CAR)

CAR, like Customer Closing Ratio, is another useful measure of your site's or email's ability to persuade someone to take action. In the case of CAG above, you subtracted Customer Acquisition Cost from Cost Per Visitor. With Customer Acquisition Ratio, you divide your cost per visitor by your cost per customer (CPV/CAC), then multiply by 100 to get a %. The resulting percentage allows you to measure how your persuasion efficiency and your marketing efficiency work together. As you lower your Customer Acquisition Cost, your Customer Acquisition Ratio will increase.

CUSTOMER EXPERIENCE

The customer's (possibly only the prospect's) overall experience of pleasure during the sales encounter.

CUSTOMER RETENTION RATE (CRR)

An essential ingredient of your long-term profitability is the ability of your website or your emails to generate repeat business. In pursuing that goal it is important to realize today's online shoppers, whether B2B or B2C, expect much more than they did even a year ago. To get repeat business you have to do more than satisfy your customers, you have to delight them. If you do, they'll not only come back, they'll recommend your site to colleagues, friends, and family. The result: more sales with zero additional marketing expenses.

To calculate your CRR you determine the total number of repeat customers within a given time frame and divide that by your total number of unique customers.

CUSTOMER SERVICE

Both online and offline, a business must be available to respond to its visitors' concerns, frustrations and questions with service that is not merely satisfying, but delightful. Options include offering a fax number, a toll free number, email contact and online help (FAQ and information boxes). Whenever possible, customer service issues should always be handled in a personalized manner, ideally by a human rather than an autoresponder.

DELIGHT FACTOR

The degree to which the overall experience leaves the customer feeling it is worth repeating and worth telling others about.

DEVELOPMENT

From the moment you decide to create or redesign a website, you are starting to develop something. But as the fifth phase in planning for Persuasion Architecture, development specifically refers to the task of coding the prototype into a fully functional website.

DRIVING POINT

The starting point of a scenario – home page, landing page, etc. where a persona starts their interaction.

ECOMMERCE/RETAIL SITE

One of four ebusiness categories. The basic objective of this category is to increase sales and decrease marketing expenses.

EMAIL HEADERS

The documentation that accompanies the body of an email message. Headers contain information on the email itself and the route it's taken across the Internet. Recipients can normally see the "to" (identity of recipient), "from" (identity of sender) and "subject" (information in the subject line) headers in their inbox. You can modify these to influence their decision to open or delete an email.

ERROR PREVENTION

Exhaustive testing of the site prior to "going public" should determine that the programming is bug-free, the conversion process is designed to help the visitor avoid making errors that encourage the visitor to leave and that any necessary error messages are clear, friendly and do not suggest the visitor is stupid.

EXPECTATION

The ability of the design to employ the basic conventions that online users have come to associate with ebusiness (i.e., hyperlinks are blue and underlined). Limiting though conventions might seem, when an ebusiness provides through its design and layout exactly what the visitor expects, it helps that visitor accomplish her task more efficiently and with much less frustration.

EXPLICIT ACTION

Occurs when a visitor takes a measurable action — clicking on a hyperlink, submitting a form, etc.   (see Implicit Action)

EYE TRACKING

The characteristic path the visitor's eye takes when first arriving on a Web page. Before deciding to fully engage with the information, the visitor starts in the upper left, scans across the top, drops to the central area of the screen, then casts left and right before returning to center. Placing elements with an understanding of what the visitor's eye is looking for improves the readability of a site and encourages the visitor to engage with the information.

First Mental Image

The opening scene in a mental sequence. Must capture attention and engage interest.

Font

A complete set of type of one style and size. For example, all the characters associated with 12 point Arial constitute a font.

Format (Appearance)

Emails currently can be delivered in plain-text format or HTML format. Consider the target audience to determine which is the more appropriate format for any specific campaign.

Frequency

The intervals at which email marketing efforts are repeated: weekly, bi-weekly, monthly, bi-monthly, etc.

From / To / Signature

From: Indicates the sender. People prefer to buy from people, not robots, autoresponders, or even websites. The sender should be a person — not a company or a department within the company.

To: Indicates the receiver. People like to feel emails are addressed to them, rather than posted to "undisclosed recipients" (or somewhere other than to your name or email address), and like to feel they are something more than "valued customers."

Signature: An email signature is the text that you see at the bottom of the body of an email message. It provides another opportunity to create a call to action.

Fulfillment

Everything that makes up timely and delightful delivery of the product or service, including confirmations, packaging and presentation, shipping notification, the ability to track shipments, etc.

Get the Cash (GTC)

The sales axiom that describes the business's goal to move the customer toward a completed transaction. In e-commerce, GTC can refer to a completed purchase (get the cash), a completed action such as subscribing or registering (get the customer) or simply getting the visitor to take the next step in the conversion process (get the click).

Goal (Objective) of Emailing

The coherent, defined purpose, which allows targeting recipients appropriately, creating a unified and effective message and measuring the results. Each email, as well as the overall campaign, should have a clear goal.

Graphic versus Text

Speed of page delivery is critical. Slow-loading graphics will frustrate visitors and persuade them to leave. When images are called for, they must appear as quickly as possible on the computer screen. Using thumbnails to speed delivery can be advantageous; using high quality copy that engages your visitor while they are waiting for images can also make the download time seem faster.

GREYSCALE

The first stage of design is done in black and white. Preliminary storyboards should appear in grayscale, so you can evaluate the composition, layout and scale without the emotional influence of color. You then proceed to a color mockup.

HARD BOUNCE/SOFT BOUNCE

A hard bounce is the failed delivery of an e-mail due to a permanent reason like a non-existent address. A soft bounce is the failed delivery of an e-mail due to a temporary issue, like a full mailbox or an unavailable server.

HEADERS

In body copy, headers and sub headers are important headlines that help visitors scan and skim copy. Headers and sub headers should be keyword rich.

HEADLINE

The opening announcement that greets recipients once they have opened the email. Ideally, this immediately communicates the company's unique selling proposition and encourages the recipient to penetrate further into the email.

HOME PAGE

In theory, the entry portal to your business's website, although very often, visitors arrive on a home page through the back door – by navigating from one of your landing pages that they discovered as the result of a search or surfing links. The home page has three basic responsibilities: to let visitors know they are in the right place; to provide them with your unique value proposition; to qualify their needs and move them quickly and easily into the persuasive process of your site.

HOUSE LIST

A permission-based list that you built yourself. Use it to market, cross sell and up-sell, and to establish a relationship with customers over time. Your house list is one of your most valuable assets.

IMPACT QUOTIENT

An email's ability to persuade people to save it, talk about it, remember it, refer to it and forward it to their sphere of influence.

IMPLICIT ACTION

Something has to happen. For example, if a visitor downloads a whitepaper, the implicit action would be to send a follow up email within a certain amount of time. (see Explicit Action)

INCENTIVE

A reason to take action, which might include discounts, bonuses, free shipping, bundle pricing, etc.

INFORMATION ARCHITECTURE

The layout, organization, labeling, navigation, and searching systems that help people find and manage online information.

INSTILLS TRUST

The ability of the online effort to create trust and confidence in the mind of prospects, which increases their propensity to take action.

INTERVALS

The times between emails in a campaign. They should be optimized for maximum results.

INTUITIVENESS

At the level of details, intuitiveness refers to choices the designer makes in using graphics, symbols and icons, and the ability of the visitor to quickly apprehend their meaning and how to use them. In a broader sense, intuitiveness refers to the general placement and organization of information such that the visitor does not have to work hard to figure out how to use the site. In Web design for ebusiness, the cardinal rule is: Don't make me think!

JARGON

A word or term that is unique to a particular business or area of knowledge and not generally known to the public at large. In most cases, avoid the use of jargon.

KEY PERFORMANCE INDICATOR (KPI)

The critical Web metrics you should be monitoring to evaluate the effectiveness of your site. Key performance indicators differ depending on the business topology (ecommerce/retail, lead-generation, content or self-service/support). The two most important indicators for all ebusiness sites will be conversion rate and page reject/abandonment rates.

KEYWORDS (AND KEY PHRASES)

The words and phrases users type into search engines that shape the nature of their queries. Keywords are critical elements that must be included "behind the scenes" to help search engine spiders that crawl your site and in the body of your copy. Keyword research and planning is essential to search engine optimization.

KISS

"Keep it Simple, Stupid" — a directive to keep the conversion process clear, concise and intuitive to improve the likelihood prospects will take action.

LANDING PAGE

The page on a website where the visitor arrives (which may or may not be the home page). In terms of an email campaign, one can think of the landing page as the page to which the email directs prospects via a link. A landing page must satisfy all the requirements pertaining to a home page.

LAST MENTAL IMAGE
The closing scene in a mental sequence. Creates desire, hints at satisfaction and encourages action.

LAYOUT
The arrangement of elements designed to optimize use of screen real estate. Layout may need to take into account the fact that only a small portion of the content will appear in the visible window ("above the fold") or preview pane, and further reading requires prospects to scroll.

LEAD
A prospect who is engaged actively in the buying decision for a product or service and has identified him- or herself.

LEAD-GENERATION SITE
One of four ebusiness categories. The basic objective of this category is to increase and segment your ability to generate leads and close the transaction.

LINKS
Text links, hyperlinks, graphics or images which, when clicked or when pasted into the browser, direct the prospect to another online location. To be most effective in motivating action, links must be obvious to the visitor or recipient. When images or graphics are used as links, or when hyperlinks are used, always provide a corresponding text link as well.

LIST HOST
A service providing users with tools and facilities for distributing high volumes of email and managing a list of email addresses.

LIST HYGIENE
The process of updating a list to remove unsubscribes, duplicate names, bad debts, names on the DMA Mail Preference Service, prison ZIPs and undeliverable addresses.

LIST MAINTENANCE
The ongoing process of keeping a list up-to-date.

LOAD TIME
The length of time it takes for a page to open completely in the browser window. Generally this is a measure of raw speed, although it is possible to affect the visitor's perception of load time by making sure critical elements that engage attention load first.

LOOK AND FEEL
The degree to which design, layout and functionality are appealing to prospects and fit the "image" the business is trying to portray.

MAILING LIST

A set of email addresses designated for receiving specific email messages.

MAP™ (MINERVA ARCHITECTURAL PROCESS™)

Future Now, Inc.'s patent-pending methodology for designing and developing a website based on the principles of Persuasion Architecture. The phases of MAP™ include Uncovery, Wireframing, Storyboarding, Prototyping, Development and Optimization.

MARKUP LANGUAGE

Html coding will influence the degree to which search engine spiders are able to gather critical information from the website for placement in search engine responses. Designs that include tabular layouts and keyword-sensitive, text-rich pages will typically place higher in the rankings.

MOOD & MEANING

The style of the design and the implications of the message are revealed through the characteristics of each element. In particular, mood and meaning is communicated through font styles, color choices, and the shapes and sizes of elements in their relationships to one another.

MOVEMENT

Movement refers to the organizational flow of information and design elements in persuasion architecture so they reflect and acknowledge the needs of both the selling process and the buying process.

MULTIMEDIA / PLUG-INS

Using elements on your site that require your visitor to download plug-ins that are not typically a part of their browser will generally encourage them to leave — the visitor must completely disengage from the sales process to perform a technical function. Whenever your visitors disengage from the process, the risk they will simply leave is huge. Even waiting for Flash presentations to appear or media downloads to finish can frustrate visitors. Be sensitive to this issue when you offer these to your visitors: information about file sizes and typical download times can be helpful.

NAVIGATION

The tabs, text and graphic hyperlinks that always let prospects know both where they are and where they can go. Navigation elements must always be available and obvious. Well-designed navigation will lead the prospect in the intended direction.

nTH SAMPLING

When a subset of the list is constructed based on every *n*th individual. For example, if one is doing Ninth-Testing, every ninth person on the list is sent an email.

OPENING SENTENCE

The first complete sentence of the email communication.

OPTIMIZATION

The final and ongoing phase in planning for Persuasion Architecture is optimization. The persuasively architected website is a starting point for testing and measuring that will allow you to adjust your tactics to maximize your effectiveness. Through optimization, you establish and consistently follow a disciplined strategy for monitoring your Web analytics, which allows you full accountability, the ability determine how closely you have met or will meet your objectives, and how you can improve your results on every page that doesn't meet its responsibility.

OPT-IN / OPT-OUT

Opt-In is the action a person takes when he or she actively agrees, by email or other means, to receive communications. It requires tactics and mechanisms to encourage and allow people to become recipients. Opt-Out is the action a person takes when he or she chooses not to receive communications. It requires tactics and mechanisms by which people can ask to be removed reliably from an email list.

PARAGRAPH LENGTH (AVERAGE)

The average number of sentences in a paragraph, determined by dividing the total number of sentences in a document by the total number of paragraphs. Shorter paragraphs encourage readers to stay focused and move through the document.

PERCENT BOUNCED BACK

The number of emails that were returned as undeliverable divided by the total number of emails sent, multiplied by 100.

PERCENT OPENED

The number of emails opened divided by the total number of emails sent, multiplied by 100.

PERCENT REMOVES

The number of requests for opt-out or removal divided by the total number of emails sent, multiplied by 100.

PERCEPTION

Related to Speed. The visitor's impression of how quickly the site and each subsequent page appear on the screen. While a site can load with an absolute speed, it is possible to give the visitor an impression the site is loading faster by prioritizing and loading critical information first. The visitor ideally will engage with that information while the secondary information is still loading. Actual speed and perception of speed are often inversely related, because the ultimate influences are the users' experiences and their ability to complete the tasks they came to accomplish.

Related to Time. The visitor's impression of the length of the persuasive process from start to finish. Structural designs that use five pages when three would do will needlessly waste their visitors' time. At a smaller level, forms that "look" long — even though they may not request more information — are often perceived as requiring more time to complete. In general, the longer the visitor perceives it will take her to accomplish her task, the more frustrated and disinterested she becomes.

Related to Confidence. Beyond issues of security, privacy and trust, a design can communicate the impression that the business understands the needs of its visitors and is sincerely interested in not merely satisfying those needs, but delighting the customer as well. Careful attention to the design elements: layout, color, and the momentum of the process will promote a visitor's feeling of confidence in the online business.

PERMISSION
The idea of only sending email messages to those recipients who have agreed (or asked) to receive them. The definition of permission is the subject of considerable debate in the email marketing community.

PERSONA (PERSONAS)
A comprehensively fleshed-out archetypical construct that uncovers motivation and facilitates the development of persuasive navigation scenarios. A meaningful persona profile includes names, personality attributes, personal concerns, communication styles, time management qualities, employment, passions, even images and faux quotes written in the persona's own "voice." The goal is to create someone with whom you can imagine carrying on a substantive, persuasive conversation that answers the questions they would ask of you. Persona development relies on an understanding of demographics, psychographics and topographics.

PERSONALITY
The tone your website or email communicates through design elements and content: excited, cheerful, playful, serious, concerned, helpful, etc. The personality of the document should be consistent with the personality of the business and the offer. It should remain consistent throughout any one email and consistent across all emails in a campaign. (For "personality" as it pertains to your prospects, see WIIFM.)

PERSONALIZATION
The practice of writing the email to make the recipient feel it is more personal and was sent with him or her in mind. This might include using the recipient's name in the salutation or subject line, referring to previous purchases or correspondence, or offering recommendations based on previous buying patterns.

PERSUASION ARCHITECTURE
The creation of an intentional structure, the purpose of which is to persuade visitors to take action. Persuasion Architecture combines the management of information and design with the principles of the "buying" and "selling" processes.

PERSUASION FACTOR
The ability of the copy to persuade the recipient to take action.

PERSUASION PROCESS
The intentional mapping of the sales process to the buying process using persona-based navigation scenarios.

PERSUASIVE MOMENTUM
The consequence of well laid out scent of information trails that motivate visitors to continue to move further into the sales process because they are engaged by the relevance and desirability of the end goal.

PLACEMENT

Placement is the exact location of an element on the Web page, and hence, affects exactly where it will appear on the visitor's computer monitor. Placement of elements needs to reflect knowledge of eye-tracking principles and the expectations visitors bring with them to the online medium. When a visitor can quickly find the elements she expects and needs, she is far less likely to be distracted from the persuasion process.

POINT OF ACTION (POA)
(see also Calls to Action)
Specific locations in a presentation that offer the opportunity and encourage the prospect to take action by providing assurance, as in "We value your privacy" or "You can remove the item later."

POINT OF RESOLUTION

A link or even a Web page that provides information or answers a question specific to a visitor's buying process, located where the visitor is most likely to require the information or ask the question.

POSITION

Position refers not to the absolute, but to the relational properties of the elements included on the Web page. No element stands in isolation, but is affected by the elements that surround it. For example, a large, dark element may functionally obscure the presence of an adjacent small, light element. It is important to evaluate the positional relationships — including size, shape, color and proximity — of all elements so that each is visually "available" to the visitor.

PRESENTATION

The manner in which the conversion process describes and displays the products or services.

PRIORITIZATION

Determining the relative importance of all the elements that will comprise a Web page is the act of prioritization. Not all elements are of equal importance, and to be most effective, the resulting layout must take this into account. Important elements may need to be given specific placement on a page or handled in a manner that makes them more visually available to the visitor. Prioritization is the functional bridge that brings discrete elements into functional relation through the layout.

PRIVACY

The condition of being free from unsanctioned intrusion. Web sites and emails need to reassure the prospect through clear, accessible and enforced assurances so he/she can feel comfortable about providing personal information and transacting business.

PROSPECT

A suspect who actively expresses interest in the product or service.

PROTOTYPING

As you iteratively storyboard in planning for Persuasion Architecture, you get to the point where you have a finished prototype of your website that will be identical to the actual final product – but is not fully functional. It will satisfy the various personas who visit your site, offering them meaningful paths through the various scenarios that reflect their needs in the buying and selling process.

QUALITY

Successful design exhibits evidence of a superiority of kind — a degree of excellence — in the quality of the icons, symbols, type and graphics chosen to communicate the website's message. Poor quality negatively impacts consumer confidence and trust, and contributes to an unsatisfying online experience.

READABILITY

The degree to which the copy is well-written as well as optimized for reading on the web. The readability of text is affected by many factors including, but not limited to: the color of the text in relation to the background color, the font, the spacing between words and between lines of text, the length of lines of text, how blocky and dense the paragraphs appear, text justification, the complexity of the grammar and the education level of your audience.

READER EXPERIENCE

The reader's overall experience of pleasure during the encounter.

RELATIONSHIP BUILDING

Undertaking strategies and tactics aimed at developing a positive and ideally long-term relationship with the prospect or customer.

RELATIONSHIP RECOGNITION

The email should be written in a tone and style appropriate to the nature of the relationship that exists between the business and the customer.

RELEVANCE

Content, copy, images and any other elements that have true value and speak to the desires, wants, and motivations of your personas have relevance. It's about speaking to the dog, in the language of the dog, about what matters to the dog – a message that has relevance is the "meat" that draws your visitor to your website and creates persuasive momentum.

RENTAL LIST (OR ACQUISITION LIST)

A list of prospects or a targeted group of recipients who have opted-in to receive information about certain subjects. Using permission-based rental lists, marketers can send e-mail messages to audiences targeted by interest category, profession, demographic information and more. Renting a list usually costs between $.10 and $.40 per name.

RESOLVING DOOR

Links a visitor uses to gather information and answer the questions that are necessary to his or her buying decision process. These links are non-hierarchical, non-linear and very often circular in nature. They allow the visitor to navigate the path that best satisfies his or her needs.

SALES FUNNEL

The sales funnel is a metaphor first articulated by Robert Miller and Stephen Heiman in their book Strategic Selling. Although the concept had existed before in such expressions as "moving prospects through the pipeline" or "sales is a numbers game", they were the first to give definition to it. The sales funnel illustrates two important ideas. The first idea is sales is a social process and the second is that most prospects will drop out of the process before buying.

SALES METRICS

Parameters that help you evaluate and track the success of your business. While it is the most powerful, Conversion Rate is but one of many sales metrics a business can employ to track the efficiency of the conversion system. For a suite of free downloadable calculators, visit Future Now, Inc. at http://www.futurenowinc.com/digitalsalescalculators.htm.

SALES PER VISITOR (SPV)

Keep in mind that when we talk about "sales," we always mean it in the wider sense of "taking action." SPV is another way of measuring your marketing efficiency. It's similar to Customer Conversion Rate, except that instead of showing you the percentage of visitors you persuade to take action, the SPV shows you the actual average amount purchased per visitor (not per order). Obviously, you can improve your SPV by increasing your Customer Conversion Rate, increasing your Average Order Size, or both.

SALES PROCESS

A multi-step persuasion process that begins with Prospecting (largely a Marketing function), continues through establishing Rapport, Presenting, Qualifying and culminates in the Close. While it is linear to the extent that the Close is the goal, the process itself typically operates in an iterative fashion. Sales process involves giving individuals information the seller wants them to have. (The buying process involves individuals gathering the information they want to have, which is sometimes different.

SCANNABLE TEXT

Highlighted, bolded, bulleted or otherwise visually-distinguished content that allows the reader to quickly scan a Web page, orient themselves, and determine if the page contains information of interest.

SCENARIO (PERSUASION SCENARIO)

The predicted navigation path a segment of visitors or persona will take to find the key information they need (buying process) and the key information you want them to have (selling process) in order to achieve a specific goal.

SCENARIO NARRATIVE

The story of what thoughts and decision making processes go through the head of a persona: how they define their need; get to your site; and the information they seek in order to feel comfortable enough to take the action you want them to take as well as accomplish their goals. This is done at the end of uncovery, before you start wireframing.

SCENT OF INFORMATION

Personas will search for information that answers their questions and is relevant to them. They will follow that sent of information by clicking on hyperlinks or images that speak to their motivation and goals. How they follow the scent of information is how they navigate the website.

SECURITY

The ability of the website to communicate to visitors that it is a secure environment, from both a technological and emotional point of view.

SEARCH ENGINE ADVERTISING

Pay strategies — specifically pay-per-click — that advertise your business to the millions of people typing their search queries into a search engine, based on the keywords of their queries.

SEARCH ENGINE MARKETING

This is an umbrella label for the constellation of efforts you direct toward both site optimization for search engines and search engine advertising.

SEARCH ENGINE OPTIMIZATION

All the structural tactics you use behind the scene — including attention to title, keywords, alt tags and meta tags — that allow search engine spiders to crawl your site effectively and identify the critical information that will help you achieve higher rankings in the search engines.

SELF-SERVICE/SUPPORT SITE

One of four ebusiness categories. The basic objective of this category is to increase customer satisfaction and decrease support inquiries.

SENTENCE LENGTH (AVERAGE)

The average number of words in a sentence, determined by dividing the total number of words in a communication by the total number of sentences. In general, shorter sentences capture and retain a reader's interest best. Long sentences can be confusing.

SEQUENCING

The order in which different emails are delivered in the course of a campaign. Each should build on the ones before and lay a strong foundation for the ones to follow.

SHAPE

The characteristic surface configuration of an element — its outline or contour — defines its shape.

SIGNATURE FILE (SIG FILE)

A tagline or short block of text at the end of an e-mail message that identifies the sender and provides additional information such as company name and contact information. Use it to convey a benefit and include a call-to-action with a link.

Site Penetration Index (SPI)

SPI is a measure of how deep your website draws your visitors in. It's a measure of the strength of your overall persuasion or sales process. The deeper you draw them in, the more likely they will be to make it all the way through to taking action. Calculate your SPI by determining the average number of click-throughs your average visitor makes before leaving your site. You do this by dividing the number of hits beyond the home page by the number of visitors. Bigger is better.

Site Penetration Rate (SPR)

It comes as a surprise to many e-commerce website owners, but most visitors to most websites never get past the home page. There are many potential causes, but the result is the same: you spend money driving traffic to your site and they leave almost immediately. Clearly, this is something you want to measure and track. You can do so simply by dividing the number of unique visitors who click to any interior page by the total number of unique "hits" to your home page. As you work to improve the persuasive power of each page, your visitors will click on more pages, going deeper into your sales process and closer to becoming a buyer, and you will be able to measure your progress by whether, in response to any change you make, your SPR goes up or doesn't.

Size

The physical dimensions, proportions or extent of an object comprise its size. While size can be considered an absolute quality, its importance in Web design is based more on the viewer's perception of size. Appropriate sizing of elements aids categorization, readability, and visual availability. Size is a critical quality to consider when dealing with the essential communication media of the Web page: type and graphics.

Skimmable Text

Text written in such a way, and perhaps enhanced with bolding or other visible features, that enables the reader to distill the main points and essential features of the communication quickly, allowing them to decide if they want to read the entire thing.

Spacing

The amount of "white space" a design uses affects the viewer's perception of the spacing of elements and the resulting perception of clutter or lack of coherence. Designs that pack elements together too tightly or spread them too loosely often discourage the visitor from engaging with the information. Appropriate spacing allows the design to cohere, yet helps individual elements stand out in a way that engages the visitor and promotes readability.

This is especially true for type line heights (leading) in blocks of text — even adding one increment of line height can produce a more readable layout.

SPAM / UCE

Unsolicited commercial email. The term normally given to commercial email sent without the recipient's permission. Those accused of sending UCE can run into trouble, ranging from impolite responses through loss of Internet access accounts to destruction of reputations and infrastructure.

STICKINESS
Content's ability to retain the visitor's interest and attention.

STORYBOARDING
Storyboarding focuses on HOW you go about accomplishing the WHAT – it's the third phase in planning for Persuasion Architecture. Storyboarding begins the process of filling in the wireframe. When you storyboard, you develop your persuasive copy and the graphic mockup. Preliminary storyboards should appear in grayscale, so you can evaluate the composition and process without the emotional influence of color. You then proceed to a color mockup and finally, an HTML mockup in which you also consider download speeds, browser compatibilities, style sheets and tabular formats that help search engine spiders crawl your site.

SUBHEADS (OR SUBHEADINGS)
Titles within the body of the email communication or on a Web page that distinguish discrete sections, topics, offers, promotions, etc. Subheadings aid scanning and skimming, allowing readers to more quickly organize and apprehend information.

SUSPECT
Any one individual from the universe of potential customers for the product or service.

TARGETING
Tailoring of the message to the audience or segments within the audience. Timing may or may not be a factor.

TEASER
A message, or part of a message, designed to arouse curiosity and interest without revealing too much detail in itself. You can use appropriate teaser copy in the subject line to encourage prospects or customers to read the email.

TERMINOLOGY
Words that communicate specifics about the features and benefits of the product or service, or features and benefits of the sales process. Content needs to communicate effectively in language that avoids jargon, does not require insider knowledge and is understood easily. In email campaigns, it is particularly important that terminology avoid clichés and "spam words" such as "free," "limited time offer," etc.

TIME TO BUY (TTB)
How long it takes the average buyer from the time they reach your site to the time they have completed their purchase. No matter what else is going on, if it takes too long, your visitors will lose patience and leave. As a point of reference, the best sites persuade visitors to complete a purchase in less than 3 minutes and are getting closer to 2 minutes.

   The same is true for emails. No matter how good your offer may be and how well targeted and timed your email may be, if your email can't persuade your recipient to "buy in" and take action quickly, you have wasted most, if not all, of your money. There are exceptions to this, but only a professional web copywriter would know when or how to bend the rule.

You should get the data from your logs of actual customer visits, not from employee or contrived focus group experiments.

TIMING

1. Scheduling the email campaign to reach the audience at the most opportune time so it is most likely to be read. Timing might be seasonal (for example, vacation or school), dependent on holidays, etc. or mailings might go out on a standard schedule. Even the day of the week and what time of day the mailing goes out are important considerations. For example, a Friday afternoon mailing may be great for retailing customers, but bad for business-to-business customers.

2. Choosing the most appropriate interval between emails in a campaign, to maximize overall effectiveness.

TOOLS

Websites use a variety of "tools" to enhance the shopping experience. These can include shopping carts, immediate online authorization of credit cards, wish lists, forms, etc. To be beneficial elements in the conversion process, all tools must be efficient, intuitive (and come with help information), and truly helpful.

TRACKING

Collecting and evaluating the statistics from which one can measure the effectiveness of an email or an email campaign.

TRAFFIC

People directed to your site through the various marketing and advertising programs a business employs to "drive traffic."

TRIGGER WORDS/VALUED WORDS

Trigger words capture the attention of your visitors and motivate them to take action – they are a valuable part of your site's internal hyperlinking strategies to help visitors get to the information that meets their needs. Trigger words will certainly include, but are not limited to, keywords. For example, a detail-oriented, methodical individual who types "conversion rate" into a search engine will want to see those words on the landing page, but finding a hyperlink on the word "methodology" on that same page may persuade him to remain on that site and investigate further.

TRUST

The condition of having built rapport with your prospects in such a way that they respect your integrity and have confidence you will keep your promises as well as meet, if not exceed, their expectations.

TYPE

A size or style of typewritten or printed character. For example, a serif type (or typeface), a sans-serif type, 10 point type, 14 point type.

UNCOVERY

The first phase in planning for Persuasion Architecture, uncovery is responsible for mapping objectives, developing strategy, understanding the customer's buying process, understanding and refining the sales process, researching keywords and key phrases and defining the key business metrics you will use.

UNIFORMITY

The consistency or uniformity of elements on a Web page and across the website allow the visitor to quickly categorize the information presented and move through the persuasive process with an increased sense of confidence. Attention to uniformity improves readability and contributes to the satisfaction of the visitor's expectations. Repetition of styles, sizes, shapes, colors, position, proximity and other design features reinforces the visitor's perception of a site's uniformity.

UNIQUE FORWARDERS

The number of unique individuals who forwarded an email.

UP-SELLING / CROSS-SELLING

Presenting customers with an opportunity to purchase related products, services or accessories to products they have shown an interest in or previously purchased.

USABILITY

The ability to implement effectively the body of knowledge concerning the human-computer interface in order to remove any obstacles impeding the experience and process of online interactions.

VALUE

The overall appeal and usefulness of the product or service to the prospect. Rarely is value simply a function of price (which typically ranks fourth among purchase considerations).

VALUE PROPOSITION

The concise and memorable phrase that concisely and powerfully describes the value of your business and creates excitement in the prospect. The value proposition is not a slogan or a phrase designed for advertising, although that is one potential use for it. Instead, its purpose is to answer the prospect's implicit question, "Why should I do business with you and not somebody else?"

VALUED WORDS

See Trigger Words.

VIRAL DESIGN

Elements and functions included in a communication that encourage and allow recipients to pass the offer along to others, thereby leveraging the marketing effort ("tell a friend," "please forward," etc.).

VIRAL EFFECT

A measurable outcome of the degree to which recipients of a communication refer the offer, products, services or company to others.

Viral Forwards

The number of referrals sent.

Viral Marketing

Taking advantage of the visitor's inclination to tell others about the online experience. Websites can actively encourage viral marketing by offering tell-a-friend or email-this-page options, or by offering incentives. Even when a website does not make a conscious effort to support viral marketing, the "grapevine" effect still takes place, although it is important to understand that visitors are likely to tell more people about a negative online experience than a positive online experience.

Viral Responses

The number of recipients who received the referral, opened it and clicked on a link.

Visual Availability

While an element may appear on the page, or while critical information may be presented on the site, if a visitor cannot "see" it, the element is functionally not there. Layout and eye-tracking techniques suited to the online environment help visitors quickly distinguish important information.

Visual Clarity

A function, in large part, of layout and design: Pages are easy to scan; text and graphics are clear; prospects can find what they are looking for quickly and easily.

Voice

(see Active Voice)

Voice is the way in which your copy is written. Active voice, present tense, and strong verbs all add to persuasive momentum. NOTE: "Voice" also can refer to the personality of your business in your emails and on your website.

WeWe Test

Developed by Future Now, Inc., this metric provides a general measure of the degree to which your communication is customer-centered. It compares the number of customer-oriented words (you, your, etc.) in the communication to the number of self- or company-referential words (we, our, I, me, etc.). http://www.futurenowinc.com/wewe.htm

WIIFM

"What's In It For Me?" This question always underlies and informs a prospect's decision whether to take the suggested action. Beyond addressing the critical value propositions and benefits that will interest prospects, all messaging must accommodate the deeply-felt, emotional needs and take into account the different personality profiles that influence prospects' different shopping styles. (Amiable, Methodical, Expressive and Assertive are our categorizations for the personality profiles – there have been many other representations of these four groups).

WIREFRAMING

Wireframing defines the WHAT of the creative process – it's the second phase in planning for Persuasion Architecture. A wireframe is a structural representation of every click through possibility and path your personas can take. No pictures, no graphic design, just bare bones text and hyperlinks. You can click the links and see where you go; you can get a feel for the process of the site and help generate useful feedback at a time when changes and multiple iterations are a snap.

Wireframed pages will contain the answers to the three questions essential to the persuasive process:

- What actions satisfy the objective?
- Who needs to be persuaded to take action?
- How do you persuade them most effectively to take action?

WORD LENGTH (AVERAGE)

The average number of letters in a word, determined by dividing the total number of letters in a communication by the total number of words. Unless meaning is compromised, choose the shorter word over the longer word.

About Future Now, Inc.

Founded by Bryan and Jeffrey Eisenberg in 1998, Future Now, Inc. is a New York City based consulting firm focused on helping clients persuade and convert their website's traffic into leads, customers and sales by applying our patent pending Persuasion Architecture methodology, and proven conversion rate optimization methods.

Future Now, Inc.'s products and services include free and low-cost resources for the do-it-yourselfer (see our website), mid four-figure assessments, special projects and strategic consultations, and assistance with tactical implementations to long-term engagements.

Future Now, Inc. publishes GrokDotCom, the weekly ROI Marketing column in ClickZ.com and has published three books: "The Marketer's Common Sense Guide to e-Metrics" (currently licensed and distributed by WebTrends), "What Converts Search Engine Traffic" (with exclusive WebSideStory/StatMarket data) and "Persuasive Online Copywriting".

Future Now, Inc.'s team members have been featured speakers at numerous industry events: DMDAYS, Adtech, Search Engine Strategies, Internet World, Net.Marketing, DMA Annual, eMetrics Summit, Electronic Retail Association, Wizard Academy & ClickZ Email Strategies. Their work have been featured in publications such as The Wall Street Journal, Forrester Research, Publish, Internet Advertising Report (IAR) Chicago Business Tribune, Inc Magazine, Entrepreneur, Target Marketing, DM News, Microsoft's bCentral, EDP the Business, MarketingSherpa, the Toronto Star, Ecommerce-Guide.com, InternetDay & Internet Retailer.

Future Now, Inc.'s memberships include:

Founders and Chairman of the Web Analytics Association
Charter member of the WebTrends Insight Network
Members of the Asilomar Institute for Information Architecture
Members of the Usability Professionals Association
Members of the American Society for Quality

Future Now, Inc.'s experienced Conversion Rate Analysts and Persuasion Architecture specialists help you achieve results that are dramatic, quick and permanent. Visit us at http://www.futurenowinc.com or call us at (877) 643-7244.

Business Blogs: A Practical Guide

By: Bill Ives and Amanda G. Watlington, Ph.D.
ISBN#: 0-9766180-0-1

Blogs are hot, but what do they really bring to business and how are successful early adopters using them? This is a question the authors asked 70 well-known bloggers at firms ranging from IBM, Microsoft, Yahoo!, and SAP, to many small businesses in a variety of industries. In addition to a detailed case study with the insights gained from each interview, Business Blogs: A Practical Guide addresses all the business, technical, writing, and publishing issues you will face as a business blogger. The authors provide practical guidance on everything a manager needs to decide from how writing a blog will support the business to how to successfully integrate blogging into the marketing communications mix. Business Blogs: A Practical Guide will be available Spring 2005. For more details see http://www.businessblogguide.com .

What is Wizard Academy?

Composed of a fascinating series of workshops led by some of the most accomplished instructors in America, Wizard Academy is a progressive new kind of business and communications school whose stated objective is to improve the creative thinking and communication skills of sales professionals, internet professionals, business owners, educators, ad writers, ministers, authors, inventors, journalists and CEOs.

Founded in 1999, the Academy has exploded into a worldwide phenomenon with an impressive fraternity of alumni who are rapidly forming an important worldwide network of business relationships.

"Alice in Wonderland on steroids! I wish Roy Williams had been my very first college professor. If he had been, everything I learned after that would have made a lot more sense and been a lot more useful... Astounding stuff." —Dr. Larry McCleary, Neurologist and Theoretical Physicist

"...Valuable, helpful, insightful, and thought provoking. We're recommending it to everyone we see." —Jan Nations and Sterling Tarrant, senior managers, Focus on the Family

"Be prepared to take a wild, three-ring-circus journey into the creative recesses of the brain...[that] will change your approach to managing and marketing your business forever. For anyone who must think critically or write creatively on the job, the Wizard Academy is a must." —Dr. Kevin Ryan, President., The Executive Writer

"Even with all I knew, I was not fully prepared for the experience I had at the Academy... Who else but a wizard can make sense of so many divergent ideas? I highly recommend it." —Mark Huffman, Advertising Production Manager, Procter & Gamble

"A life-altering 72 hours." —Jim Rubart

To learn more about Wizard Academy

Visit www.WizardAcademy.com or call the academy at (800) 425-4769.